To Brieg

Every blessing for
the future!

NEW ECCLESIAL MOVEMENTS

Tony Hanny

NEW ECCLESIAL MOVEMENTS

TONY HANNA

ST PAULS

Alba House

Library of Congress Cataloging-in-Publication Data

Hanna, Tony (Stephen Anthony).
  New ecclesial movements / Tony Hanna.
    p. cm.
  ISBN 0-8189-0996-X
1. Laity—Catholic Church. I. Title.

BX1920.H28 2006
267'.182—dc22

                          2005015472

North American edition published by
Alba House, 2187 Victory Blvd., Staten Island, NY 10314-6603
www.alba-house.com
ISBN 0-8189-0996-X

Australian edition published by
ST PAULS PUBLICATIONS - Society of St. Paul
60-70 Broughton Road - PO Box 906 - Strathfield, NSW 2135
www.stpauls.com.au
ISBN 1-921032-15-4

Produced and designed in the United States of America by the
Fathers and Brothers of the Society of St. Paul,
2187 Victory Boulevard, Staten Island, New York 10314-6603,
as part of their communications apostolate.

ISBN: 0-8189-0996-X

Printing Information:

Current Printing - first digit   1   2   3   4   5   6   7   8   9   10

Year of Current Printing - first year shown

2006   2007   2008   2009   2010   2011   2012   2013   2014   2015

TABLE OF CONTENTS

ACKNOWLEDGMENTS

This book has been gestating for quite some time and it came to fruition through the prompting and the support of many people. It emerged out of doctoral studies I undertook on the question of the new ecclesial movements at St. Patrick's Pontifical University, Maynooth, Ireland. Dr. Tom Norris, my doctoral director deserves sincere thanks for his patient probing and astute guidance around critical directions, not to mention his warm friendship. Sr. Briege Murphy has been a long time friend and mentor and I owe a huge debt to her for much of my own formation and for helping me to shape my thinking on this subject. The Redemptorist Community in Dundalk, Ireland, offered me the use of their library facilities and this was a huge practical resource. My own community, The Family of God, has been a constant support and inspiration and my daily interaction with these brothers and sisters has shaped and moulded many of my ideas now expressed in this book. I wish to acknowledge with grateful thanks the support of my bishops, past and present. Cardinal Thomas Ó Fiaich (R.I.P.) supported the launch of our fledgling community in 1979. His successor Cardinal Daly approved the community provisionally as a Private Association of the Faithful on July 11, 1995 entrusting us to the patronage of St. Benedict, the patron saint of Europe. Archbishop Sean Brady, the current Primate of Armagh, has written an informed foreword to this work and I am indebted to him for his kindness and ongoing support.

My four daughters and son-in-law have been constant encouragers but my greatest advocate and supporter has been my wife, Jacinta and it is with deep love and gratitude that I acknowledge her contribution to the writing of this book.

FOREWORD
by Archbishop Sean Brady

The arrival of the new ecclesial movements has come as something of a surprise to the Church. Their emergence has coincided largely with the Second Vatican Council and the subsequent reforms and impetus that the council desired to bring to the Church and to the world. The late Pope John Paul II was one of the first to recognize the potential of the new movements and his generous and consistent pastoral support was a key factor in shepherding them to the heart of the Church at a time when their emergence was not universally welcomed.

One thing that alerted the Church to the possibilities inherent in the new movements was their particular attraction to young people, many of whom have been challenged and missioned by the rigorous formation and demanding expectations of these movements. It was noted also that a significant number of the current vocations to priesthood and religious life were emanating from membership of these very movements.

The Church also noted the interesting way in which the various walks of life, celibate, religious, married, lay and clerical all come together to share the richness of a truly communal spirituality and how exciting it is when the gifts and the charisms of the whole community are shared in a generous and wholesome way.

This book written by Dr. Tony Hanna is based on doctoral

studies undertaken by him at St. Patrick's Pontifical College, Maynooth. Apart from his academic research, Dr. Hanna speaks from his own personal engagement with one such movement which was an offshoot of Charismatic Renewal. The Family of God, a community of which he is a co-founder, was established in 1979, in the Archdiocese of Armagh with the permission of Cardinal Ó Fiaich and which later received provisional canonical approval by my predecessor, Cardinal Daly, in 1991. The Family of God Community is a council member of the Catholic Fraternity established by the Pontifical Council of the Laity and is recognized as a Private Association of the Faithful. I am delighted to have this Community within the Archdiocese of Armagh and am very aware of the many blessings its presence has bestowed on the people it serves.

New Ecclesial Movements is one of the first major examinations in English of an exciting, new gift of the Spirit to the Church. The book is a wide-ranging and extensive overview of the who, what, how and where of this new phenomenon. Its author points out in a very readable style some of the wonderful possibilities that the new movements offer to the Church but he also articulates some of the dangers that lurk behind the potential. His wise advice to bishops is that we "test everything and to hold fast to the good," but he also warns us not "to stifle the Spirit" (1 Th 5:19).

One of the most interesting features of the new movements is that they are to the fore in the debate around the relationship between the universal and local church and some of the perennial tensions that, of necessity, exist around this reality. As Bishop of a particular diocese, I am called to have a profound concern for the welfare of the local flock under my care but I also am equally aware of the need to be solicitous for the welfare of the whole Church. It is at times suggested that some new movements could threaten the cohesion and the pastoral plan of the local church when they seek to be independent of the local ordinary. This has not been my experience but there is no doubt that these new movements call for vigilance and sensitivity on the part of the bishops. The time also calls for servant leadership on the part of the new ecclesial movements as together we humbly seek the will of God.

The ecclesial movements described in this book are incredibly diverse and in many ways the Church is still grappling to have a full comprehension of what the Spirit is saying to us through their appearance. Dr. Hanna looks in particular at three of the major movements to highlight this diversity, namely Communion and Liberation, the Neo-Catechumenal Movement and Charismatic Renewal. Their distinct origins, their varied foci, their leadership structures and outreaches all provide fascinating material for reflection. While they have much in common their diversity is remarkable and this is part of their fascination.

There have been a number of fora in recent years around this new phenomenon but there is a need for more solid and ongoing research into this reality. Undoubtedly, theologians and church historians will produce more extensive research into these new ecclesial movements over the coming years. However, Dr. Hanna has produced a scholarly, timely and challenging introduction to this phenomenon. *New Ecclesial Movements* is a wide-ranging and informative volume which addresses a significant and innovative aspect of ecclesiology. I hope it reaches a wide audience and that it stimulates debate about the shape and direction of the Church as she enters into the new millennium under the dynamic and often surprising impulse of the Holy Spirit.

INTRODUCTION

Pentecost 1998 witnessed a plenary gathering of representatives of fifty-six invited ecclesial communities in Rome with the Pope. This was an epic moment in the historical development of the new movements most of which have swept through the Church in the final decades of the last millennium. A host of new ecclesial movements, with an astonishing array of charisms and committed members have sprung up all over the world. Most surprisingly of all, the main human protagonists in this new development have been lay people.

Historical Context

Yet these new movements have not suddenly sprung up in isolation from already existing roots and it is important to situate their emergence in the Church within an historical context. Given the reality that the vast majority of those involved in the life and animation of the new ecclesial movements are lay people, an important factor that needs to be considered, as part of the historical milieu which has enabled the birth of these new ecclesial communities, is the re-awakening of the laity to their proper role in the Church. Such a re-awakening of the laity has been fostered by a number of key figures who prophetically helped to re-orient the Church back to its apostolic roots where all the baptized considered themselves as equals and all saw themselves as evangelists.

However, laity are not the only members of the new ecclesial communities and the various states of life represented in the movements is one of their riches. As J. Beyer has pointed out,

> the notion itself of communion, which is a distinctive feature of the Church, in the way Vatican II contemplates her mystery, remains incomprehensible if it is not made visible in the living Church herself. These new forms of communion [the movements] seem to have been created precisely to enable people to understand and experience this communion.... What the Spirit illuminated in the Council, was expressed by the Spirit with this new gift to the life of the Church.[1]

However, notwithstanding the various expressions of community life to which the new ecclesial movements bear eloquent testimony, the emergence of a vibrant lay spirituality is hugely significant and warrants some detailed analysis and explanation. Undoubtedly Vatican II had a huge impact on the Church's understanding of the lay apostolate and this was pivotal in enabling the new movements to secure a place in the heart of the Church.

Another factor which helps to clarify the place of the new movements in the Church is to situate them within the historical tradition of renewal movements that have been a perennial feature of the life of the Church. In reviewing some of these historical incidences one can detect clearly the tension between conflicting concepts of the Church, concepts which lead to an examination of the relationship between the local and the universal, between the Petrine ministry and the collegiality of the episcopacy, between the institutional and the charismatic, between the Marian and the Petrine. I believe the research clearly indicates that not only did this phenomenon of "movement" stimulate a constant renewal trend within the tradition of Church but it also pro-

---

[1] J. Beyer, "I movimenti ecclesiali," *Vita Consecrata* 23 (1987): 156.

voked controversy. The problems and the promise associated with the new twentieth-century ecclesial movements can best be assessed by examining them within an historical framework. Then one can better appreciate their place in the ongoing dynamic plan of the Holy Spirit who continues to animate a constant renewal of the Church. As Karl Rahner has lucidly explained,

> the charismatic is essentially new and always surprising. To be sure it also stands in inner though hidden continuity with what came earlier in the Church and fits in with her spirit and her institutional framework. Yet it is new and incalculable and it is not immediately evident at first sight that everything is as it was in the enduring totality of the Church. For often it is only through what is new that it is realized that the range of the Church was greater from the outset than had been previously supposed and so the charismatic feature, when it is new, and one might almost say it is only charismatic if it is so, has something shocking about it. It can be mistaken for facile enthusiasm, a hankering after change, attempted subversion, lack of feeling for tradition and for the well-tried experience of the past.[2]

The arrival of charisms has always, inevitably, involved a certain disturbing of the peace. One also needs to be aware that the skeptical voices currently raised against the liberty afforded to some of these new ecclesial movements is also part of their historical evolution. An historical sweep of lay spirituality and the legacy of previous "movements" in the history of the Church is a necessary prerequisite to provide a backdrop which situates the new movements in the life of the Church. Likewise, the crucial role

---

[2] K. Rahner, *The Dynamic Element in the Church* (Freiburg: Herder; London; Burns and Oates, 1964), 83.

played by the new ecclesiology of Vatican II is critical in assisting the acceptance of the new ecclesial movements within the Church. The deeper appreciation of charisms and the role of the Holy Spirit is central to this new ecclesiology. I attempt to situate the new movements within a theology of charisms and understand this new reality as another surprise of the Spirit. As Cardinal Suenens wrote in *A New Pentecost?*,

> The Spirit is the living breath of the Church leading it on its pilgrimage, as long ago the pillar of cloud by day and the pillar of fire by night led the people of Israel in the desert; He is at once continuity and freshness, "new things and old" (Mt 13:52), tradition and progress.[3]

> The Spirit is living Tradition and he binds successive generations to the Lord Jesus "who is, who was, and who is to come" (Rv 1:4). It is he who explains to the disciples of Jesus those things in the teachings of the Master that up to now they were not able to bear. He heals them little by little of their "incredulity and obstinacy" (Mk 16:14). He draws from the one word of God that which will quench the thirst of each generation: "You will draw water joyfully from the springs of salvation" (Is 12:3). He calls to mind the word of God giving it a freshness and a capacity to shed light on what is actually happening at the moment. He never repeats himself: each time his teaching of the word confers a new resonance and a new urgency. The Spirit recalls to the Church in a living and practical way the teaching of Christ. In order to understand its true and actual message, the Spirit must teach us.

> The Spirit is also a living movement forward. He is reaching out to what is yet to come, carrying the past in order to propel it into the future. He is at the source of the great decisions that have determined the course

---

[3] Leon Joseph Cardinal Suenens, *A New Pentecost?* (Collins Fountain Books, 1975), 229.

of the Church's mission. The Acts of the Apostles mentions him at the Council of Jerusalem (Ac 15:28), and attributes to him Paul's decision to cross over into Europe. The Spirit is always at work to prevent the Church from taking itself as an end in itself and finding complacency in self-satisfaction. He wants Christians to set out on the journey each morning, and with a minimum of baggage.[4]

The overall aim of the book is to introduce the phenomenon of the new ecclesial movements to a wider audience. Just as the Second Vatican Council was a significant surprise to the Church and the world, so too the emergence of these new ecclesial movements has caused more than a little stir. Almost like an unexpected pregnancy (perhaps even an unwanted pregnancy), their arrival has brought a mixture of joy and dismay. Some see them as a hope for the Church in the midst of difficult times, others see them as usurpers and divisive at a time when the Church needs unity and clarity.

---

[4] Suenens, *A New Pentecost?*, 230.

Biblical Abbreviations

OLD TESTAMENT

Genesis	Gn	Nehemiah	Ne	Baruch	Ba
Exodus	Ex	Tobit	Tb	Ezekiel	Ezk
Leviticus	Lv	Judith	Jdt	Daniel	Dn
Numbers	Nb	Esther	Est	Hosea	Ho
Deuteronomy	Dt	1 Maccabees	1 M	Joel	Jl
Joshua	Jos	2 Maccabees	2 M	Amos	Am
Judges	Jg	Job	Jb	Obadiah	Ob
Ruth	Rt	Psalms	Ps	Jonah	Jon
1 Samuel	1 S	Proverbs	Pr	Micah	Mi
2 Samuel	2 S	Ecclesiastes	Ec	Nahum	Na
1 Kings	1 K	Song of Songs	Sg	Habakkuk	Hab
2 Kings	2 K	Wisdom	Ws	Zephaniah	Zp
1 Chronicles	1 Ch	Sirach	Si	Haggai	Hg
2 Chronicles	2 Ch	Isaiah	Is	Malachi	Ml
Ezra	Ezr	Jeremiah	Jr	Zechariah	Zc
		Lamentations	Lm		

NEW TESTAMENT

Matthew	Mt	Ephesians	Eph	Hebrews	Heb
Mark	Mk	Philippians	Ph	James	Jm
Luke	Lk	Colossians	Col	1 Peter	1 P
John	Jn	1 Thessalonians	1 Th	2 Peter	2 P
Acts	Ac	2 Thessalonians	2 Th	1 John	1 Jn
Romans	Rm	1 Timothy	1 Tm	2 John	2 Jn
1 Corinthians	1 Cor	2 Timothy	2 Tm	3 John	3 Jn
2 Corinthians	2 Cor	Titus	Tt	Jude	Jude
Galatians	Gal	Philemon	Phm	Revelation	Rv

SECTION ONE

THE PHENOMENON

CHAPTER ONE

Features

Who are these new Ecclesial Movements?

The new spiritual movements are groupings, mostly comprising laypersons, but also clerics and religious, who are striving for an intense religious life in the community and a renewal of the faith in the Church. They are mostly organized on a trans-local level and have a varying regional distribution. Coda dislikes the prefix "lay" before them because he sees such a definition as "reductive."[1] Both he and Beyer, who has analyzed the evolution of the movements and the forms they take in a number of articles, agree that the term "movements" indicates that these groups already differ in their structures from the conventional forms of communities of the Church.[2]

The appearances of these movements are extremely diverse and manifold so that the common denominator with regard to their makeup is not easy to find. The distinction from other groups is not always easy. They differ from the classical religious orders and modern forms of religious orders, since they are not founded

---

[1] Piero Coda, "The Ecclesial Movements. Gifts of the Spirit," *Laity Today* (2000), 95.

[2] See J. Beyer, "I Movimenti Ecclesiali," *Vita Consecrata* 23 (1987): 156; "Il Movimento Ecclesiali: Questioni Attuali," *Vita Consecrata* 26 (1990), 483-494 and "I Movimenti Nuovi Nella Chiesa." *Vita Consecrata* 27 (1991), 61-77.

on so radical a life decision, which — as in religious orders — is sealed with lifelong vows and because they, therefore, have less institutional and constitutional elements. They show some similarity to secular institutes, which after World War II were established officially in the Catholic Church, but they tend not to be as tightly structured. The term "movements" is appropriate because it implies well the flexible form of the communities. Yet, they are more structured and more committed than groups formed spontaneously. However, official statements and documents of the Church repeatedly point out that the new spiritual movements are most closely connected with the great basic forces of the post-Conciliar renewal and with many other movements of present-day ecclesiastical life.

The statement of the German Bishops' Conference regarding the Guidelines for the Bishops' Synod of 1987 mentions the classic Catholic federations, the spiritual movements and base communities as important basic forms of communities in the apostolate of the laity.[3] The post-synod apostolic publication *Christifideles laici* encourages alliances of the laity to promote the richness and the diversity of the gifts, which the Spirit keeps alive in the Church.[4]

The Bishops' Synod of 1994 conferred on *The Consecrated Life and Its Mission in the Church and in the World*. Already in the preparatory documents "new communities and renewed forms of life according to the Gospel" had been defined. In its definition of the new communities, the post-synod apostolic publication *Vita Consecrata*, which was presented on March 25, 1996, points out that the new associations are not alternatives to the earlier institutions but rather are a gift of the Spirit, which manifests itself through the signs of the times and is the origin of the community and of perpetual renewal of life.[5]

---

[3] Cf. "Guidelines" 45. Ed. Secretariat of the German Bishops Conference, May 2, 1986, 18ff.

[4] Cf. Pope John Paul II, *Christifideles laici*, § 29.

[5] Cf. Pope John Paul II, *Vita Consecrata*, §62.

What is an Ecclesial Movement?

In a letter to the World Congress of Ecclesial Movements in May, 1998, Pope John Paul II defined a movement as "a concrete ecclesial entity, in which primarily lay people participate, with an itinerary of faith and Christian testimony that founds its own pedagogical method on a charism given to the person of the founder in determined circumstances and modes."[6]

This definition highlights three traits of the new movements: They are primarily lay, their work is to evangelize, and their charism comes from their founder. In essence they are vibrant Christian communities with predominantly lay membership who are aware that they are on a journey of faith; they exemplify a Christian witness based on a precise charism given to the person of the founder or founders in specific circumstances and ways.

Rather than give a specific definition of what constitutes an ecclesial movement, Joseph Cardinal Ratzinger, then Prefect of the Sacred Congregation for the Doctrine of the Faith and presently Pope Benedict XVI, chose to indicate a "number of criteria," chief of which is "being rooted in the faith of the Church."[7] Without unity with the apostolic faith, one cannot lay claim to apostolic activity. Such a desire for unity gives rise to a second criterion, namely, to be "incorporated into the living community of the whole Church" and "to stand at the side of the successors of the apostles and the successor of Peter who bears responsibility for the harmonious interaction between the local Church and the universal Church as the one People of God."[8]

As Bishop Cordes pointed out, "Movements originate only if they have a different level than that of their surrounding environment."[9] They are different from the norm in the way that they

---

6   Pope John Paul II, "Movements in the Church," *Laity Today* (1999), 18.
7   Joseph Cardinal Ratzinger, "The Ecclesial Movements; a Theological Reflection on Their Place in the Church," *Laity Today* (1999), 25.
8   Ibid.
9   Paul Josef Cordes, *Charisms and New Evangelisation* (St. Paul's Publications, 1991), 23.

live and act. However, in the teachings of John Paul II, the movements are a normative form of life for the Church, an expression of the life of the Church.

> If on 30 May 1998, I spoke in St. Peter's Square of "a new Pentecost," referring to the growth of charisms and movements which has occurred in the Church since the Second Vatican Council, with this expression I wished to acknowledge the development of the movements and new communities as a source of hope for the Church's missionary action.[10]

The Pope said in this regard that it is significant to see how the Holy Spirit has continued to work throughout the Church's history, and today has called forth many varied forms of movements.

> Ecclesial movements, inspired by a desire to live the Gospel more intensively and to announce it to others, have always been manifest in the midst of the People of God.... In our day and particularly during recent decades, new movements have appeared that are more independent of the structures and style of the religious life than in the past.[11]

They are new things that need to be fully understood in their full form as a work of God in our day. The Pope provoked further debate and reflection on this whole issue when he stated that the

> Church herself is a movement and above all she is a mystery, the mystery of the eternal love of the Father from whose paternal heart the mission of the Son and the mission of the Holy Spirit derive their origin. The

---

[10] Pope John Paul II, "Message to the participants in the Seminar on 'The Ecclesial Movements in the Pastoral Concern of the Bishops,'" *Laity Today* (1999), 17.

[11] Pope John Paul II, "Directives on Formation in Religious Institutes," §92.

> Church born of this mission, is in *statu missionis;* she is a movement and penetrates hearts and minds. The mission of the Father, Son, and Holy Spirit is the mission of the Church. It is therefore the mission of the movements. The movements are an expression of God's diversified plan in the Church. The mission has its origin in the Father, Son, and Holy Spirit. This is a movement of the Church throughout time.[12]

This declaration is a restatement of something that he had underlined earlier in his pontificate:

> In fact, one of the most important fruits produced by the movements is precisely that of knowing how to release in so many lay faithful, men and women, adults and young people, an intense missionary zeal, which is indispensable for the Church as she prepares to cross the threshold of the third millennium. However, this objective is only achieved where "these movements humbly seek to become part of the life of local Churches and are welcomed by Bishops and priests within diocesan and parish structures" (*Redemptoris missio,* n. 72).[13]

Church, Institution or Charism?

With the emergence of the movements in the Church some have tried to set up a dialectic between "institution and event, or institution and charism."[14] As Ratzinger points out, such a concept is flawed. The fundamental institutional reality that charac-

---

[12] Pope John Paul II, "Homily at the Mass for participants at the congress of 'Movements in the Church,'" *Insegnamenti* 4/II (1981), 305-306.

[13] Ibid.

[14] Ratzinger, "The Ecclesial Movements; a Theological Reflection on Their Place in the Church," *Laity Today* (1999), 25.

terizes the Church is her sacramental ministry in its varying degrees. Ultimately, the "sacrament, that significantly bears the name Ordo, is, in the final analysis, the sole permanent and binding structure that forms so to say the fixed order of the Church."[15] As it is a sacrament, it must be perpetually created anew by God and it is primarily called into existence by Him, at the charismatic and pneumatological level.

The Church is not our institution, but the irruption of something else; that it is intrinsically *iuris divini* has as its consequence that we can never apply institutional criteria to her; and the Church is entirely herself only where the criteria and methods of human institutions are transcended.[16] Of necessity, the Church has institutions of purely human right to enable administration and organization but there is always the danger that if they become too powerful they can jeopardize the order and the vitality of her spiritual reality.

Other Models

Another dialectical pairing proposed is that between a christological and pneumatological view of the Church. It is argued that the sacrament of Church belongs to the christological-incarnational aspect which then needs to be supplanted by the pneumatological-charismatic element. A distinction does need to be drawn between Christ and the Holy Spirit but they are also united as a *communio* with the Father and with one another. Christ and the Spirit can only be rightly understood together. "The Lord is the Spirit," says Paul in the Second Letter to the Corinthians (3:17).

A third model suggested is the relation between the permanent order of ecclesial life and new irruptions of the Spirit on the other, sometimes characterized in terms of Luther's dialectic be-

---

[15] Ibid.
[16] Ibid., 26.

tween Law and Gospel which leads to a tension between the cultic-sacerdotal aspect and the prophetic aspect of salvation history. In this outlook the movements would be ranged on the side of prophecy.

Each of these three outlooks indicate a desire or a tendency to treat the movements as something parallel to the Church; often they are seen as separate entities to the more traditional structures of diocese, institution and parish. It can even lead to the accusation that the movements want to create a parallel Church.[17] In Scola's view time has erroneously been wasted on examining this dualistic presupposition that is flawed from the outset.[18]

Theological Definition of Movement

However, we can make some theological analysis to differentiate the word "movement" from its sociological meaning. In the history of theology it has been used to designate phenomena which were characterized by a strong sense of renewal. According to Fernandez,[19] the characteristics of the ecclesial movements are that they emerge as a result of a charism which "makes itself present in the reality of the local and the universal Church."[20] This new charism often helps other older charisms or existing ecclesial forms which have become somewhat muted from age or exhaus-

---

[17] E. Barcelon, "Las asociaciónes y movimientos laicales en la vida y misión de la Iglesia," *Teologica Espiritual* 36 (1992), pp. 193ff.

[18] Angelo Scola, "The Reality of the Movements in the Universal Church and the Local Church," *Laity Today* (1999). See P. Mullins, "The Theology of Charisms: Vatican II and the New Catechism," *Milltown Studies* 33 (1994), 123-162. J. Beyer, "Le Laïcat et des Laïcs dans L'Église," *Gregorianum* 68 (1987), 157-185. M. de Merode, "Théologie du Laïcat Aujourd'hui," *Lumen Vitae* 41 (1986), 379-392. G. Grouthier, "'Église Locale' ou 'Église Particulière'; Querelle Sémantique ou Option Théologique?" *Studia Canonica* 25. Jean Marie Tillard, "L'Église Locale: Ecclésiologie de Communion et Catholicité," (1995).

[19] Fidel Gonzalez-Fernandez, "Charisms and Movements in the History of the Church. The Ecclesial Movements in the Pastoral Concern of the Bishops," *Laity Today* (2000), 71-103.

[20] Ibid., 103.

tion to rediscover the energy and vitality of their gift and mission. Moreover, charisms are of their very nature "catholic" in that "they transcend the local frontiers in which they were born."[21] They tend to manifest spontaneously the catholic nature of the Church, and an "immense ecclesial fertility"[22] is unleashed. Not only is the ontological and missionary sense of baptism energized in the laity but various forms of consecrated virginity and religious life, as well as vocations to the priesthood, are fostered. The lessons of history are that such springs of renewal have always had a "profound Marian and Petrine sense,"[23] the latter in various ways supporting them to spread in catholicity.

Ratzinger sees the movements as sharing in the universal apostolic responsibility of the successor of Peter.[24] Scola sees them as a particular realization of Church, which is itself a "movement." For him, "Movement" means mission; apostolate, and identity is in mission; the particular and the universal are aspects of the same Church.[25]

Bishop Albert de Monléon eloquently portrays the movements as places of a transfigured humanity which is founded on a personal encounter with the Living Christ revivifying the grace of baptism.[26] Giovanni Magnani notes that the whole Church has a "lay character." It is a permanent, practical and stable way that he sees indicated in the conciliar affirmation of a *proprium* (or "distinctive character," "although not an exclusive one") of the laity which finds its full justification here.[27]

---

21 Ibid.

22 Ibid.

23 Ibid.

24 Ratzinger, "The Ecclesial Movements; a Theological Reflection on Their Place in the Church," 35.

25 Ibid.

26 Bishop Albert de Monléon, "The Movements as Places of a Transfigured Humanity," *Laity Today* (1999): 149-163.

27 Giovanni Magnani, "Does the So-Called Theology of the Laity Possess a Theological Status? Vatican II Assessments and Perspectives, Twenty-Five Years Later (1962-1987)" (1988), 621-622.

All the states of life, whether taken collectively or individually in relation to the others, are at the service of the Church's growth. While different in expression, they are deeply united in the Church's "mystery of communion" and are dynamically coordinated in its unique mission. The new ecclesial movements remind all of us, regardless of our state of life, that we are called to a deep unity in Christ.

Criteria of Ecclesiality

Pope John Paul II in his first Encyclical, *Redemptor Hominis*, identified the emergence of new lay groups with "a different outline and an excellent dynamism"[28] as one of the fruits of the post conciliar period. He saw them as a providential response because "they represent one of the most significant fruits of that springtime in the Church which was foretold by the Second Vatican Council but which unfortunately has been hampered by the spread of secularism."[29] As formulated in *Christifideles laici,* there are "clear and definite criteria for discerning and recognizing lay groups, also called 'Criteria of Ecclesiality.'"[30] These criteria call for:

(1) The creation of schools of holiness which promote a unity between faith and life;

(2) An inescapable responsibility to confess the Catholic faith and to clearly show fidelity to the Church's *magisterium* in matters of faith and doctrine.

(3) Witness of communion, steadfast and convinced with the Pope, who is the center of unity between the universal Church and the Bishop. *Ubi Petrus ibi Ecclesia — ubi Episcopus ibi Ecclesia.* (This principle is expressed at the diocesan level in

---

[28] Pope John Paul II, Encyclical Letter *Redemptor Hominis,* §5.

[29] Pope John Paul II, "Message to the World Congress of Ecclesial Movements, 1998," *Laity Today* (1999), 222.

[30] Pope John Paul II, *Christifideles laici,* §30.

obedience to the Bishop and in willing collaboration with other associations and movements. Moreover, Church communion demands both an acknowledgment of a legitimate plurality of forms in the associations of the lay faithful in the Church and at the same time, a willingness to cooperate in working together).[31]

(4) Compliance with and participation in the apostolic aims of the Church. Therefore each community should have a strong missionary thrust to the whole world and guard against closing in on oneself or one's circle.

(5) A committed presence in society, to build it according to the spirit of the gospel; this requires solidarity, defense of human rights and the dignity of persons: the Christian is called to "work for the sanctification of the world from within as a leaven."[32]

(6) A renewed commitment to making Christ present in our world through solidarity, service and charity.

Movements as Response to Need

In a thoughtful presentation to the Bishops, gathered by Pope John Paul II in the year 1999 to reflect on the phenomenon of the new ecclesial movements, Guzman Carriquiry (Sub-Secretary of the Pontifical Council for the Laity, the married lay person with the greatest level of responsibility in the Vatican), elucidated how the movements respond to certain needs which are core aspects of the mission of the Church.

In his view, one of the salient characteristics of the new movements is that they are a charismatic reality which "responds to a deeply felt need today for a rediscovery and revitalization of

---

[31] Cf. *Christifideles laici,* §30.
[32] Cf. *Lumen Gentium,* §31.

the Christian experience in the life of the Church."[33] For him this is crucially important because some ecclesiastical structures and programs have become somewhat jaded or insipid in proposing Christ.

By means of the charisms "of the new movements, the presence of Christ becomes a living reality, a real presence, a source of newness, of capacity for affection and persuasion, just as the person of Jesus was for the apostles and the first disciples two thousand years ago… the movements are ways in which the event of Christ and his mystery in history, namely, the Church, encounter the life of persons, full of joy and hope, without reservations or inhibiting quibbles, of the truth that Jesus is Lord."[34]

Moreover, the charisms enable an existential dynamic of communicating the faith in persuasive, convincing forms consolidated by a life of faith. Given the erosion of much of the Christian environment, which heretofore had been the norm in many societies, the encounter "with witnesses who are walking testimonies of the presence of Christ"[35] is both fascinating and attractive. This is a vital characteristic of the new ecclesial movements which seek to meet man in the heart of his own milieu with a joyful witness to the living Lord.

Movements as a "Providential Response"

The poet T.S. Eliot characterized the society of the last century as being a "rootless generation"[36] and in such an environment it is difficult if not impossible to build community. Some see the arrival of the new movements as a "providential response."

---

[33] G. Carriquiry, "The Ecclesial Movements in the Religious and Cultural Context of the Present Day," *Laity Today* (2000), 55.

[34] Ibid., 55.

[35] Carriquiry, 56.

[36] T.S. Eliot, *The Waste Land and Other Poems*, Faber and Faber, 1964, 33.

Through the charism which calls individuals to follow Christ in a radical way, they are also infused with a "spiritual affinity" which bonds them into communities and movements, living representations of the Church, mysteries of communion in the very heart of humanity. They are "signs of the freedom of forms"[37] which Pope John Paul II alluded to when addressing the Communion and Liberation Movement in 1984.

One of the great emphases of Vatican II was the call, not only to deepen the awareness of the ecclesiology of communion, but to steadfastly work for its realization.[38] The movements embody the mystery of communion and propagate it on the basis of the strong appeal exerted by their community experiences. They seek to provide an antidote to the impersonalism and the fragmentation of many of the societies in which we live. The witness of authentic Christian love can be as compelling a testimony to communion today as it was in the lives of the first Christians.

Fraternity, a Core Characteristic

Characteristic of the new ecclesial movements is the conviction of being believers on the way together. Fraternity and fellowship are core elements of the new ecclesial movements. For some communities, the passage in the Sacred Scriptures, "Where two or three are gathered together in my name, there am I in the midst of them" (Mt 18:20), has become their primary text; only through Christ and in Him is true community and mutual fraternal like-mindedness possible. The experience of community life in the name of Jesus, however, is not an end in itself. It is from the beginning open to others. So the group, that is, the concrete

---

[37] Pope John Paul II, "Address to the Communion and Liberation Movement," *Insegnamenti* VII/2 (1984), 696.

[38] Cf. *Lumen Gentium*, §11.

spiritual community, can also be understood as a "Church in miniature."[39] In this way, the designation of the Church as *Communio* can be translated into an experiential and visible reality.

Such a life in spiritual community is, therefore, stamped with a different sense of brother-sister fraternalism. This, by necessity, has a broad spectrum. It has the security and closeness of a small group, it also has the solidarity of larger communities, particularly in the Church; this means all embracing Catholicism and internationality. Brother-sister fraternalism becomes ministry to others. The way to God leads through the brother and the sister. With that purpose in mind, the various group meetings are intended to be an aid and encouragement. The personal discussions, corrections and encouragements, but especially the experience of not being alone in this endeavor, of being connected to others and of being supported by them, gives to the individuals new strength for their different duties. It can be argued that for today's materialistically minded and consumer oriented society, the orientation towards poverty, as it is being lived by the members of the spiritual communities, is a particularly up-to-date testimony.

The experience of a vibrant community life, which is a hallmark of the new movements, prompts a renewed consciousness and experience of the sacramental, Eucharistic source as the only one capable of building the *communio* that the world is unable to create. They seek to confirm a fundamental precept of *Christifideles laici* that "in order to reconstruct the fabric of human society what is needed first of all is to remake the Christian fabric of ecclesial communities themselves."[40]

---

[39] Cf. *Lumen Gentium*, §11; *Gaudium et Spes*, §48; *Apostolicam Actuositatem*, §11; *Familiaris Consortio*, §49.

[40] Carriquiry, 61.

Catechesis

Another aspect of the new movements is that they have become places of education in the faith, authentic schools of catechesis where "fidelity to Christ and to the Tradition are supported and comforted by an ecclesial environment truly conscious of this necessary fidelity."[41] The movements are places of education which propose Christ as the key to meaning and fullness in every aspect of life. As Vatican II has stressed, "In reality, it is only in the mystery of the Word made flesh that the mystery of man truly becomes clear."[42] The pedagogic methods of the movements bridge the gap between gospel and culture, between faith and reason. They are a "providential response" in that they "educate persons whose Christian experience grows in a more faithful and systematic intelligence of faith as the key to a deeper intelligence of the whole of reality."[43]

Zeal to Evangelize

One of the clarion calls of Pope John Paul II's pontificate was *"Duc in altum"* ("put out to sea" cf. Lk 5:4), which is an appeal to undertake a new evangelization, one which is "new in ardor, in its methods, in its expression."[44] The urgency of the situation was highlighted by Pope John Paul in *Christifideles laici* where he spoke of the masses who live "as if God did not exist.... Whole countries and nations where religion and the Christian life were

---

[41] *Christifideles laici,* §34.
[42] *Gaudium et Spes,* §22.
[43] Carriquiry, 64.
[44] John Paul II, "Address to the Assembly of CELAM," *Insegnamenti* VI 1 (1983), 698. The term "re-evangelization" was first used by John Paul II in Latin America. See also the "Message for the opening of the 'novena of years' promoted by CELAM in preparation for the fifth centenary of the evangelization of America," *Insegnamenti* VII 2 (1984), 896.

formerly flourishing... are now put to a hard test, and in some cases, are even undergoing a radical transformation, as a result of a constant spreading of an indifference to religion, of secularism and atheism."[45] As he pointed out in *Redemptoris Missio*, the numbers of those who are ignorant of Christ has virtually doubled since the Council.[46] Hence the need for mission, something which has joyfully been accepted by the new movements whose members "seek to make the faith present in an explicit and visible way, without fear or calculation, in all the spheres and situations of life as communicators of the extraordinary gift of the meeting with Christ."[47]

New Evangelization

The new evangelization has as its point of departure the certitude that in Christ there are "'inscrutable riches' (Eph 3:8) which no culture nor era can exhaust, and which we must always bring to people in order to enrich them.... These riches are, first of all, Christ himself, his person, because he himself is our salvation."[48]

Fr. Avery Dulles, S.J., in an important essay has identified this focus on evangelization as one of the most significant and surprising shifts in Catholic tradition.

> In my judgment the evangelical turn in the ecclesial vision of Popes Paul VI and John Paul II is one of the most surprising and important developments in the Catholic Church since Vatican II.... All of this constitutes a remarkable shift in the Catholic tradition. For centuries evangelization had been a poor stepchild....

---

[45] *Christifideles laici*, §34.

[46] *Redemptoris Missio*, §3.

[47] Carriquiry, 66.

[48] Pope John Paul II, "Address to Bishops of Latin America," *L'Osservatore Romano*, English Edition (October 21, 1992), 7.

Today we seem to be witnessing the birth of a new Catholicism that, without loss of its institutional, sacramental, and social dimensions, is authentically evangelical.... Catholic spirituality at its best has always promoted a deep personal relationship with Christ.... Too many Catholics of our day seem never to have encountered Christ. They know a certain amount about him from the teaching of the Church, but they lack direct personal familiarity.... The first and highest priority is for the Church to proclaim the good news concerning Jesus Christ as a joyful message to all the world. Only if the Church is faithful to its evangelical mission can it hope to make its distinctive contribution in the social, political, and cultural spheres.[49]

It is in this area of evangelization that the new ecclesial communities have made a huge impact. Central to their work has been a personal encounter with God which has given to them a unique dynamism. As Ralph Martin points out,

the movements can help us remember the catechumenate of the early Church, the preparation for baptism, the exorcisms, the teachings, the community of faith, the meaning of Christian marriage, the need for preparation, for support, for practical teaching and vision; the awesome gift of the Holy Spirit and all his varied ways of working, all his charisms; the mission of Jesus in all its dimensions, teaching, preaching, healing the sick, casting out demons, raising the dead, baptizing in the Holy Spirit, reaching out to the poor and outcast; the universal love of the Father that reaches out to everyone, saint, sinner and non-Christian.[50]

---

[49] Avery Dulles, *John Paul II and the New Evangelization* (New York: Fordham University, 1992), 13-17.

[50] Taken from a talk given by Ralph Martin to National Conference of Catholic Bishops / United States Conference on 26th October 1999. Published by ICCRS.

Considering what the New Evangelization ought to look like concretely in order to be successful, Cardinal Karl Lehmann, says:

> In the future we need places, groups, movements, and communities in which people with a determined will for life come together, learn together, and mutually help each other. That strengthening of faith, hope and charity is becoming ever more necessary today when Christianity is finding itself in the condition of *diaspora*. Only that way is faith able to become recognizable again and obtain a clear profile.[51]

The new ecclesial movements attach importance to the realization of the mission of preaching the gospel, especially in areas where the Church can become the salt of the earth only through the apostolic testimonies of the laity.[52] For example, the Neo-Catechumenate and the Cursillo, which are especially open to committed Christians as well as to the so-called less committed, came into being because of the lack of a true catechesis. In order to credibly put the evangelization into effect, the spiritual movements, according to their particular charism, emphasize and promote interior unity between practical life and the faith of their members.

Missionary Formation

In missionary formation, the movements seem to have generated extraordinary fruits: they have exhibited missionary courage and dynamism, helping many lay people to overcome a certain shyness and inferiority complex when confronting the world.

---

[51] Karl Lehmann, "Was heisst Neu-Evangelisierung Europas?" *Internationale katholische Zeitschrift* (1992), 312-318. Cf. *Lumen Gentium*, §33.

[52] Ibid.

They have also brought creativity and originality to the methods of evangelization.

Their process of formation is demanding. They insist that Christ requires radical choices from his disciples. Unashamedly, they posit the belief that the whole gospel needs to be taken seriously and lived to the fullest. Sweetened forms of Christianity in the long run do not convince anybody. They have the courage to aim high, especially with the youth. One of the secrets of success of the movements is that they do not restrain from requiring decisive choices from people. The movements are not afraid of placing high demands.

The first Christian communities had a strong awareness of being sent out with a mission. Toward the end of Mark's gospel, the Risen Lord says to the disciples: "Go into the whole world and proclaim the good news to all creation" (Mk 16:15). After he very briefly reports on Jesus's ascension into heaven, the evangelist then concludes, "They went forth and preached everywhere. The Lord continued to work with them throughout and confirm the message through the signs which accompanied them" (Mk 16:20). Matthew likewise finished his gospel with the same command, although he somewhat modified it in keeping with the spirit of the theological concept of his work: "Go therefore and make disciples of all nations…" (Mt 28:19).

An additional promise shows that this is an unlimited mission for all times, which the disciples need not be afraid of: "I am with you always even to the end of the world" (Mt 28:20). In light of his view of salvation history, Luke interprets that proclamation as the fulfillment of scripture which has to take place beginning from Jerusalem. The new ecclesial movements situate themselves firmly in this missionary zeal for the gospel to be spread "to the end of the world."

Agents of Human Dignity

The last point which Carriquiry presents is the role of the movements in promoting more dignified forms of life in the midst of the technological world of science, the global economy and the all pervasive world of communication. One of the most negative aspects of this new world order is the sense of *'ennui'* as captured by Camus in his epic novel *L'etranger*.[53] Alienation and an acute sense of non-belonging is a sad and pervasive characteristic of the modern era. Again the work of the movements has proven to be a "providential response." Central to their approach is the conviction that it is necessary to begin with the person, to reawaken faith in him or to introduce him to faith. If a person is a new man in Christ, this newness has an impact on his whole life, his family, his affections, his work. He is able to make Christ present in the various forms and contexts of social life. Like-minded people bond together to form charitable initiatives to promote improvements in the social fabric of society. In this way, the principles of the dignity of the person, of subsidiarity, of solidarity that the social doctrine of the Church propounds for an authentic reconstruction of the social fabric are put into practice, beyond any absolute ideological faith in the hand of the State and the power of the market.[54]

Unity of the Movements

Having come to some understanding and acceptance of the new ecclesial movements in the first phase of their evolution the Church is now in the second phase of recognizing the "substantial unity of the charismatic realities and the institution."[55] Pri-

---

[53] Albert Camus, *L'Étranger* (Penguin, 1967).

[54] Carriquiry, 68.

[55] Ratzinger, "The Ecclesial Movements; a Theological Reflection on Their Place in the Church," 37.

mary in this second phase has been the clear and deep desire for unity. Undoubtedly, one of the interesting developments within the life of the movements has been a drive towards unity not just with the institutional Church but also with each other. On January 17th, 2000, for the first time ever, the founders and directors of new movements and ecclesial communities met in Rome to spend some time together, and exchange ideas, experiences, and good times. The meeting, an initiative of Chiara Lubich, foundress of the Focolare Movement, took place at the Pontifical Athenaeum, "Regina Apostolorum," the university directed by the Legionaries of Christ. The meeting was a follow-up to the commitment made by the movements in the presence of John Paul II during the historic 1998 Pentecost encounter, which gathered some 400,000 members of these new communities in St. Peter's Square.

On that occasion, Lubich had publicly assumed the responsibility to become a link of unity and communion among all these movements, a responsibility she carried out by calling this meeting. In addition to Chiara Lubich, professor Andrea Riccardi, founder of the St. Egidio Community; Fr. Marcial Maciel, founder and general director of the Regnum Christi Movement; Fr. Michael Marmann, president of Schönstatt; and Salvatore Martinez, general coordinator of Renewal in the Spirit in Italy, attended the meeting. Following this event, the participants committed themselves to work together for the building up of the Church.[56]

Undoubtedly the inspiration and the prompting of Pope John Paul II have been hugely influential in encouraging this ongoing work of unity. However, it can also be seen as yet another authentic action of the Holy Spirit who empowers men to reconcile differences and come together in unity. Perhaps in the past there was the all too human tendency to seek self-affirmation and personal

---

[56] "One Spirit At Work," *Newsletter of the Council of Ecclesial Movements and New Communities of the Archdiocese of New York*, 1 (Spring 2001), 1.

supremacy. Like the Apostles, before the Spirit's coming at Pentecost, the communities also succumbed to the temptation to debate "who among them was the greatest" and petty arguments and contests ensued (see Mk 9:34, 10:41). After Pentecost, the Spirit enabled the Apostles to form a "community... of one heart and mind" (Ac 4:32) among themselves and with other disciples.

The new language that they are called to learn, one which everyone comprehends, is the language of Christian humility. Through the Spirit all are enabled to realize the "need in us to be in some way the whole and not just scattered fragments of it."[57] The prayer of Christ is realized, "that they may all be one, as you, Father, are in me and I am in you, that they may also be in us" (Jn 17:21).

One of the Fathers of the Church, Cyril of Alexandria, describes it beautifully.

> Since we have all received one and the same Holy Spirit, we are all, in a certain specific way, united both to one another and with God. In fact, even if, taken separately, we are many and in each one of us Christ makes dwell the Spirit of the Father, nevertheless, the Spirit is one and indivisible. By means of his presence and his actions he reunites in unity spirits that among themselves are distinct and separate. He makes of all, in himself, one and the same thing.[58]

Archbishop Miloslav Vlk of Prague, one of the Cardinals attending the Seminar for Reflection and Dialogue on the Movements, spoke of the witness of unity now in evidence among the new ecclesial movements.

---

57 Raniero Cantalamessa, *The Mystery of Pentecost* (Collegeville, MN: Liturgical Press, 2001), 12.

58 Cyril of Alexandria, "Commentary on John." This is taken from the only collected edition of Cyril's *Opera* produced by J. Aubert, Canon of Notre-Dame, Paris (6 vols. Paris, 1638; reprinted with additions, J.P. Migne, PG 74: 560. Trans. by R.M. Tonneau, 1953).

The Synod for the Laity was held in 1988; at that time, the movements were discussed. There were a number of criticisms and doubts expressed. The movements were regarded with fear, uncertainty, and a degree of rejection by some pastors. As we enter the new millennium much has changed, because, exactly on the tenth anniversary of the Synod for the Laity, in 1998, the Holy Father convoked a meeting of the movements and stated clearly that they "are the fruits of the Holy Spirit." The commitment of the leaders of these movements to get to know one another, to come closer to each other, and to act together seems to me an authentic sign of their genuineness. Unity is the sign of the Church. If the movements can achieve this, it means they have overcome their own limits and expressed a sign of their authenticity, because the Holy Spirit favors unity in the Church, even in diversity.

With this end in view, I think it is important to point out that over the last few years, there have been a number of meetings among the movements. For example, a significant meeting took place in Speyer, organized by the movements, with the participation of local Bishops, as well as Bishop Stanislaw Rylko, the Holy Father's delegate, and many lay persons. This meeting gave a beautiful picture of the Church. I am convinced that the movements are a result of Vatican Council II. If you study the characteristics of some of the movements and read what the Council requested, you will see the harmony. In my opinion, both phenomena — the Council and the movements — are phenomena encouraged by the Holy Spirit.[59]

---

[59] See Internet ref. <http://www.legionofchrist.org/eng/articles/en99100802.htm>.

The new movements, like all the great spiritual reforms of the Church, encourage their members to give personal and communal prayer its proper place. In this challenge they are observing an essential principle of the Christian view of life: the primacy of grace. There is a temptation which perennially besets every spiritual journey and pastoral work: that of thinking that the results depend on our ability to act and to plan. God of course asks us really to cooperate with his grace, and therefore invites us to invest all our resources of intelligence and energy in serving the cause of the Kingdom. But it is fatal to forget that "without Christ we can do nothing" (cf. Jn 15:5).

Four States in the Church?

Such has been the impact of the new movements on the life of the Church that one cardinal (at the seminar of the bishops convened in Rome in 1999 by the Pontifical Council for the Laity to examine the phenomenon of ecclesial movements), asked Cardinal Ratzinger if there would be in the future "a separate Congregation for the movements."[60] Specifically he wondered if, in the future, there would be four classes in the Church: priests, religious, members of the movements, and laity.

In his reply Ratzinger expressed his own view that the traditional tripartite division of priest, religious and laity would remain as a fundamental dimension of the structure of the Church. However, given the close relationship between these three sectors within the movements, it raises serious issues for the Curia who now have to deal with a situation which often presents the "three states under the same roof."[61] Crucially, Ratzinger acknowledged

---

[60] Adriadnus Cardinal Simonis (Archbishop of Utrecht) posed this question in the dialogue with Cardinal Ratzinger which followed some of the presentations made at the seminar "The Ecclesial Movements in the Pastoral Concern of the Bishops," 228.

[61] Simonis & Ratzinger, "The Ecclesial Movements in the Pastoral Concern of the Bishops," 228.

that "organization must follow life"[62] and not the other way around. Indeed, he felt that the "intercommunication between the three states of life within the movements may also represent a stimulus for closer collaboration among the various offices of the Curia."[63] This could be seen as one example of how the Spirit brings life-giving change to the institution through the emergence of an unexpected charismatic development. The Church is waiting not passively but patiently for the role of the ecclesial movements to emerge. Bishops and theologians, together with the leaders of the new movements, are seeking to understand what exactly it means to be an ecclesial movement.

The role of Pope John Paul II in all of this was absolutely crucial. He sought to re-orient the Church to a more correct understanding of the movements by reminding us that "the Church herself is a movement."[64] The term needs further unpacking and theologians and bishops as well as the movements themselves are endeavoring to grasp the full import of the word.

Undoubtedly, the different spiritual awakenings and renewal movements are largely a wholesome disturbance of the traditional order and often, in practice, it is difficult for the institutional authorities to absorb and integrate completely the spiritual impulses. The new ecclesial movements have a legitimate right to be able to develop within the Church but perhaps not in already existing structures.

The Holy Spirit, who guarantees the unique solidarity of the Church with the Lord, grants unity and multiplicity at the same time. He guarantees much more freedom of spiritual effects, of ways of life and also of knowledge than we would allow ourselves. But, in the end, this multiplicity serves a new form of unity. This does not consist in the abolition of plurality, but rather in its free collaboration toward a whole, as St. Paul expressed in his First

---

[62] Ibid.

[63] Ibid.

[64] John Paul II, *Insegnamenti* II, 2 (1981): 305.

Letter to the Corinthians.[65] For this collaboration, it is decisive that spiritual renewal is consciously done and credibly practiced as an enduring mission of all Christians.[66]

In spite of their different histories of origin, outward appearances and spheres of activities, the objectives of the new spiritual movements are to a large extent coming to a profound convergence: the responsible participation in the mission of the Church, to proclaim the gospel of Christ as the source of hope for mankind and renewal for society.[67] The Second Vatican Council emphasized the dignity, importance, and mission of Christian laymen in today's world. In the Dogmatic Constitution on the Church we read: "Therefore the laity, since they are consecrated to Christ and anointed by the Holy Spirit, are wonderfully invited and instructed for all the more abundant gifts of the Holy Spirit to be brought forth in them."[68]

In this way, the Council confirmed what was already happening in the Church, and at the same time gave a still greater impetus to new movements. Besides the already existing movements such as Focolarini, Cursillo, Opus Dei, Communion and Liberation, Marriage Encounter, other different forms of renewal in the Spirit also appeared after the Council. Some were about individual renewal, or the various states of life through the renewal and the enlivening of the grace of the respective sacrament, or about renewal of parish communities.

Common and Diverse Elements

What is common to all these movements is the endeavor to create a style of spirituality suitable to our time, spirituality as an impetus for the renewal of human ways of thinking and willing

---

[65] Cf. 1 Corinthians 12:8-12.
[66] Cf. *Christifideles laici*, 18ff., especially §24, the remarks concerning charisms.
[67] Ibid., §29.
[68] *Lumen Gentium*, §34.

in the spirit of the Gospel, connected with an aspiration for experiencing faith in communion which opens up new approaches to prayer, the word of God, and the sacraments.[69] One can also begin to appreciate the wide range of spiritualities they embrace. They are in many ways very different, each to the other. One can readily see an incredible diversity in the range of movements that have sprung up in every continent of the world over the last few decades.

Community of the Beatitudes

At one end of the spectrum there is a community like the Community of the Beatitudes[70] which was first recognized as a Private Association of the Faithful, established in the archdiocese of Albi (France) in 1985. In 2002 the Holy See further extended this recognition; to approve the community as an "International Private Association of Faithful of Pontifical Right with Juridical Personality." It was founded in France in 1973 by Ephraïm Croissant and his wife Josephine. It is one of the new communities expressing new forms of "consecrated" life. Its members seek to answer God's call by consecrating their lives to God and committing themselves in a community life, both contemplative and apostolic.[71] The community, as the People of God, drawn from the various states of life, gather in a spirit of chastity. Together as married couples, brothers and sisters, celibates, deacons and priests they live according to the principles of the first Christian Community. All the brothers and sisters of the Community of the Beatitudes make commitments of prayer, obedience and poverty. All members strive to live the Beatitudes in a spirit of contemplative

---

[69] M. Tiggs, *Geistliche Gemeinschaften und Bewegunen* (Freiburg-Basel-Wien: Herder, 1992), 473ff.

[70] David Scott, "Community of the Beatitudes," *St. Anthony's Messenger* (March, 2002).

[71] Regina Doman, "Interview with the Beatitudes Community, Quebec," *Our Sunday Visitor* (July 6, 1997).

prayer and solicitude for the poor, donating themselves with joy and enthusiasm in their apostolate in the service of the Roman Catholic Church: parishes, youth, families or media.[72] Currently the community is active in thirty-two countries. It has forty-six houses in Europe, eleven in Africa, seven in Asia, three in Latin America, three in North America, two in Oceania, and three in the Middle East. In total, one and a half thousand religious brothers and sisters live in residential community. Associated with them is a community known as the Family of the Beatitudes. The community's spirituality is a call to live the mystery of the Transfiguration through union with Jesus in his paschal mystery. Based on the charism of St. Thérèse of Lisieux the community emphasizes a life of prayer (especially Eucharistic adoration), obedience and poverty. It is essentially a monastic lifestyle as one of its Denver members, Christine Meert, stated in an interview with David Scott, "We are a family living like monks."[73]

Cursillo

At a different end of the spectrum there is a movement like the Cursillo Community. The Cursillo movement is an interesting example of how movements can be initiated to renew the Church.[74] The Cursillo movement was deliberately begun in 1949 in Mallorca by a pastoral team of priests and laymen under the direction of a bishop. They set out to solve the problem of the

---

[72] See Internet ref. <http://www.catholic.org/cathcom/worldnews>.

[73] Scott, 11.

[74] Cf. Dominic Wiseman and Chris Bryden, *Cursillos in Christianity*, Catholic Truth Society, 2001. Richard Bord and Joseph E. Faulkner, "The Anatomy of a Modern Religious Movement," *American Journal of Sociology* 90, no. 5 (March 1985), 1140-1144. Gilbert Coxhead, "What is the Cursillo Movement?" (1991), 1-6. Luke Jong-Hyeok Sim, "Founder's Charism and Its Outlook. Cursillo Movement and Theology of Conversion," Ed., *The 15th Asia-Pacific Encounter: Cursillos in Christianity, October 11-14, 2001*. Keith Fred Larkin, "A Critique of the Cursillo Movement and a Manual for a Presbyterian Cursillo Programme," Columbia Theological Seminary, 1990.

alienation of the young from the Church and the problem of the lack of Christian commitment in Christian organizations. They developed a method that has since given rise to a powerful international movement. In other words, the Cursillo movement was a movement that was started by Church leaders to make headway in an environment which was resistant to the Christian message and to overcome what was perceived to be an imbalance in a previous movement in the Church (the Catholic Action movement).

It came to birth in the movements of renewal that preceded the Second Vatican Council. Vatican II was such a major event in the history of the modern Catholic Church that there is a certain tendency to date everything from the Council. But Vatican II was itself born out of an effort of spiritual and pastoral renewal that had begun years beforehand. It is telling that many of the new movements were prophetic of Vatican II. Founded in the decades preceding the Council, they anticipated the Council Fathers' call for "the laity to take a more active part, each according to his talents and knowledge in fidelity to the mind of the Church, in the explanation of and defense of Christian principles and in the correct application of them to the problems of our times" (*Decree on the Apostolate of the Laity*, 1:6). The liturgical movement, the scriptural renewal, Catholic Action and other movements of the lay apostolate had begun years before the Council. Everywhere in the Church, people were seeking to find ways of bringing the Church to life in the hearts of men. The Cursillo movement came from the work of such individuals.

Today, it is a worldwide movement with centers in nearly all South and Central American countries, the United States, Canada, Mexico, Portugal, Puerto Rico, Great Britain, Ireland, France, Germany, Austria, Italy, Yugoslavia, Australia, Japan, Korea, Taiwan, the Philippines, Sri Lanka and in several African countries. The movement is a member of the International Catholic Organizations of the Pontifical Council for the Laity in Rome. The goal of the Cursillo movement is that Christ be the prime influence in society. It seeks to develop in adult Christians a consciousness of their power and mission to become leaders in their work of Christian renewal, and to sustain them as they provide a Christian leaven in civic, social, and economic life.

Conclusion

These two movements indicate something of both the variety and the complexity of this new phenomenon. Clearly the ecclesial movements are a complex reality. Neat categorizations are not an option. They have caused the Church more than a little difficulty in terms of definition because they differ so radically in their charisms and in their spirituality. Yet, despite the huge diversity in the range and type, there appear to be a number of common features that characterize their lifestyles and orientation. Their members have a personal relationship with Christ which is usually attributed to a conversion experience through the power of the Holy Spirit; they are committed to the cause of evangelization both by word and action; they are dedicated to a life of prayer; they often subscribe financially to assist the outreaches of their movements; they have a deep affinity with the Church; they adopt a lifestyle which is often counter cultural; they exhibit a joy and dynamism which is infectious and particularly appealing to young people; they have mostly lay leaders and their own statutes and they have their own formation programs; they have their own internal life within their respective movements as well as external missionary outreaches. The various groups and movements are held together by their interest in spirituality. The primary concern is not actions and programs, efficiency and strategy, but rather a renewal of human thinking, a reshaping of the human heart and the human will, according to the spirit of the Gospel. This spirituality is often based on great ideals and masters of spiritual life and uses often traditional but also new techniques and practices of meditation and prayer. The new ecclesial movements also seem to have in common an impetus toward experiences in faith. They want to experience God from within.

Analyzing the various elements that are successfully used by these movements to help bring people to conversion one can cite the use of personal testimony by lay witnesses, the shaping of the message in a kerygmatic manner, the use of small groups to help assimilate the message, the focus on an individual, personal response, and the strong undergirding with prayer and sometimes fasting. In the next chapter I will look more closely at the history and the salient features of three of these new ecclesial movements.

CHAPTER TWO

Three Movements Examined

To begin to examine this new phenomenon of new ecclesial movements in more depth I propose to examine more critically three of the better known to elicit some common trends and characteristics. I have chosen one that had its origins prior to the Second Vatican Council (Communion and Liberation), and two that have emerged since the Second Vatican Council (the Neo-Catechumenal Way and Charismatic Renewal). My method of enquiry will be to outline a short history of each, indicate their main characteristics and missionary activities, their spheres of influence, their spirituality, their association with the Church, their impact on their environment, their weaknesses and strengths, and an overall conclusion on each of them.

A. COMMUNION AND LIBERATION

Communion and Liberation (hereafter abbreviated as CL)[1] is an ecclesial movement founded by Msgr. Luigi Giussani (+2005). Born in Desio, Lombardy, Italy, Msgr. Giussani had his priestly formation at the Seminary of Venegono, where his teachers

---

[1] Luigi Giussani, *Why the Church?*, Queens University Press, 2001. Luigi Giussani, and Robi Ronza, *Communione e Liberazione*. Jaca Books, 1976. Davide Rondoni, *Communion and Liberation, A Movement in the Church*. Queens University Press, 2000.

were Giovanni Colombo, Carlo Colombo and Gaetano Corti, important figures in the Ambrosian Church. The earliest manifestations of the movement date to 1954 but it was only in 1982 that the Pope gave official recognition to the Fraternity of CL.[2] Originating in Milan and spreading rapidly throughout Italy, it is now present in some seventy countries all over the world.

Overview

CL defines itself as a movement because it does not, first of all, take the form of a new organization or structure (there are no membership cards) nor as a special insistence on some particular aspect or practice of the life of the faith, but as a call to live in the present the Christian experience as defined by tradition. The aim of life in CL is to propose the presence of Christ as the only true response to the deepest needs of human life in every moment of history. In the person who encounters and adheres to the presence of Christ there is generated a movement of conversion and witness, which tends to leave its mark on the environment in which he or she lives (family, work, school, neighborhood, society, etc.). Born in the schools where it was first proposed to young people, CL today extends its call to everyone, irrespective of age, occupation, or social position. The aim of CL is the education of its members towards Christian maturity and collaboration in the mission of the Catholic Church in present-day society. In essence they see themselves with three core charisms.

(1) The announcement that God has become man (the wonder, the reasonableness and enthusiasm of this fact). "The Word became flesh and dwelt among us" (Jn 1:14).

(2) The affirmation that this man — Jesus of Nazareth died and is risen — is an event in the present in the "sign" of "com-

---

[2] Luigi Giussani, "La Fraternità di Comunione e Liberazione, L'opera del Movimento," San Paulo: 2002. See also Internet ref. <"http://www.comunioneliberazione.org">

munion." That is a unity of a people guided by a living person, ultimately the Bishop of Rome.

(3) Only in God made man, therefore only in the tangible form of His presence (therefore ultimately only within life in the Church), can man be more truly man, and humanity more truly human.

In recent years, the presence of CL in society has become more specifically attuned to its educational, cultural, and social nature. At a time when politics and the confrontation of ideas seem to have lost their ability to involve people on a personal level, the movement is concentrating on the crisis at the root of all the social and political crises: the crisis in education.

Incarnation as Central

The CL movement, through its publications and the action of committed lay people in the mass media, sets out to reaffirm the centrality of the method of the Incarnation against any pseudo spiritualistic, gnostic, or Pelagian reduction. Moreover, it consciously proposes the Incarnation against every dualistic separation between what is regarded as the temporal and what belongs to faith.

CL's contribution to the Church and the world is thus distinguished by three words: education, fraternity, and works. These are the three factors on which CL spends most of its energy with the aim of contributing to the human glory of Christ in history. Education to maturity in the faith takes place in Christian communities that are present in the various "environments" (school, university, work). Their community life is founded on obedience to authority, on frequenting the Sacraments and on listening to the Word of God. Thereby a person deepens the fundamental dimensions of the Christian event and is called to engage in culture, charity, work and mission.

Origins

The CL movement was born in Italy in 1954, when Msgr. Luigi Giussani initiated a Christian presence called *Gioventù Studentesca* (GS — Young Christian Students), starting from the Berchet High School in Milan. The present name, CL appeared for the first time in 1969, in order to express the conviction that the Christian event lived out in communion is the foundation of man's authentic liberation. The guiding idea of the movement is that Christianity is an event that invests and tends to determine the whole of man's life, as John Paul II affirms in his first Encyclical, *Redemptor Hominis*, in which he set out the program for his pontificate:

> The Redeemer of man, Jesus Christ, is "the center of the cosmos and of history"; faith is therefore the source, the criterion of judgment, and the fully adequate motivation for action.[3]

The fundamental instrument of formation of the members of the movement is a weekly catechesis called "School of Community" or "Community School," in the form of texts, personal meditation and community gatherings. The movement's official publication is the monthly "*TRACCE — Litterae Communionis.*" The whole life of the movement is sustained economically by free voluntary contributions from members. Within the experience of the movement, and as a development of this, was born the lay association called *Memores Domini*, officially recognized by the Pope in 1988. It is made up of persons who commit themselves before God to live, in virginity, the Memory of Christ in the work environment, giving rise to a missionary presence in order to bring the faith into men's lives.

Adults in the movement have initiated works of a cultural,

---

[3] *Redemptor Hominis*, §3.

charitable and entrepreneurial nature, according to the Church's social doctrine, and in line with Catholic social tradition. Many of these adults have collaborated in the birth of the *Compagnia delle Opere* (Companionship of Works), an association of more than 9,000 charitable and business initiatives that try to put into practice the Church's social doctrine.

CL began by organizing study groups, various entertainments, prayer meetings, Masses and cultural presentations. The group consolidated itself and divided responsibilities by sectors, each with its special emblem: universities, workers, families, educators. During university elections, CL's student party *Cattolici Popolari* ("The People's Catholics") attempted to absorb even non-CL Catholic groups. The party founded its own publishing house, Jaca Books, and Italy's universities became a productive field for CL recruitment. *Cielini* (a nickname by which the members are called) began running university cafeterias, student apartments and various other public services throughout Italy. CL's militant anti-Communism made it appealing to Italy's major political party, the (Catholic-based) Christian Democrats and, by 1972, CL was already suggesting planks for the Christian Democrats' political platform. Thwarted in its struggle to defeat Italy's divorce and abortion referendums, CL nevertheless was becoming known as a formidable political force. In 1975, CL's political arm, *Movimento Popolare* ("The People's Movement," or MP) was founded. Vehemently attacked by the Italian left for both its program and its methods, MP became the leader in the struggle for the political unity of Italian Catholics.

Organizational Structure

The organizational structure of a movement like CL is elastic by nature. At its top is the General Council (commonly called the "Center") presided over until his death by Fr. Giussani and uniting the directors in Italy and abroad for every sphere — school,

university, work, culture, etc. — in which the movement oper-
ates. Each of these spheres is led by its own group of leaders. On
the local level — national, regional, or city — the movement is
guided by *"diakonias,"* that is, groups of leaders available for service (as their name indicates) to the life of the community. The
leaders are chosen from among those who show the clearest awareness of the movement's aims and who offer the most generous
witness and dedication of service to the community.[4] Although
CL does not register members, it does have an organizational
structure, with deacons at local, regional, and international levels, and a National Council of representatives from the different
regions and branches of activity, presided over until his death on
22 February 2005 by Don Giussani. He was succeeded by Fr.
Julián Carrón of Spain.

Some 500,000 attend its annual Summer Meeting in Rimini,
and around 80,000 receive its publications. The group has 2,400
business enterprises, managed by *La Compagnia delle Opere* ("Association of Works"), with combined total revenues in excess of
$1 billion. The university cooperative, *Studio e Lavoro* ("Study and
Work") numbers over 200,000 members. Today CL also has
branches in Africa, Latin America, the US and other European
countries.

The CL movement is based on the belief that salvation is
possible for everyone. It requires only that Christ be recognized
as immediately present. They attempt to communicate the awareness that Christ is the one true response to the deepest needs of
people at every moment of history. The person who encounters
and welcomes the presence of Christ undergoes a conversion that
affects not only the individual but also the surrounding environment.

---

[4] Information about the movement as shown on Internet ref. <PRIVATE HREF
="<www.comunioneliberazione.org>." MACROBUTTON HtmlResAnchor
www.comunioneliberazione.org>.

The Religious Sense

The philosophy underpinning the movement is articulated in *The Religious Sense*,[5] a book written by Giussani and the fruit of many years of dialogue with students. Giussani undertakes an exploration of the search for meaning in life. He shows that the nature of reason expresses itself in the ultimate need for truth, goodness, and beauty. These needs constitute the fabric of the religious sense, which is evident in every human being everywhere and in all times. So strong is this sense that it leads one to desire that the answer to life's mystery might reveal itself in some way.

Giussani challenges the reader to penetrate the deepest levels of experience to discover our essential selves, breaking through the layers of opinions and judgments that have obscured our true needs. Asserting that all the tools necessary for self-discovery are inherent within us, he focuses primarily on reason, not as narrowly defined by modern philosophers, but as an openness to existence, a capacity to comprehend and affirm reality in all of its dimensions. Although it is situated within the so-called new religious revival, *The Religious Sense* avoids any sentimental or irrational reduction of the religious experience. In many ways it is a forthright and refreshing call to reassess our lives.

Criticisms

It is quite difficult to give a clear idea of CL's theological orientation, since the movement responds to contemporary reality, according to the guidance of its charismatic leader, Don Giussani. In fact, it is for its nature as a charismatically-guided movement that CL has been most vehemently criticized. Certainly, CL's most characteristic trait is its insistence on the centrality of Jesús Christ, the pivot upon which all must turn — his-

---

[5] Luigi Giussani, *The Religious Sense* (tr. John Zucchi), McGill, Queens University Press, 1997.

tory, society and culture. The message of Christ's centrality is hammered home by CL on every possible occasion.

For CL, Christ is never a merely verbal announcement or moral example, but a concrete, personal reality, who must be the unifying "cement" for Catholicism, imparting immediate relevance and meaning to all life. CL members embrace the words "concrete," "fact" and "presence" — always understood in the sense of a real and living witness in the world. They dislike words like "abstract" and "theory," seeing them as "dis-incarnating" true Christian witness, which must be real in schools, in the workplace, in politics, and in the general culture.

This fierce commitment to being a *real* Catholic "presence" in post-modern society (a society which seems to ask of Christians only that they not be too Christian), lived out during four decades of spiritual and political crises, has been sharply criticized by many as the sign of an "integrist" or "fundamentalist" Catholic mentality.

In the *Cielini* vocabulary, "fact" and "event" are words used to describe Christ. He is the "fact" who has changed and still changes human history, for the individual, and for society as a whole; his life was — and is — the "event" which transcends all merely human theories and philosophies and pours living water on those thirsty for it. It is CL's radical interpretation of the requirements of this unity between faith and life, however, along with the movement's almost dualistic interpretation of the last 500 years of Western history, which have exposed CL to the charges that it is "fundamentalist." CL tends to idealize the Middle Ages as a time of unity between faith and life, and to reject entirely the Enlightenment, the French Revolution, and modern culture, as having interrupted that unity.

Medieval Man as Model

Msgr. Giussani has been asked what he considers the ideal human being. He replies without hesitation: the medieval man.

For the Middle Ages, faith was not a cage to keep out the new and unexpected, and freedom was not the most essential element in every undertaking, but rather participation in God's divine plan for history.[6]

Medieval culture was not concerned with *having*, affirms Giussani, but with *being*. Exactly the opposite is true of contemporary man, victim and prisoner of modern ideology, he says. "Do not think we are nostalgic for the past," Giussani explains. "We are and intend to remain in the forefront, even the *avant-guard....* But our concentration on the future does not mean that we forget our Christian past..., our common inheritance, and the origins of our movement. For that reason we study the history of Christianity and sainthood, and try to rediscover our roots."[7]

While many Catholics see a consistent testimony of faith in the work of such unpredictable religious geniuses as St. Francis of Assisi and Mother Teresa of Calcutta who found that their societies afforded ample opportunity for self-denial and Christian witness, the *Cielini* seem to insist that the faith is life — unity become dogma, obedience, order — one might even say, conformity.

Political Engagement

A characteristic element of Giussani's group is its political commitment. In contrast to many other Catholic movements, which focus solely on spiritual renewal, CL confronts the world as an "alternative" culture, and consolidates its positions in political activity. *Cielini* defend themselves against the charge of "integrism" by stressing their aim as political crusaders is not to

---

[6] Cited in an article by Antonio Gaspari, "Communion and Liberation, Crusaders for Catholic Integrity," *Inside the Vatican* (July 1992): 26. This article is part of a series, "Onward: The Divisions of the Pope," which focused on religious movements in the Church.

[7] Gaspari, 26.

impose a Christian culture and Christian values on recalcitrant, de-Christianized modern men and women, but to fully live out their own profound Christian vision.

The Over Exaltation of Reason

Moreover, Giussani believes that in the Church today there circulates a hodgepodge of old heresies, presented as new ideas. There is a constant emphasis on reason, according to the principles of the Enlightenment, that is, the validity of my "opinion," or what seems to me at that moment to be true. This is a process which is insidiously eating away at Catholicism, a type of subtle Protestantism, infiltrating here and there. Giussani adamantly criticizes those Christians who rely solely on spreading the "word": "A Christianity reduced to words alone, a Christianity which is not reflected and lived as an ontological reality, touching our profound nature, is only a superficial Christianity."

The aggressive and direct manner in which CL confronts those it considers enemies of Christianity, whether within or outside the Catholic community, has generated a barrage of fierce attacks. Many critics of CL say the movement's lack of emphasis on the "word" reflects indifference towards the Gospels. Christianity is, for *Cielini*, an encounter with the Risen Christ — not a moral code, not a set of Church laws, but a life-transfiguring "encounter." Many of the *Cielini* are thus, like many charismatics and Protestant evangelicals, "born again" — they have experienced a profound conversion during their teenage or early adult years. The boldness with which the *Cielini* then call on other Catholics to leave behind a sterile faith for a living one can seem to be the boldness of an initiated "elite," and this explains why some leaders of the Italian Church, including Cardinal Carlo Maria Martini of Milan, have been critical of CL's "sectarian" tendencies — in spite of Pope John Paul II's expressed admiration.

Critical Church Figures

CL, secure in its own Christian "integrity," seems to relate to the political world with a certain arrogance, sparking resentment and antagonism. Many CL-based political figures have been investigated in Italy's "Clean Hands" anti-corruption program. The weekly *Il Sabato*, which for many years mirrored CL thought and policy (it is now out of business), was often criticized by bishops and Catholic intellectuals for assuming an attitude, similar to that of supreme judge.

During the October 1987 Synod of Bishops, Cardinal Martini advised a group of *Cielini* to "practice the Gospel values of poverty and justice" and to "resist the temptations of power." Later that year, Martini's spokesman, Fr. Roberto Busti, wrote to *Il Sabato* in response to accusations against another Catholic newspaper, *Il Resegone* of Lecco: "What is the source of this fiery defense of orthodoxy? This conviction of being in exclusive possession of the truth? This fierce crusade against brothers in the faith?"[8]

Controversy

Antagonism toward CL intensified all during the 1980's as the movement grew and prospered. *Il Sabato* launched ever more intense criticisms of Italian and Western society, suggesting a huge conspiracy, involving Communists, Protestants, secular humanists, progressive political parties, liberal Jesuits, and Catholics committed to ecumenical dialogue, was "selling out" true Christianity.

One of the targets of these accusations was Gianfranco Svidercoschi, former Vice-Director of the Vatican's semiofficial daily *L'Osservatore Romano*, accused of involvement in a secularist-Masonic plot to remove Catholic presence from society. The accusations and counter-accusations became so heated that three

---

[8] Ibid.

Il Sabato journalists were called in to the Milan Archbishopric on March 4, 1988 to respond to infringement of Article 220 of the Code of Canon Law, against unjustified libel. *Il Sabato*, however, continued its virulent attacks against "unorthodox" groups and individuals, until Msgr. Giussani himself withdrew his support from the journal. The weekly finally closed in November 1993.[9]

Criticism of CL's political activity has been widespread. In the January 1, 1988 edition of the Italian daily *La Repubblica's* weekly, *Venerdi*, the sociologist Giovanni Tassani ignited an uproar by blasting the "noisy and spectacular" way in which CL's political arm, the People's Movement, engaged in politics. The article criticized the "privileged" relationship between politicians and CL's business enterprises. To these criticisms, Giussani responded:

> We are attacked for our "culture," which is identical to that of the Pope. Many Italian Catholics are Church-oriented in appearance, but secular in their thought and culture. We are the opposite — secular in our style, and religious in our content. We are accused of being dogmatic, intolerant, and even Fascist, because we believe in the truth as expressed by Christ, and because we oppose all who try to impose untruth.[10]

Giussani believes that engagement with the political process is a risk which the true Christian must take. However, in the wake of Italy's 1993-94 corruption scandals, in which several members of CL's political arm, MP (*Movimento Popolare*) were implicated, CL underwent a complete reorganization. At the present time, CL's Milanese group is attempting to distance itself from politi-

---

[9] Cf. February 1996 issue of *Inside the Vatican* provided by the Eternal Word Television Network; see Internet ref. <PRIVATE HREF="<http://www.ewtn.com>." MACROBUTTON HtmlResAnchor http://www.ewtn.com>.

[10] Luigi Geninazzi, "Interview of Luigi Giussani," *Avvenire*, Sunday Supplement: Agora (1995), 6.

cal activity, renewing itself as an authentic spiritual movement. CL's Rome branch is still heavily involved in politics. Recently, the group committed its efforts to the defense of former Prime Minister Giulio Andreotti, on trial on charges he assisted the Mafia. He, and his *Cielini* supporters, maintained his innocence.

Papal Support versus Episcopal Unease

Another element which has caused disarray in the Italian Church, is the manner in which CL pits the Pope's teachings against statements by certain bishops. The Italian Catholic writer Vittorio Messori once asked Giussani if he ever thought other opinions could possibly be right, and his wrong. CL's founder replied: "I have never experienced that type of doubt. Why should I tire myself in such a manner, when it is so much easier to obey the Holy Father?"[11]

The extremely close relations between Pope John Paul II and CL, particularly at the beginning of Wojtyla's papacy, were confirmed by the Pope himself. During a May 13, 1984 meeting with CL members, the Holy Father said: "We, as the Church, as Christians, as *Cielini*, must be visible in society. Thus we must search for our rightful space (in society), in order to realize this visibility." Wojtyla's phrase "we *Cielini*," was even cited by the Vatican's semiofficial daily *L'Osservatore Romano*. A short time before, the Pope had told another group of *Cielini*: "Your manner of approaching humanity is similar to mine. I can even say, it is the same."[12]

Although derided as "Stalinists of God" and "Wojtyla's Monks" because of their fervent devotion to Papal hegemony, the Milanese priest and his organization enjoyed an unparalleled as-

---

[11] Vittorio Messori, "Interview of Luigi Giussani," *Jesus*, June 1985, 9-10.

[12] Cited in article on the Pope's talks to CL on <PRIVATE HREF="<http://www.comunioneliberazione.org">" MACROBUTTON HtmlResAnchor http://www.comunioneliberazione.org>

cendancy under John Paul II.[13] The Holy Father's sympathy was reciprocated by Giussani. The CL leader once said of John Paul: "We serve this man; with our very existence, we serve Christ in this great man. This Pope is the event which God has brought about; his human figure is the concrete phenomenon which we must observe, hear, follow, and whose mentality we must make our own."[14]

CL's relations with Popes John XXIII and Paul VI were not that warm. It was with the advent of John Paul II that Msgr. Giussani's movement really took off. On February 11, 1982, with the papal decree, *Consilium Pro Laicis*, John Paul II established the Fraternity of Communion and Liberation as a "secular institute" under papal jurisdiction. Thereby the group could operate in any diocese in the world without specific episcopal authority. On December 8, 1988, the Council for the Laity recognized the CL group *Memores Domini* (those who remember the Lord) as a private ecclesial association.

The Fraternity and the *Memores Domini* are the two official structures within which CL functions as a recognized Church organization. The Fraternity is a public association of laymen, and can include married persons. *Memores Domini*, on the other hand, is a private organization which requires its members to profess the religious vows of poverty, chastity and obedience. In fact, the community life of *Memores Domini* members is comparable to that of a religious congregation, in some cases even stricter.

Summary

In a very real sense the reality of Communion and Liberation disturbs the peace. It certainly does not leave people neutral. At this point in time in Italy, Communion and Liberation has ap-

---

[13] Cletus Nelson, "Vatican Shock Troops: John Paul's Holy War" found at < PRIVATE HREF="mailto:<cletus@disinfo.net">," MACROBUTTON HtmlResAnchor cletus@disinfo.net>, written on October 18, 2000.

[14] Gaspari, 26.

proximately 100,000 members, from just about every class, profession and geographical area. CL does not register its members; individuals participate freely in CL activities, whenever and however they wish. Moreover, CL has members in about 60 other countries. In Europe these include Germany, Spain, Portugal, Switzerland, Belgium, France, Great Britain, Ireland, ex-USSR, Poland, ex-Yugoslavia, Hungary, Czech Republic, Slovakia, Romania. In the Americas these include United States, Canada, Mexico, Chile, Argentina, Paraguay, Brazil, Peru, Colombia. In Africa these include Uganda, Kenya, Nigeria. In the Middle East they are active in Lebanon and in Israel while in Asia they have members in Japan and Taiwan. It has become a significant voice not only in the local Church but in the Church universal. Perhaps, at times, it can be accused of an over-aggressive approach in its methods of evangelization. Some have gone as far as branding it a cult.[15] Nevertheless, it has called people to a radical and committed Christian lifestyle and it challenges in a very forthright manner the secularism which is so pervasive in our society. CL enjoyed the unqualified support of Pope John Paul II who enabled its existence and influence to spread throughout the universal Church.

B. THE NEO-CATECHUMENAL WAY

The founder of the Neo-Catechumenal Way[16] is Kiko Argüello. In the late 1960's this Spanish painter *cum* itinerant troubadour experienced an existential crisis. He discovered in the suffering of innocent people the awesome mystery of the crucified Christ present in the "least" of the earth. Such a discovery made

---

[15] Gordon Urquart, *The Pope's Armada* (New York: Prometheus Books, 1999). See also by the same author "A Dead Man's Tale," *The Tablet* (March 22, 1997), 367-370.

[16] K. Walsh, "An Exclusive Presence," *The Tablet* (July 2, 1994), 831-832. G. Gennarinn, "The Role of the Christian Family in Announcing the Gospel in Today's World," *L'Osservatore Romano*, English Edition (October 19, 1987), 18-19. See also Ricardo

him abandon all things and, following in the footsteps of Charles de Foucauld, he went to live among the poor people of the slums of "Palomeras Altas" in the outskirts of Madrid. It was there that a Spanish woman, Carmen Hernàndez, a graduate in chemistry, came to know Kiko Argüello. She had come in touch with the renewal of the Second Vatican Council thanks to Monsignor Farnés Scherer (a liturgist) and had been called by her bishop while trying to gather together a group of people with a view to evangelize the miners of Oruro (Bolivia).

The environment of the slums was one of the most degraded in society, mainly made up of gypsies and "quinquis" (white nomads) as well as illiterate people, tramps, thieves, prostitutes, young delinquents, etc.... Kiko's artistic temperament, his existential experience, his previous formation as a catechist of the "Cursillos de Christianidad,"[17] Carmen's thrust for evangelization — formed in the Institute of the "Misioneras de Cristo Jesùs" — her theological preparation (she has a licentiate in theology), her knowledge of the Paschal Mystery and the liturgical renewal of the Vatican Council, together with the environment of "these poorest of the poor" of the earth, were the elements that created the "*humus*," "*the laboratory*" in which a kerygmatic, theological and catechetical synthesis came into being.

For the Church and with the Church

This kerygmatic synthesis touched the hearts of the poor people of the slums who responded with immense gratitude and

---

Blazquez, *Neo-Catechumenal Communities: A Theological Discernment*, St. Paul Publications, 1987. Cf. Ezekiel Pasotti, ed. *The Neo-Catechumenal Way According to Paul VI and John Paul II* (Maynooth, Ireland: St. Pauls, 1996). In this book there is an appendix that outlines a brief synthesis on the Neo-Catechumenal Way which Kiko Argüello and Carmen Hernández gave to Paul VI in 1974. See also an interview given by Kiko Argüello to *30 Days Magazine* in November 1997. It can be found at <www.members@aol.com/fatherpius/neo5.html>.

[17] See pages 29-31 for an account of the Cursillo movement.

thus the first Christian community of the Neo-Catechumenal Way was born. It is this community that gave birth to the first seed, the first "*mustard seed*" which mushroomed beyond all imaginings. That "seed" came to the notice of the Archbishop of Madrid, Bishop Casimiro Morcillo (one of the General Secretaries of the Second Vatican Council) on the occasion of his visit to the slums. There he personally witnessed the action of the Holy Spirit and consequently defended it, blessed it and identified it as a true realization of the Council. He then sent this seed to the parishes of Madrid with the recommendation that the parish priest should always be at its center. At the same time he approved "*ad experimentum*" some necessary liturgical adaptations for a Christian initiation centered on the Word, the Liturgy and the Community.

Some Important Statistics

After more than thirty years of the work of evangelization, this complex reality of the Neo-Catechumenal Way has spread to one hundred and five countries and five continents. Up to the year 2001 the Communities were present in five thousand parishes of eight hundred and eighty dioceses with a total of sixteen thousand, seven hundred communities of which eight thousand are to be found in Europe, seven thousand three hundred in the Americas, about eight hundred in Asia and Australia and six hundred in Africa. About one and a half thousand seminarians are preparing to become priests for the new evangelization in forty-six "*Redemptoris Mater*" missionary diocesan seminaries that the Neo-Catechumenal Way has helped open, of which thirty-two are already canonically erected. Born of an explicit request by their respective bishops, they are presently distributed in the following way: twenty in Europe, fourteen in the Americas, six in Asia, one in the Middle East, three in Africa and two in Australia. Since 1989, seven hundred and thirty-one priests formed in the "*Redemptoris Mater*" seminaries have been ordained. Moreover, two thousand young people in various vocational centers, helped by their respective catechists and priests are making a first serious verification of their vocation. In this way they prepare to enter one of the *"Redemptoris Mater"* seminaries. Likewise, numerous young girls (about four thousand) from the Neo-Catechumenal Communities have entered convents, especially of enclosed orders.[18]

Fruit of the Second Vatican Council

While the Council, and then the Magisterium, were rediscovering the centrality of the catechumenate in the process of evangelization for the non-baptized, and, in a certain way, also of the baptized, Kiko Argüello and Carmen Hernàndez had discovered, in the suffering of the innocent, the mystery of Christ crucified, present in the least ones of the world.

As already mentioned, their rediscovery in concrete form of doing a post-baptismal catechumenate came to the attention of the hierarchy first through the Archbishop of Madrid, Casimiro Morcillo, who discerned the action of the Holy Spirit in their work and blessed it, seeing in it the fulfillment of the Council. Then, in 1972, the Neo-Catechumenate was studied in depth by the Congregation for Divine Worship, which was in the process of publishing the RCIA. After two years of study on the liturgical-catechetical praxis of the Neo-Catechumenal Way, they published in *Notitiae*, the official journal of the Congregation, a note of praise for the work that the Neo-Catechumenal Way was doing in the parishes, recognizing in the Way a gift of the Holy Spirit for implementing the Council. Together with the Congregation, the name was agreed upon: "Neo-Catechumenate," or "Neo-Catechumenal Way."

---

[18] Information obtained from the official Neo-Catechumenate Internet site at <www.camminone.com>.

Aims

Theoretically, the movement aims to recreate the lengthy period of training and teaching that catechumens underwent in the early Church. This necessitates an intimate knowledge of biblical texts, a powerful experience of the Church as a small accepting community, the revitalization of the Easter Vigil as the central Christian feast, and participation in Saturday evening Eucharist and sacraments with a degree of commitment exceeding what is expected in the average parish. It sees the Church ideally as consisting of small communities with members being held together by strong communitarian bonds; lay catechists have a central position and members are expected to be generous in giving of their time and income to the group's activities. They may be required to go as missionaries of the Way to any part of the world at any time decided by the Way's authorities. The Way is not concerned with any particular social or political programs. Their task, they claim, is verbally to proclaim the Word of God. Little or no cultural knowledge of the area to be evangelized is necessary; all that is needed is zeal and dependence on the power of the Holy Spirit.[19]

What is the "Way"

The most comprehensive written document explaining the Neo-Catechumenate Way is a fifty-five page transcript based on a presentation given by Kiko Argüello to the Bishops of Denver in 1993. In this he points out that there are three phases: Pre-Catechumenate, Catechumenate and Election. The Catechumenate begins with the first scrutiny. Afterwards there is a second scrutiny where a sign with respect to goods must be given. Then there is an Initiation to Prayer; then the *Traditio*, the *Reditio*,

---

[19] See A. Oresanz, "Spanish Catholicism in Action," *World Catholicism in Transition* (1988), 141ff.

the Our Father and the Election. After the Election, there is the renewal of baptismal promises (with the white tunic). This process is known (by Kiko) as the rite of baptism of adults by stages involving three phases: Humility, Simplicity and Praise. In other words, the people realize that it is necessary to be small in order to be a Christian and that such simplicity can only be given by the Lord in prayer.

The success of the movement has depended greatly on the role of the late pope, John Paul II. His affirmation of the Neo-Catechumenate culminated in a decree of the Pontifical Council for the Laity whereby the Statutes of the Neo-Catechumenal Way were approved on the 29th of June, 2002. In the audience granted to the initiators and those responsible for the Neo-Catechumenal communities throughout the world on the 24th of January 1997, on the occasion of the commemoration of the thirtieth anniversary of the Way, the Holy Father had expressly urged that the Statutes be drafted, "a very important step which opens the way towards its formal juridical recognition by the Church, giving you a further guarantee of the authenticity of your charism."[20] From that moment onwards, the initiators, accompanied by the Pontifical Council for the Laity, began the process of articulating statutory norms to regulate the praxis and the insertion of the Neo-Catechumenal Way into the ecclesial fabric.

On the 5th of April 2001, with a personally signed letter addressed to His Eminence Cardinal James Francis Stafford, president of the Pontifical Council for the Laity, Pope John Paul II, reaffirming the above mentioned request, reconfirmed this Dicastery as competent to approve the Statutes of the Neo-Catechumenal Way and entrusted to its solicitous care the future accompanying of the Way itself.[21]

It was the Pope himself who in 2004, with his letter of the 5th of April, addressed to Cardinal James Stafford, President of

---

[20] *L'Osservatore Romano,* 25 January 1997, 4.

[21] *L'Osservatore Romano,* 17-18 April 2001, 4.

the Pontifical Council for the Laity, entrusted to that Dicastery of the Roman Curia the work of bringing to a conclusion the process of juridical approval of the Statutes of the Way. By doing so he assigned to the Pontifical Council for the Laity the necessary competence in relation to other interested Dicasteries of the Curia. The drafting of the Statutes of the Way was concluded, therefore, in close dialogue and collaboration between the Pontifical Council for the Laity and those responsible for the Way. Interestingly, in the above letter, John Paul II expressed his wish that, once the Statutes were approved, even if in this case it was not a question of an international association of the faithful, it would be the role of the Pontifical Council for the Laity, as distinct from other organisms of the Holy See, to continue to accompany the apostolic activity of the Neo-Catechumenal Way.[22]

Distinctive Nomenclature

In these Statutes, the Neo-Catechumenal Way is considered neither as an association, nor as a movement, nor as a grouping of persons who establish among themselves a special formal link for achieving particular objectives in the Church. Rather than describing a juridical entity already codified in the Law of the Church, these Statutes limit themselves to presenting the juridical expression of the reality lived in the Way. The Statutes are nothing other than the synthetic expression of a reality that already has a life in the Church. Again they have made present a

---

[22] *The Statutes of the Neo-Catechumenal Way, Canonical observations* by Prof. Juan Ignacio Arrieta as quoted on Internet site <www.camminoneocatecumenale.it/en/statuti6.htm>. Prof. Arrieta is a professor of Canon Law in the Pontifical University of the Holy Cross, Judge of the Ecclesiastical Tribunal of the Vatican City State, Referendario of the Segnatura Apostolica, Consultor of various Dicasteries of the Roman Curia, including the Pontifical Council for Legislative Texts, Member of the International Association of Canonists "Consociatio Internationalis Studio Iuris Canonici Promovendo." Ezekiel Pasotti, ed. *The Neo-Catechumenal Way According to Paul VI and John Paul II* (Maynooth, Ireland: St. Pauls, 1996), 127-135.

vital fact in the life of the Church, namely that life precedes law. The approval of their Statutes represents above all the confirmation of an apostolic praxis lived and consolidated in recent years.

A Program of Formation, not an Association

According to the synthesis given by Kiko and Carmen, the Neo-Catechumenal Way is lived out within the existing structure of the parish, and in communion with the Bishop, in small communities each composed of people who are different in age, social status, outlook and culture. The synthesis explains that the Neo-Catechumenate is not a group formed spontaneously, neither is it an association, nor a spiritual movement, nor an elite within the parish. Rather, it is a group of people who wish to rediscover and to live Christian life to the full; to live the essential consequences of their Baptism by means of a Neo-Catechumenate divided into different stages, like that of the early Church, but adapted to their condition as baptized persons.

Language School Analogy

In trying to explain this new phenomenon and to emphasize that this phenomenon of the Way is not of an associative type, Professor Arrieta used the analogy of a language school to try to clarify the relationship among the members. In a language school or any other kind of school there certainly appears a system of stable relations among the students who follow the courses over a period of years. However, this does not mean that the students establish relationships of a juridical nature among themselves, however intense these human relations may be. On the other hand, for example, in such schools, a definite program of teaching has to be followed, and those responsible for carrying it out, the professors and the directors of the school, must keep to a methodology already clearly established, accepting the obligations which follow from the respective positions of formation or of direction which each occupy.

> In the same way, in the itinerary of formation repre-
> sented by the Neo-Catechumenal Way, no new juridi-
> cal relationships are established, other than those that
> each of the faithful already has in virtue of his belong-
> ing to the Church. Therefore, in these Statutes a list
> of rights and duties of those who benefit from this ac-
> tivity will not be found. Instead, there is a fairly pre-
> cise indication of the tasks that the catechists, or those
> who, in complete freedom, make up the various teams
> of *responsibles*, must perform. All of this, as I have said,
> is a direct consequence of the nature of the Way, which
> in no way corresponds to the characteristics of an as-
> sociation.[23]

Although they have been at pains to deny the nomenclature of "movement" the fact that the Holy Father invited them to the Pentecost Meeting of Ecclesial Movements in Rome in 1998 and that he regularly referred to them as an ecclesial movement, all of this brings them under the scope of this book.

Moreover, Kiko himself, in a testimony he gave to a significant number of Bishops, reflecting on the reality of the new movements seems to have become more comfortable with this description.

> What is the Neo-Catechumenal Way? A religious con-
> gregation? Certainly not. A Movement? In some sense,
> without doubt; the Pope said that even the Church is
> a movement. But if we wish to sum up more than thirty
> years in the life of the Way throughout the world, we

---

[23] Arrieta, *The Statutes of the Neo-Catechumenal Way, Canonical observations.*

can say, as indeed the name suggests, that it is a *neo-catechumenate*, a new catechumenate, a Christian initiation in adult faith.[24]

The difficulty over categorizing them and the limits of language specification merely highlight the range and diversity of this new phenomenon which has impacted the Church in the latter part of the twentieth century.

Redemptoris Mater

A key element within the Neo-Catechumenal Way is the number of priests who are members. Among the articles of the second section of their Statutes, detailed reference is made to the "Initiation and Formation to Priestly Vocation," and to the "*Redemptoris Mater*" diocesan seminaries. Article 18 begins by quoting a passage from the *General Catechetical Directory* (no. 86), where it notes that, like any other catechetical itinerary, the Way is also "a means for awakening vocations to the priesthood and of particular consecration to God in the various forms of religious and apostolic life and for enkindling a special missionary vocation in the hearts of individuals." Their only unique characteristic is that a specific element of their formative *iter* is participation in the Neo-Catechumenal Way. In summation then one can say that the Neo-Catechumenal Way aspires to be a theological-catechetical synthesis, a catechism, a catechumenate for adults, an itinerary of Christian formation for modern man.[25]

---

[24] Kiko Argüello, "The Neocatechumenal Way: Testimony to the Bishops," *The Ecclesial Movements in the Pastoral Concern of the Bishop: Laity Today* (2000), 160.

[25] Ricardo Blazquez, *Neo-Catechumenal Communities: A Theological Discernment*, St. Paul Publications, 1987. See also an extensive Internet site <http://www.christusrex.org/www2/ncw>. This site has a comprehensive series of articles and background information on the Neo-Catechumenate, all of which are very supportive of its ministry.

Catechumenate in History

In the Early Church, the Catechumenate was formed by a synthesis between Word (*Kerygma*), Liturgy and Morality. The early Church had above all a *Kerygma*, that is an announcement of salvation. This announcement of the Gospel that was made by apostles like Paul and Silas, brought about a moral change in those who heard it. Empowered by the Holy Spirit, the auditors began to change their lives. This moral change was sealed and encouraged through the sacraments, concretely, through the reception of Baptism which was given in stages. In this way the primitive catechesis was a "gestation" to divine life. The Baptism instituted by Jesus was from the very beginning the rite of initiation into the community of his disciples (Ac 2:41-42; 19:1-7; Mt 28:19). Early reflection saw it as incorporation into the death and resurrection of Jesus (Rm 6:3-4), an incorporation into Christ (Gal 3:27). New Testament teaching also insisted on the necessity of Baptism (Mk 16:16; Jn 3:5).

When the Catechumenate disappeared over the following centuries, this synthesis of *Kerygma* — Change of Life — Liturgy was lost. The *Kerygma* as a call to faith that implied a moral decision no longer existed; it was transformed into a scholastic doctrine. Morality became an internal forum, a private act. The Liturgy became the same for all. In a profound way the Neo-Catechumenal Way seeks to recover this period of gestation, this synthesis between *Kerygma*, Change of Life and Liturgy.

A Witness to the Secular World

Pope John Paul II stated that the Neo-Catechumenate is an "itinerary of Catholic formation valid for our times and our society."[26] He saw it as one of the providential actions of the Holy Spirit. In the letter of 12 April 1993 to bishops, priests, itinerants

---

[26] Pope John Paul II, *Letter of Recognition*, 1990.

and families of the Neo-Catechumenal Way assembled in Vienna, Pope John Paul II praised their missionary activity. After recognizing that the Neo-Catechumenal Way is able to respond to the challenges of secularism, the diffusion of sects and the shortage of vocations he stated:

> This Way appears particularly qualified to contribute in deChristianized areas to the necessary *reimplantio ecclesiae* leading man in his moral behavior towards obedience to revealed truth and even contributing to the very fabric of society, which is decayed due to a lack of knowledge of God and His love.[27]

Community Initiation

Communities of thirty to fifty people, well grounded in the Catholic faith, establish further communities within the parish and charisms such as catechists, missionaries and vocations to the religious life normally appear with the passage of time. These communities are meant to establish adult Christians and, eventually, the aim of the Neo-Catechumenate is to bring lapsed Catholics back to a sacramental life and convert people of other denominations to the Catholic faith.

Neo-Catechumenal communities are never established within a diocese without the approval of the local ordinary. With his permission, the itinerant catechists approach priests, often by simply knocking on parish rectory doors, and preach the *Kerygma* to them. They will often be given an opportunity to describe their own experiences of the Risen Lord through the Neo-Catechumenal Way and priests may be invited to have this same experience in their own parishes. Those priests who accept this invitation are told of some of the practical aspects of the Neo-Catechumenate and a

---

[27] Ezekiel Pasotti, ed. *The Neo-Catechumenal Way According to Paul VI and John Paul II* (Maynooth, Ireland: St. Pauls, 1996).

catechesis is arranged for a suitable time. The catechesis itself is usually given on two nights of the week for approximately eight weeks. At the end of this period, those present are asked to attend a weekend away, called a *convivence*. Further catecheses on certain aspects of faith are provided at the *convivence* to prepare those in attendance for what they can expect. On the Saturday morning the catechists describe at some length the development of the Mass from patristic times to the present day. The primitive liturgy is presented in a positive light, whereby the catechists emphasize the Passover aspect of the sacred meal.

The addition of different elements of the Mass throughout the centuries, up until the Second Vatican Council, are viewed by the catechists as things which detract from the essence of the Eucharist. They go on to state that the new order of Mass promulgated since the Council is more in line with primitive liturgical practice and that the Neo-Catechumenate liturgy (which is celebrated on the Saturday evening), itself a derivative of the new Mass, allows the Eucharist to shine in all its glory once again. At the conclusion of the *convivence*, the catechists ask whether anyone would like to continue this way of conversion they have already begun with the catechesis itself. Although most do not know exactly what this may entail, many do take up the offer and, if the catechesis has been particularly successful, a community will have been established. This being so, "*responsibles*" are elected for the community who will be left to organize practical matters within the community itself and provide a link between the community and the catechists, who are forever vigilant to ensure that the new community is faithful to the Spirit.

Community Formation

A community is formed when a group of people embark on a program of catechesis called the Neo-Catechumenal Way. It is a course that can take twenty or more years to complete. Led by a catechist, it is marked by six successive stages, culminating in the renewal of the promises of Baptism, usually at the Easter Vigil. A priest is said always to be present during the catechesis. A close bond develops between people on the course who share their thoughts and problems on the spiritual journey. But members of the same family are very often in different communities as they will have embarked on the Way at different times and are at different stages.

The communities usually meet weekly and celebrate the Eucharist on a Saturday night. They attend Mass on Sundays with the rest of the parish, but the Neo-Catechumens tend to keep to themselves. They may be active in parish life but their Eucharist is not always listed in parish bulletins. The liturgy of the Neo-Catechumenate takes three basic forms: the "Celebration of the Word," the "Penitential Celebration" and the "Celebration of the Eucharist."

1. Celebration of the Word

The celebration of the Word takes place once a week, normally on a Tuesday or a Wednesday night. Prior to the night itself, a designated group of the community, normally three to five people, meet to prepare the celebration. This involves a study of a particular theme in the Bible, typically based on a reading of Xavier Leon-Dufour's *Dictionary of Biblical Theology*. At the end of this meeting readings are selected (one each from the historical books, the prophets, epistles and Gospels) for the meeting of the entire community. The celebration of the Word normally takes place in a room of suitable size such as a classroom or a parish hall. If a priest is present he will preside over the celebration itself. Otherwise, the head responsible of the community will lead the liturgy. The celebration begins with an introduction to the theme of the night, a procession song, and an invocation to the Holy Spirit: "O my Lord, send your Spirit to renew the face of the earth." The first three readings are introduced and proclaimed in turn, followed by a song. The Gospel is then introduced by a member of the preparation group and proclaimed by the priest (or the head responsible in his absence). A time of prayerful response follows the proclamation of the Gospel. The brothers and sisters of the community are invited, either by the priest or head responsible, to respond to the Word of God in view of their own experience. The priest will begin his homily after the contributions are completed. Following the homily, everyone is invited to stand for spontaneous prayers of the faithful and the priest (or responsible) ends this time with the sign of peace (a kiss on each cheek). A final blessing is given and the final song is sung.

2. Penitential Celebration

This is essentially a celebration of the Word which climaxes in a penitential rite. Following the proclamation of the Word the president often gives a homily and then begins the penitential rite itself with an opening prayer. If more than one priest is present, these will hear one another's confessions while the cantors begin singing songs of a penitential nature. Private confessions are then heard by the priests in the midst of the community. Each recipient of the sacrament of Penance then goes back to his or her place and, if possible, does the penance prescribed and then continues to sing with the community. At the completion of individual confessions, the president sings the "Penitential Anaphora" and the sign of peace is given. The celebration ends with a final prayer and blessing and the priest(s) process out with a final song.

3. Celebration of the Eucharist

The Neo-Catechumenate celebration of the Eucharist is loosely modeled on the *Novus Ordo Missae* but has a number of elements that are peculiar to the Neo-Catechumenate. Certain parts of the New Mass have been either deleted or placed in a different location. The Sunday liturgy is celebrated on the Saturday night because, we were told, the Jewish Passover was always celebrated from the evening before the Sabbath. In addition, the Neo-Catechumenal liturgy is rarely celebrated in the normal place of

Catholic worship because most churches, being built prior to the Vatican Council, do not necessarily accommodate the communal nature of the celebration. Community members are arranged in a horseshoe shape around three sides of a large central "altar" (which often consists of a number of tables joined together, covered with altar cloths and adorned with side candles, a candelabra and flowers). Behind the altar is a lectern from which introductions are made, certain songs are sung and the Word of God is proclaimed. The celebrant sits behind the lectern and may be flanked by an acolyte. The credence table is normally located to one side of the celebrant. The celebration of the Eucharist is prepared in a similar manner to that described above for the celebration of the Word, with the exception that the readings used are taken directly from the Missal.

Criticisms

One of the most prevalent criticisms of the Neo-Catechumenate is that it offers an exclusivist model of Christianity focused entirely on the Way with an excessive focus on sin. This was certainly one of the findings of the Clifton enquiry which reported that the Way was represented as the only means of salvation. Since this enquiry stirs up and examines many of the issues pertaining to the tensions that arise when the Neo-Catechumenate arrives in a parish, I have decided to look at this in some detail.

The Clifton Enquiry[28]

At the beginning of January 1996, the Right Reverend Mervyn Alexander, Bishop of Clifton, established a panel of Enquiry to consider the claim made by some parishioners in at least

---

[28] Report into the presence and activities of the Neo-Catechumenal Way in the Diocese of Clifton, November 1996 taken from Internet ref. <www.ourworld.compuserve.com/homepages/Ronald-haynes/nc-erpt.htm>

three parishes in the Diocese that their parishes had suffered harm and neglect through the presence and activities of the Neo-Cat-echumenate. These views were made known to Bishop Alexander in accord with Canon 212.1.2 which states:

> Christ's faithful, conscious of their own responsibility, are bound to show Christian obedience to what the sacred Pastors, who represent Christ, declare as teachers of the faith and prescribe as rulers of the Church.
>
> Christ's faithful are at liberty to make known their needs, especially their spiritual needs, and their wishes to the Pastors of the Church.
>
> They have the right, indeed at times the duty, in keeping with their knowledge, competence and position, to manifest to the sacred Pastors their views on matters which concern the good of the Church. They have the right also to make their views known to others of Christ's faithful, but in doing so they must always respect the integrity of faith and morals, show due reverence to the Pastors, and take into account both the common good and the dignity of individuals.[29]

The task of the Enquiry was to determine whether the presence and activities of the Neo-Catechumenal Way had caused harm in each parish and to what extent. The Enquiry sought information from those who were members of the Neo-Catechumenal Way, from parishioners of the three parishes who were not members and from persons outside of the parishes or outside of the Clifton Diocese who wished to offer their views. The panel appointed for the Enquiry included: Mr. Tom Millington (chair) a Member of the Lord Chancellor's Panel of Independent Inspectors assisted by Mrs. Valerie James, a Member of the Diocesan

---

[29] The Canon Law Society of Great Britain and Ireland, *The Canon Law, Letter and Spirit* (Dublin: Veritas, 1995).

Trustees and a former National President of the Union of Catholic Mothers and by Fr. Barnaby Dowling, Parish Priest of Wells.

According to the Enquiry panel, all those beginning the Neo-Catechumenate program had to undergo a process of conversion in which a team of catechists from outside the parish would publicly castigate their commitment to God and suggest they had little or no faith. Great emphasis was placed on the sharing of the "inner self" with their brothers and sisters.

There were periodic scrutinies by catechists that caused people "considerable stress." The panel said there was little doubt that the Way had caused "some spiritual, personal and mental anguish for people." It also heard evidence to show that no members of the Neo-Catechumenate anywhere in Britain had at that time reached the end of the Way, which is supposed to culminate in the renewal of baptismal vows and the wearing of a white tunic. This was despite the fact that the first community at the parish of St. Nicholas of Tolentino had existed for about 16 years.[30]

The panel expressed disquiet about the lack of full cooperation by the Neo-Catechumenal Way in their investigation and they expressed misgivings about how the Neo-Catechumenate had used letters of papal support to justify some of their behavior. Indeed, the panel took specific aspects of the papal letters from Pope John Paul II to challenge the integrity of some of their behavior. Specifically they cited a number of key extracts from the Pope's address to priests of the Neo-Catechumenate. In the view of the panel this was "unequivocal guidance from the Holy Father."[31]

> It is the task of the pastors to make an effort to see that the parishes benefit from the positive values that these communities can bring and as a result be open to the communities. However, it must be very clear that the

---

[30] Elena Curti, "Who Are the Neo-Cats?" *The Tablet* (January 6, 2001).

[31] Report into the presence and activities of the Neo-Catechumenal Way in the Diocese of Clifton, November 1996 taken from Internet ref. <www.ourworld.compuserve.com/homepages/Ronald-haynes/nc-erpt.htm>

communities cannot put themselves on the same plane as the parish community itself, as a possible alternative. On the contrary, they have the duty to serve the parish and the local Church. It is precisely this service given in conjunction with the parish and the diocese, that the validity of these experiences within the Movements and Associations can be seen.[32]

Secondly:

Here I offer another point for reflection: Exercising your ministry for the guidance of the Neo-Catechumenal Communities, you do not feel sent only to one particular group but to serve the whole Church.... The spiritual gift which priests have received in ordination, the Second Vatican Council reminds us, does not prepare them merely for a limited and circumscribed mission, but for the fullest, in fact the Universal, mission of salvation....[33]

Cogently the pope states:

The first demand that is made on you is to know how to keep faith, within the community, with your priestly identity.... It would be an illusion to believe you can serve the Gospel by diluting your charism in a false sense of humility or in misunderstood manifestation of fraternity.... Do not let yourselves be deceived! The Church wants you to be priests and the lay people you meet want you to be priests and nothing other than priests.[34]

---

[32] Private audience for 2,000 Priests of the Neo-Catechumenate Community (9 December 1985) reported in *The Neo-Catechumenal Way According to Paul VI and John Paul II* (Maynooth, Ireland: St. Pauls, 1996), ed. by Ezekiel Pasotti, p. 193.

[33] Ibid., 194.

[34] Ibid., 193.

These points were forcibly underlined because many of the movement's opponents had argued that rather than being a force for renewed dynamism and evangelization within the parish, the arrival of the Neo-Catechumenate had led to division and a form of elitism. Priests were perceived to be partial to the Neo-Catechumenal Way to the detriment of the rest of the parish. If true, this would be a betrayal of the commission that the Pope had entrusted to them when he said,

> Another delicate and irrenounceable responsibility that I hope you will undertake is to build up ecclesial communion, not only within your group, but with all members of the parochial and diocesan communities. Whatever service has been entrusted to you, you are always the representative of and the *providi cooperatores* with the bishop to whose authority you should feel particularly united. In effect, in the Church it is the right and duty of the bishop to give directives for pastoral activity (cf. Canon 381) and everyone has the obligation to conform to these. Do this in such a way that your communities, while losing nothing of their originality and richness, can be inserted harmoniously and fruitfully into the family of the parish and the diocese.[35]

In the panel's view this last reference by the Pope to the need for harmony could be regarded as a "signal of disharmony"[36] known by the Holy Father to exist in consequence of the Neo-Catechumenal involvement in parishes.

Unity Within the Diocese

In section 11 of *Christus Dominus* the following definition is given of a diocese:

---

[35] Ibid.

[36] *Clifton Report*, 2.30.

a portion of the People of God which is entrusted to a bishop to be shepherded by him with the assistance of his presbyterate so that, loyal to its pastor and gathered by him in the Holy Spirit through the Gospel and the Eucharist, it might constitute a particular Church in which the one, holy, catholic, and apostolic Church of Christ is truly present and active.

One can see that the definition is not purely canonical, but includes spiritual and theological elements. The diocese is defined as a group of people, "a portion of the People of God," gathered in the Holy Spirit through Gospel and Eucharist around the bishop and presbytery. [The French speak of the three "E's": évangile, eucharistie, évêque (gospel, eucharist, bishop).]

These spiritual constituent elements make this portion of the People of God an individual Church, in which the one whole Church is present and active. As *Lumen Gentium*, §23 said, the one whole Church exists only in and out of the particular Churches. This is another point at which the Council insists that the whole mystery of the Church is realized in individual Churches. This was one of the texts that after the Council inspired the considerable theological literature on the local Church and on the whole Church as a communion of communions in the Holy Spirit.[37] The activities of the Neo-Catechumenate were perceived by the Clifton Enquiry to endanger this communion.

Another area of concern was the relationship between the Rite for the Christian Initiation of Adults (the RCIA for short) and the Neo-Catechumenate methodology.

It is apparent to the panel that there are competing claims and competition between the Neo-Catechume-

---

[37] This is one of the tensions that the arrival of the new ecclesial movements brings to the fore. I will address this tension in some detail in Chapter VIII.

nate Way and the RCIA where these exist in a parish.[38]

These features were demonstrable in the three parishes under investigation in the Clifton Enquiry, albeit in differing degrees, influenced by the particular circumstances. The degree of
competition, difficulty or even potential conflict arises first from
the attitude of the parish priest towards the RCIA concept and
method if he is an adherent of the Neo-Catechumenate Way;
secondly, whether there is an assistant priest in the parish who
has an interest and is permitted to be involved in the RCIA but is
not part of the Neo-Catechumenate Way: thirdly whether the
leader(s) of the RCIA takes a passive stance or otherwise towards
the parish priest who is a member of the Neo-Catechumenate Way
and who at best is disinterested or at worst has antipathy towards
the RCIA. The Enquiry cited a situation from Gloucester to illustrate their concern.

Difficulties have arisen in the parishes where the RCIA and
the Neo-Catechumenate coexist. In Gloucester, a fundamental
point was raised as to how the parish could have "parallel
catechumenates." One of the more obvious problems arises from
the use of the same terminology and similar rites and stages. This
is not surprising given that the Neo-Catechumenate is described
as a "post-baptismal catechesis," and follows very closely in its ideas
and aims to the ideals laid out in the "General Instruction" of the
RCIA. In other words, two different "catechumenates" offer a path
to faith, bring people to a closer knowledge and relationship with
Jesus Christ, and yet do not share the same methods. This useful
phrase ("parallel catechumenates") highlights how confusion is
caused.[39]

---

[38] Subsequently, an article written by Ronald Haynes appeared in the Diocesan Justice and
Peace Newsletter of the Clifton Diocese (January, 1996). It confirmed many of the sus-
picions and concerns raised by the Enquiry over this issue. A copy of the Newsletter can
be found at <www.ourworld.compuserve.com/homepages/Ronald-Haynes/nc-
jpnl1.htm>.

[39] *Clifton Report*, 4.12.

Other concerns expressed at the Enquiry related to secrecy and clandestine behavior that caused gossip and disunity within the parish. One unnamed contributor to the Enquiry argued "the secrecy has in itself developed an atmosphere of uncertainty which leads to mistrust. Inevitably the parish is rife with gossip/misinformation which is divisive." Another representative explained with some apparent authority and experience that "over the years, secrecy can have an insidious effect on people and organizations, often without their being aware of it. There is suspicion, exclusiveness, division and sense of an 'elite' at my parish; I have found these barriers hurtful within the Church."[40]

The panel regarded these comments to stem from a person of "clear perception," and declared themselves deeply troubled by the words "barrier" or "division" or "elite," terms unacceptable in the context of unity. Unfortunately, such words were to be found in many other letters from the parishes; in the panel's view, "they seem to be genuinely held and by their consistency and repetitiveness they convey to the panel much more than a ring of truth."[41]

Another alarming criticism that the panel referred to was the lack of ecclesial accountability by the Neo-Catechumenal Way. The proponents acknowledged virtually no accountability to anyone outside of the movement. Once a bishop had given them permission to operate within his diocese, they functioned as a law unto themselves and it became difficult for the diocesan authorities to restrain them or bring their activities to a close without the most stringent use of authority. In the view of one contributor to the panel,

> It is highly regrettable and to many of the laity a cause for scandal that on the one hand the movement is supported and blessed by the Pope and by certain highly placed curia officials, and yet on the other hand is not subjected to any apparent ecclesiastical control. They

---

[40] Ibid., 4.53.
[41] Ibid., 4.53.

seem to have manipulated persons and institutions so that they appear to be exempt from the stringent control exercised over bishops, clergy, religious orders, theologians, colleges and other institutions. Even more seriously, the movement within the Church as a whole deals directly with the Pope and with Rome. This means that both Rome and the movement go over the heads of the bishops, thus weakening the episcopal structure of the Church and ignoring the collegiality of the bishops.[42]

The dearth of documentary evidence about the Neo-Catechumenate methodology and course content was another source of concern for the panel. The latter was apparently justified on the grounds that it is an oral tradition and is transmitted primarily in this fashion.

In its conclusions the Enquiry acknowledged the good that the Neo-Catechumenate Way had done, it recognized the papal approval it had received, and it affirmed the missionary zeal and commitment of the membership. Yet its overall assessment of the Neo-Catechumenate Way was a damning one.

However, our Enquiry has concluded that the Neo-Catechumenate has damaged the spiritual unity of the three parishes.[43]

Pursuant to this report, the Bishop of Clifton decided to discontinue the Neo-Catechumenate within his diocese. He circulated a letter to explain his decision.[44] In essence he stated that he had initially allowed the Neo-Catechumenal Way into the diocese in the hope that it would generate a new enthusiasm for evangelization. However this had proven not to be the case and there

---

[42] Ibid., 4.T.2.

[43] Ibid., 146.

[44] See appendix to this chapter which reports the full contents of the letter. This was found at Internet reference <http://www.petrus.ns.net.pl/clifton.htm>.

was significant evidence to indicate that they had actually done "spiritual harm" and caused disunity within the diocese. Hence the Neo-Catechumenate was being discontinued within his diocese.

Counter View

At least one canon lawyer who reviewed this case expressed surprise at the methodology used by the Enquiry and voiced his concern at some of the conclusions.

I feel that one must question the lack of canonical input or expertise on the part of the panel. Their report contains several dubious assumptions and recommendations. The first and most basic of these is the assertion that the unity of a Catholic diocese demands that there be one chief pastor.... However, his authority is not as exclusive as the panel appears to suggest.... The right of the bishop in regard to associations of the faithful is simply one of coordination....

A second questionable assertion in the report is that all should see Rite of Christian Initiation of Adults as the authentic way of evangelization in parish life.... Participation in the R.C.I.A. cannot be demanded of those who are already baptized ... the Neo-Catechumenate is essentially about the spiritual formation of its members, however these may be defined. As such it is entitled to its legitimate autonomy, provided that it does not interfere with the life of the parish, or other pastoral endeavors. As an international private association, even if this is not its choice of terminology, it does not need the bishop's permission to operate in his diocese, nor, in my judgment, does he have the power to order its absolute discontinuance....[45]

---

[45] Gordon Read, "The Canonical Status of Ecclesial Movements," *Canon Law Newsletter* (March 13, 1997).

However, the Clifton experience has not been an isolated incident. There has been tension between the Neo-Catechumenate and a number of bishops throughout the world.[46] Some antagonistic critics suggest that the Neo-Catechumenal Way exemplifies many of the characteristics of a cult or a sect.[47] Such critics say that it demands a total and unquestioning commitment from its members and submission to the authority of its organizers; they accuse it of being elitist and frequently divisive within parishes. Moreover, it demands an excessive time involvement from priests/ religious and it often acts without reference to existing parish structures.

---

[46] Some bishops censure the movement for trying to create "a Church within the Church." The fact of the Neo-Catechumenate liturgies taking place on Saturday evenings, perhaps several at the same time for different groups, and all outside the normal Sunday services (in which Neo-Catechumenate members apparently do not participate) upsets bishops. This situation has created a myriad of problems between bishops and the movement. For example, Cardinal Giovanni Saldarini, Archbishop of Turin, issued a Decree on May 15, 1995, in which, after praising positive aspects of the Neo-Catechumenate experience, he canceled their separate activities and restored all his parishes to normal diocesan pastoral supervision. Likewise Cardinal Hume issued a statement in 1995, after widespread consultation with his priests, that it is not appropriate to integrate further the Neo-Catechumenate into the diocese of Westminster, beyond the three parishes where the Neo-Catechumenate flourished successfully. Although the Cardinal was happy for Neo-Catechumenate seminarians to study at the diocesan seminary, he did not intend to ordain them as priests of the diocese of Westminster. The Cardinal stated his high esteem for these students but underlined the difficulty of incorporating into the diocesan priesthood in this diocese those who chose to remain priests of the Neo-Catechumenate movement. See also the Internet site at <www.ourworld.compuserve.com/homepages>.

[47] Leslie Thomas, "Catholic Sect accused of Brainwashing," *Sunday Times*, April 23, 1995. In this article Thomas cites Monsignor Buckley, the Vicar General of Clifton who stated that it could be compared to extremist cults because "it smacks too much of a sect and there is a danger of psychological damage to those who follow it. It has been divisive and has caused a lot of hurt in some parishes. Several bishops share my concerns." See also Richard P. McBrien, "The New Movements in the Church," *Essays in Theology* (February 11, 2002). See also Gerard Arbuckle, "Is the Neo-Catechumenate Way Compatible with Religious Life?" *Religious Life Review* 33, No. 164 (Jan-Feb 1994). See also Enrico Zoffoli, "The Neo-Catechumenal Way; A Fearful Danger to the Faith," *Christian Order* (April, 1995).

The Way as Anti-Inculturation?

These critics contend that the Way rejects the Gospel commitment to inculturation.[48] Inculturation is the dynamic and evaluative interchange between the Gospel and cultures, "an ongoing process of reciprocal and critical interaction and assimilation between them."[49] As evangelizers we are not free to choose or reject inculturation. It is a Gospel imperative. As John Paul II says: "The Church's dialogue with the cultures of our time (is) a vital area, one in which the destiny of the world… is at stake,"[50] and "The synthesis between culture and faith is not just a demand of culture, but also of faith." Inculturation is a complex and difficult process for it "presupposes," writes the Pope, "a long and courageous (effort)… in order that the Gospel may penetrate the soul of living cultures."[51] This is so because *inter alia* inculturation assumes:

(a) that the interaction is between two cultures. It is not a simple encounter between the Gospel and a culture, because the Gospel comes to our times as already embedded in a particular culture of the time of the evangelists. There must be an ongoing discernment to discover what is at the heart of Christ's message, and what belongs to Hebrew/Greek cultures of his time and that of the evangelists.

(b) that the Gospel message is also further encased in the centuries-old culture of the evangelizer; the Gospel can be adequately proclaimed only if the evangelizer can remove this cultural baggage and present only what pertains to Gospel faith.

---

[48] See G. Arbuckle, *Earthing the Gospel: An Inculturation Handbook for the Pastoral Worker* (London: Geoffrey Chapman, 1990), 15-25.

[49] M. de Avezedo, "Inculturation and the Challenge of Modernity," (1982): 11.

[50] *L'Osservatore Romano*, 28 June 1982, as cited by A. Shorter, *Towards a Theology of Inculturation* (London: Geoffrey Chapman, 1988), 230.

[51] Ibid.

(c) that the Holy Spirit is already acting within cultures even before evangelization begins; evangelizers are to recognize this presence through acknowledging values that conform to the Gospel. Hence, the need to approach cultures with a critical respect, even a sense of awe in the presence of the Holy.

(d) that there is to be a dialogue, sponsored by evangelizers, between the Gospel and cultures. But dialogue is impossible if evangelizers are not prepared to be open to the culture of the people being evangelized by learning as much about their way of life as is possible — the language, for example. To act otherwise is to insult the people one wishes to help. There is no shortcut to this process, unless the Holy Spirit works miracles and they are not the normal way of evangelization!

As measured by the demands of inculturation outlined above, it could be argued that the methodology of the Way is seriously flawed. In their enthusiasm to preach the Good News, the Way's followers remain uncritical of the distinction between the message of Christ and the ways it is expressed in the cultural language of the apostolic times. This is precisely the oppressive situation that Peter and Paul condemned at the Council of Jerusalem (Ac 15:1-35). The rituals and catechetical material of the Way's evangelizers are prepackaged in Europe and they are then imposed on other cultures, with no dialogue considered necessary or advisable. This inhibits the inculturation process. It appears at this stage of their development that there are no concerted attempts among the Way's evangelizers to prepare themselves for work in cultures so different from their own. Simple trust in the Holy Spirit is no substitute for the serious cultural openness and respect for diversity, discernment and pastoral competence that Paul VI considered essential for inculturation. The Way also has a tendency towards dogmatism. The Clifton Enquiry indicated that its followers were not prepared to dialogue with people questioning their pastoral assumptions and methods; they had the truth, so dialogue is unnecessary.

Delicate Problem

In April 2001, Pope John Paul II pointed out that the statutes for the Neo-Catechumenal Way posed a "delicate" problem, regarding the relations between priests and laity. The Pope wrote, in a letter to Cardinal J. Francis Stafford, the president of the Pontifical Council for the Laity, that it was crucial for the organization to indicate "submission to the pastors of the Church." Even when the Statutes were approved and the Way was validated as an authentic charism for the Church, Cardinal Stafford pointed out "four areas that require special attention in the life of the Way: the relationship with the bishops, the priests and all the dimensions of the parish and the other ecclesial communities, as well as scrupulous respect for the individual's freedom with a special emphasis on the 'internal forum'."[52]

Conclusion

The emergence of the Neo-Catechumenal Way brings in its train a host of questions and tensions. For example, questions about the status of priests in the Neo-Catechumenal Way actually involve two different issues. One question is the relationship between the movement and the hierarchy of the Church: how does the group fall within the structure of hierarchical authority? The other question involves the responsibilities of priests who are members of the movement: from whom should they take their orders? This is a critical question in the ongoing emergence of the movements within the institutional Church. Moreover, the freedom of the individual members to journey towards God without undue pressure or invasion of one's own personal interiority is of paramount importance. Hence the stress on the freedom of the "internal forum" when the Statutes were being approved.

---

[52] Address of His Eminence Card. J. Francis Stafford to the Itinerant Catechists of the Neo-Catechumenal Way, Porto San Giorgio, Sunday, 30 June 2002 available at <www.camminoneocatecumenale.it/en/st>.

Critically the relationship between the Way and the local parish is one that is fraught with danger, as the Clifton Report so clearly highlights. This central point brings to the fore the relationship between the local, particular, Catholic Church and the universal Catholic Church. It probes the delicate, multilayered, linkage between the valid authority of the Petrine, as exercised by the Pope, and the independence of the local bishop who exercises legitimately his own jurisdiction within his own diocese. There are no easy solutions to some of these issues and they raise controversy just as in the early Church the question of circumcision for the Gentiles produced heated debate.

Papal Support

Yet, Pope John Paul II was at the forefront in shepherding the Neo-Catechumenate into the heart of the Church. He believed in the authenticity of their charism and he took a very visible and personal interest in championing their cause. He entrusted them to the care of the Pontifical Council of the Laity, underlining their essentially lay state. Perhaps he also was aware of the danger of clericalizing the movement and this prompted his decision to entrust them to this dicastery. Clearly, the Pope was impressed by the vitality of their witness, lives committed to evangelization, dedicated itinerant catechists who wander the world to bring people to Christ. He welcomed with joy the number of young men and women who have consecrated their lives to God through the priesthood and religious life. Vibrant Christian families committed to the Way bear living witness to another providential action of the Holy Spirit. If mistakes have been made, perhaps through an excess of zeal, or lack of sensitivity towards parish realities, it remains clear that, on their part, there has been a very clear willingness to be under obedience to the Church, as evidenced by their consistent filial devotion to the Papacy throughout their history.

The local Church may also need to accept some responsibility for the tension between them and the Neo-Catechumenal

Way. At times, the local parish perspective can be too narrow and too comfortable; the zeal and dedication of this new movement undoubtedly challenges and upsets. Yet, their formal recognition in 2002 by Pope John Paul II confirms their ecclesial identity and it is now the responsibility of those dissenting voices within the Church to perhaps reappraise their often critical perspective.

C. Charismatic Renewal

The year before he died, Joseph Cardinal Bernardin (1928-1996), a supporter of many renewal movements, in addressing the Charismatic Renewal movement[53] in his own Archdiocese said: "It is my firm conviction that one of the greatest fruits of the Second Vatican Council is the rise of the Charismatic Renewal in the Catholic Church."[54]

The charismatic movement entered Catholic life in early 1967. At a retreat weekend some students from Duquesne University in Pittsburgh experienced a profound conversion and new power and the presence of the Spirit in their lives.[55] Gradually they were able to name the experience and to call it the "baptism of the Holy Spirit." The expression *baptism in the Spirit* refers to the experience of the past gift of the Spirit passing into present power. This experience does not replace the sacramental life of the Church but describes what should happen to people when they are bap-

---

[53] Cf. Paul Josef Cordes, "The Call to the Catholic Charismatic Renewal of the Church Universal," Ed. Franciscan University of Steubenville Press Office, 1992. Peter Coughlin, *Understanding the Charismatic Gifts*, CCSO Bread of Life Community, 1988. René Laurentin, *Catholic Pentecostalism*, DLT, 1977. Ralph Martin, *Unless the Lord Builds the House: the Church of the New Pentecost*, Notre Dame: Ave Maria Press, 1974. Kevin Ranaghan, *The Lord, the Spirit and the Church*. Notre Dame: Charismatic Renewal Services, 1973. Simon Tugwell, *Did You Receive the Spirit?*, DLT, 1972.

[54] Joseph Cardinal Bernardin, *SCRC Spirit* (May/June 1997). Homily given on Pentecost 1995, published by the Southern California Renewal Communities, PO Box 1389, Redondo Beach, CA 90278.

[55] See Internet ref. <www.spiritualitytoday.org/spir2day/823431rakoczy.html>.

tized and confirmed, although it often does not happen. It can be described in the language of classical Christian spirituality as a "second conversion," when the living of one's Christian life comes alive in ways not previously thought possible. Charismatic Renewal stresses elements which are central to Christian life: conversion and commitment to Christ. These are not past events of one's sacramental history, but a new gift of God to the believer, regardless of one's past religious experience.

Baptism in the Spirit

A key dimension of the experience of Charismatic Renewal is baptism in the Spirit. It is not a second baptism but a profound deepening and in some ways an appropriation of one's initial baptism. Much theological reflection has been given to this topic. In 1991, a leading Catholic scripture scholar, Fr. George Montague, S.M., former head of the Catholic Biblical Association, and a leading Catholic ecumenical theologian, Fr. Killian McDonnell, O.S.B., published a major study analyzing the theological and scriptural aspects of the "charismatic experience."[56] Their findings are quite significant.

In brief, they conclude that the charismatic experience of "baptism in the Holy Spirit" is in essence what Scripture and the Fathers of the Church for the first eight centuries of the Church's life describe as being integral to the experience of the sacraments of Christian initiation. Based on Patristic evidence they state:

> Thus, from Carthage in North Africa, Poitiers in Gaul, Jerusalem in Palestine, from Caesarea in Cappadocia, from Constantinople, and from Antioch, Apamea, Mabbug, and Cyrrhus in Syria, we have witnesses to the reception of the charisms within the rite of initia-

---

[56] Killian McDonnell and George Montague, *Christian Initiation and Baptism in the Holy Spirit* (Collegeville, MN: Liturgical Press, 1991).

tion.... Once again, accepting the baptism in the spirit is not joining a movement, any movement. Rather it is embracing the fullness of Christian initiation, which belongs to the Church.[57]

While the more unusual, to our time at least, features of the Charismatic Renewal such as speaking in tongues, prophecy and healing, tend to draw the most attention, the most important feature is that which is termed "baptism in the Holy Spirit," or the fundamental encounter with Christ and the filling with the Holy Spirit that the New Testament presents as normal for Christian initiation. Terminology can be debated, external expressions can vary, but the underlying reality and experience seems to be something for the whole Church. And indeed, many movements in the Church are witness to the varied aspects of this same reality. One could say that the work of the movement is to lose itself in the wider Church.

The beginnings of this can already be seen. As Archbishop Paul Cordes, President of the Pontifical Council *Cor Unum*, speaking on behalf of Pope John Paul II, said on the occasion of the twenty-fifth anniversary celebration of the Charismatic Renewal in the Catholic Church:

> The Charismatic Renewal has a great contribution to make in the years ahead to the proper understanding and renewal of the sacraments of Christian initiation so that all God's people may one day experience a greater fullness of life in Christ by being — as you call it — "Baptized in the Spirit."[58]

---

[57] Killian McDonnell and George Montague, *Fanning the Flame: What Does Baptism in the Holy Spirit Have to Do With Christian Initiation?* (Collegeville, MN: Liturgical Press, 1991), 21-22. The longer work on which *Fanning The Flame* is based, is: *Christian Initiation and Baptism in the Holy Spirit* (Collegeville, MN: Liturgical Press, 1991) by the same authors.

[58] Cordes, "The Call to the Catholic Charismatic Renewal of the Church Universal."

This conviction of the immediacy of God's presence in one's life overflows into practices of piety. Charismatic prayer is characterized by the praise of God. God is worshiped for the divine goodness. Charismatic prayer is further described by its deep trust in the power of the Spirit to answer prayer. "Believe and you will receive," is the axiom of intercessory prayer.

Charismatic life has developed a practical theology of the gifts of the Spirit. Not only are persons taught that everyone is gifted by the Spirit for service in the body of Christ, but the appearance of these gifts is expected throughout the community. Also very significant is the rediscovery of what have been termed the "spiritual gifts," for example, prophecy, gifts of wisdom and knowledge, a practical use of discernment in personal and communal settings. Although much attention has been focused on the gift of tongues throughout the history of the Charismatic Renewal because it appears to be a very unusual type of prayer, it is but one of the gifts of the Spirit. While these gifts are very important in charismatic prayer, they are actually gifts to the whole Church and should not be interpreted as only curious phenomena within charismatic prayer meetings. Even more significant in charismatic teaching is the conviction that Christians live and act in the power of the Spirit, and that this power is not abstract but concrete and definite.

Another religious element in charismatic life is love of the Scriptures. Very frequently people who receive the baptism in the Spirit find themselves almost irresistibly drawn toward the Word of God. At times this impulse to be nourished by the Scriptures has veered into a fundamentalist interpretation of the Word. Yet the desire for scriptural teaching remains.

No less important is the renewed love of the sacramental life of the Church which often follows one's baptism in the Spirit. The faith-filled and exuberant celebrations of the Eucharist which are sometimes called "Charismatic Masses" are the result of a new and intense desire to worship together in the fullest possible way, that is, in the liturgy. Rediscovery of the power of the Sacrament of Reconciliation, especially in its healing dimension, has been a continuing characteristic of charismatic religious life. In many ways, forms of the celebration of this sacrament by charismatics predate the official revisions of the rite of the sacrament.

An important element in charismatic religious life is the emphasis on healing in its physical, psychological, and spiritual dimensions. The confidence among charismatics that God will answer prayer has extended beyond mundane needs to earnest belief that God continues to make people whole at all levels of their being. Healing has been part of charismatic life from its earliest days in the late 1960's. Gradually, teachers such as Francis MacNutt,[59] Matthew and Dennis Linn[60] and Sr. Briege McKenna[61] have helped to advance the understanding of the theology of healing and to aid persons in learning how to pray with confidence for the healing power of God.

Community

Charismatic life lays stress on the importance of community life for Christian growth and development. Initiation into a prayer group or community is generally done in a systematic way, often through a series of formation instructions. The accent from the beginning is not only on personal growth but also on the importance of being part of a community. In many communities throughout the world, the informal commitment of members has gradually been institutionalized by the development of various types of "covenant communities." The covenant, which expresses the community's own understanding of commitment, is freely entered into by the new member. In some communities, commitment is for a specific time; in others, the commitment is open-ended, remaining in force until the person or the community or both feel that it is time to change or conclude one's membership.

---

[59] Francis MacNutt, *The Power to Heal* (Notre Dame, IN: Ave Maria Press, 1977).

[60] Dennis Linn and Matthew Linn, *Healing Life's Hurts* (New York: Paulist Press, 1977).

[61] Briege McKenna, *Miracles Do Happen* (Dublin: Veritas Publications, 1987).

Much more significant than community structures is the emphasis in charismatic teaching that membership in a community is part of normal Christian life. In other words, no one lives her or his Christian life alone. Whether people assemble in a prayer group of twenty members or in a large community such as the Word of God in Ann Arbor or the Emmanuel in France, the stress is the same. One lives one's life in Christ with other Christians and does not pursue sanctity as a rugged individualist. Charismatic Renewal has given birth to many types of communities with varying kinds of structure. Many persons live in households of non-related persons; others share meals, prayer, and some leisure time on a regular basis with other members of the community.

Evangelization

Charismatic life includes emphasis on evangelization and social action, though the latter has not always been pursued with the same vigor as the former. From the initial days of charismatic gatherings, there has been a stress on the need to witness to the power of the Spirit in one's life. The constant emphasis in the teaching of prominent charismatic leaders has been the Christian's mandate to preach the Gospel. Many persons involved in the Charismatic Renewal find that, before their baptism in the Spirit, they had nothing or very little to share with others about their Christian experience. Now they feel impelled to share the good news of what God has done in their lives.

Social Action

The second area, that of social action, is much more problematic in charismatic life. Although one international leader, Ralph Martin, stated publicly in September 1979, that there is no longer any choice between evangelization and social action, the practical choice in charismatic communities is usually for evangelization at the expense of social action.

By far the most common understanding of social action is that of doing the works of mercy on an individual basis. Little concern is evidenced for changing the structures of our society which produce injustice on a massive scale. This lacuna, and sometimes refusal, is due to two causes.

First is a theology of Church-world relationships that envisions a confrontation of "Christ against culture," in Niebuhr's terms. Many Catholic charismatic communities have been influenced by a Protestant evangelical emphasis that the world is corrupt and that Christians must not enter into it, lest they be contaminated. At its extreme, one can find a minor apocalyptic emphasis in charismatic teaching which presents the "end-time" as near at hand.

A second reason for the lack of interest in social justice stems from many charismatic communities' primary agenda of community building and personal renewal. This vision sees that the change of structures cannot happen in society until people's hearts are first changed. It is a restatement of the eternal dilemma of the relation between contemplation and action. The practice of many charismatic communities, which concentrates on building up small parochial Christian communities to the exclusion of all but the immediate needs of their neighbors must be challenged.

There is some evidence of change. A number of communities throughout the world such as the Community of His Kingdom in Washington, D.C., work to insure that justice, and not only the works of mercy, permeates community life. The volume by Cardinal Leon-Joseph Suenens and Dom Helder Camara, *Charismatics and Social Action: a Dialogue*, was written to urge charismatics to reflect on the necessity of working for social justice. It remains true, however, that all of charismatic life does not yet take seriously this responsibility.

The Charismatic Renewal has had a profound effect, both directly and indirectly, in five areas of Catholic Christian life. Since the Spirit is present in the whole Church, credit for these developments cannot be given only to the charismatic movement. Still, ideas and practices which are often associated with the charismatic movement and even regarded as typical of charismatic life are appearing throughout Church life.

Liturgical Renewal

The first is a more widespread emphasis on the prayer of praise. Praise and adoration of God have always been seen as the "highest" form of prayer; ironically, they also have seemed to be the least common type of prayer. One now hears in homilies, prayer services, and spontaneous prayers a greater stress on the praise of God, even from people not at all interested in "charismatic prayer." Greater appreciation of liturgical prayer as worship has helped the charismatic emphasis on praise and adoration to become more universal.

Music

A second gift of the renewal to the Church is much more obvious. That is its music. Many songs that were once first sung at prayer meetings have now entered into the standard repertoire of parishes and other communities. They have as it were become mainstream and found an authentic place in the normal liturgical life of the Church. They reinforce the first effect of the renewal in Church life.

Preaching

A third area to be influenced is that of preaching. While it is comparatively easy to chart the flow of charismatic songs into the mainstream of Church life, measuring the influence on the

Church's proclamation of the Word of God is more difficult to do. Charismatic life is most probably not the main source of the change. The accent on scripturally based homilies since the Second Vatican Council has gradually moved the themes of the Church's preaching from moralizing to proclaiming the good news of Jesus. More and more frequently, those who preach exhort persons to deeper commitment to the Lord, to a more fervent openness to the Spirit, to a greater desire for prayer. The themes may sound charismatic and were very likely judged such in 1969; today they are simply basic Christian preaching.

Healing

A fourth area is healing. There are two important developments here. The first is in the manner of the celebration of the Sacrament of Reconciliation. Three or four years before the Church officially revised the rite of this sacrament, persons involved in the renewal were finding that much more was needed in order to celebrate this sacrament more fruitfully. Not only did people find that confessing and talking on a face-to-face basis were necessary, but they also intuitively felt the need to ask for healing of the roots of their sinfulness. Laying on of hands, praying together, examination of the basis of one's sinfulness — all now parts of the official individual rite of the sacrament — seemed to come forth spontaneously from people who desired more from this sacrament. While the numerical count of confessions has declined dramatically in the last decades, it is not unusual to see very long lines of people waiting to celebrate this sacrament at charismatic conferences all over the world.

Also significant in the area of healing is prayer for actual physical, psychological, and spiritual healing. Although belief in healing has always been part of Catholic life, it has generally been relegated to shrines such as Lourdes and to the need for miracles in order to canonize a saint. In the development of charismatic life, prayer for healing was offered from the days of the earliest meetings. The language of prayer for healing has gradually ceased to be an exclusively charismatic dialect; it has once again become the common language of the Church. The renewal of the Sacrament of the Anointing of the Sick, with its emphasis on praying for physical healing and not only strength to bear one's illness, gives striking testimony to this. Healing has entered into the prayer of the Church in a more tangible way. It is no longer unusual to hear a person pray for healing who would never attend a prayer meeting, although generally there is a major difference in the degree of expectation that the healing will occur. Many persons involved in the Charismatic Renewal pray with intense expectation that God's healing gift will be evident; often people not associated with charismatic life pray for healing, believe in it, but do not profoundly expect that it will happen.

Family of God Community, Ireland

A concrete example of this is found in one of the ministries of an ecclesial community, The Family of God, which is based in Dundalk, Ireland. Each month in a large local church they animate a monthly concelebrated Healing Mass which includes the Sacrament of Anointing. This liturgy has passed its twenty-fifth year and it continues to respond to the needs of those physically, mentally, and spiritually afflicted. *De facto* there is an all-encompassing atmosphere of prayer focused on healing. In addition to the Sacrament of Anointing being made available by the priests, intercessory prayer is simultaneously led from the ambo, and Prayer Ministry Teams are available throughout the church for people to request prayer personally for themselves or others for whom they wish to pray.

The Family of God, which is essentially a lay community, has responsibility for a public Oratory in the midst of a busy shopping center from where it exercises a range of ministries including an SOS Prayer Line which has over ten thousand calls a year. The fact that a public Oratory with the Blessed Sacrament reserved has been entrusted to the care of an ecclesial community that is predominantly lay in character is a highly significant and indeed prophetic sign in the midst of our world.

Active Evangelization

A final effect of charismatic spirituality in the mainstream of Catholic life is in the area of evangelization. The word "evangelization" and the practice of evangelizing are no longer the exclusive property of the Bible Belt and various evangelical groups. What was once a strange experience for Catholics — telling the good news (and not just "making converts") — has definitely resumed its place in the heart of the Church's mission. The whole Church's mandate to spread the Gospel which was articulated again by Paul VI in 1975 in the encyclical *Evangelii Nuntiandi* resonates easily with those from within the charismatic tradition. Bishops and pastors initiating efforts to evangelize and to implement the catechumenate in their areas frequently find that some of their best personnel resources are found in the prayer groups and communities of their diocese or parish. Clearly the charismatic movement has been based upon essential elements of Christian and Catholic life, individual and ecclesial, and has promoted renewal of many facets of that life. However, there are evident shortcomings within the movement which need attention.

Criticisms

The first area of concern is sexism. This is often concealed in a theology of the gifts of the Spirit that affirms women's gifts but only in certain areas of ministry, and often only to other women. In some charismatic communities women are excluded *a priori* from leadership positions that involve authority over men.[62] Often this sexism is justified in terms of personal discernment language, for example, "The Lord has told us," or in a "Christian pragmatism" that states: "Our community (our family) is so much more peaceful now that women are in submission to their leaders (husbands)." If sexism is pervasive throughout the Church and society it is also alive and well in a number of charismatic communities.

A second concern is the continuing lack of social concern in charismatic communities. This calls forth questions about the truth of prayer which does not extend outward in service to others. Prayer is never a private action; it is always social, whether implicitly or explicitly. It is easy to "enjoy" a prayer meeting and go home satisfied that one has had "a good time praying." To refuse to allow prayer to extend beyond the borders of one's group, of one's personal intentions, to maintain that working on "good" relationships will eventually lead to peace and justice throughout the world is to ignore the oppression built into the political, social, economic, and cultural structures of the world. To proclaim consistent and constant loyalty to pope and bishops but to refuse to make the Church's teaching on social justice a part of one's very

---

[62] One of the biggest blocs of Charismatic Communities was originally known as IBOC which stands for the International Brotherhood of Communities. I was sent as a representative of the Family of God Community, Ireland to attend a conference of IBOC in Paray le Monial in 1988 and it was at this meeting that the seeds of the future Catholic Fraternity were sown. The Catholic Fraternity (I have private papers and documentation from the Catholic Fraternity, as yet unpublished, that charts its formal development from within IBOC to a recognized International Private Association of the Faithful) emerged out of this grouping and initially it had some difficulty adjusting to new styles of leadership acknowledging the rights of women to occupy leadership roles within the community. Through the efforts of Bishop Cordes (the Pontifical Council appointee charged with accompanying the Catholic Fellowship within IBOC) and the agitation of European Communities such as Emmanuel, France and the Family of God, Ireland (both of whom had female leaders *in situ*) significant change occurred, at least in principle. It is now open to women to hold such roles but *de facto* the Catholic Fraternity leadership remains largely male dominated with no female occupying any significant leadership role. Another large grouping of Charismatic Communities is the Sword of the Spirit which has a number of communities under their aegis in Ireland. These include the Community of Christ the King in Belfast and the Nazareth Community in Dublin and they too believe strongly in the male as leader.

being is to be as selective about Catholic teaching as someone who enjoys prayer but does not like the Eucharist because it disturbs his or her private prayer.

Another insidious aspect of the prayer life of Charismatic Renewal is that there is a real danger of devotionalism. Raniero Cantalamessa points out that

> Charismatic Renewal was born with a powerful drive to return to the essentials of the Christian Life: the Holy Spirit, the lordship of Christ, the Word of God, the Sacraments, the charisms, prayer, evangelization. This is the secret of its explosive power. This characteristic of the Renewal is clearly shown by the fact that it has no recognized founder, nor any particular "spirituality," but that it simply accentuates what should be common and "normal" for every baptized person.... The basic work of the Spirit is his sanctifying activity (See 2 Th 2:13: 1 P 1:2), by which he transforms human beings, giving them a new heart, not the heart of a slave but the heart of a child of God's family. Next comes his charismatic activity, by which he distributes a variety of gifts for the good of the community. This is what he did at Pentecost: he transformed the apostles, making new men of them, then he had them speak in tongues and prophesy, and he gave them all the gifts they would need for their mission. In the Charismatic Renewal too, we need this hierarchy: personal sanctification must come first, and only then, in second place, the experience of the charisms.[63]

Cantalamessa believes that the Renewal has become sucked into what is optional, into a "whirlpool, to such an extent that in some places it has become identified merely by association with

---

[63] Raniero Cantalamessa, "Remember Those Early Days; a Reflection on Charismatic Renewal," Rome: ICCRS, September 28, 1999:1-4.

certain devotions, apparitions, individuals and particular messages."[64]

While some of these may be legitimate and a sign of the richness of the Catholic Church, "they need to be kept within their proper sphere and not imposed on all and sundry as a measure of the greater or lesser extent of their 'catholicity'."[65]

In the same article, he presents the task of leadership as being that of "spiritual guide to help our brothers and sisters to be open to the great mysteries of faith and never to shut themselves up in any short-lived devotionalism, which can never serve to evangelize the world."[66]

A further problem that is linked to the previous one outlined above, is that, for the most part, charismatic communities are led by the laity. That is both an asset and a liability. Its gift is to foster genuine development of lay leadership in the Church. Its drawback is that, not infrequently, persons with very little training are made leaders of communities. Their insecurity is disguised by an authoritarianism that uses a personal discernment language ("The Lord told me that we should do this") as the norm of community direction. Effective leadership development, including sound theological and pastoral formation, needs to become a more significant part of charismatic life.

A number of other difficulties infect charismatic life. Lack of communication with other Church bodies can weaken the impact of decisions made through various forms of communal discernment in charismatic communities. There can be a tyranny over the life of a group which, when expressed in religious language, using terminology of the Spirit, is oppressive. Sometimes leaders in the renewal, including those with theological education, deride theological reflection and appeal to their communities in language that is strongly anti-intellectual. Nor is Charismatic Renewal or the Church as a whole served well by those who refuse to take

---

[64] Ibid., 1.

[65] Ibid., 2.

[66] Ibid.

modern biblical scholarship seriously (because they may judge the faith of the scholars deficient) and warn charismatics away from sound scholarly understanding of the Bible towards biblical fundamentalism.

Many of those involved in charismatic communities still struggle for a recognition and legitimacy that would give their prayer and community's life a firmer basis in their parish, religious order, or diocese. There is a tendency to want to be "different" because the difference has made such a profound impact on one's life. Charismatic life is still developing, although prayer groups are growing more slowly in the last few years. Some persons in charismatic communities want to receive approbation of their life as a legitimate, alternate way of living Christian life, especially Catholic Christian life and often this is not forthcoming.

At the same time the Church as a whole evidences a great ambivalence about charismatic life. Although today only a few bishops and priests would attack the renewal, most clergy and most Catholics still see charismatic life as a particular way of being a Catholic, a way that can be observed with interest and then set aside as "just not my style of prayer."

Overview

As one can see from this review of the charismatic movement, it has assumed several characteristics of a distinct spirituality. It calls for reform, for a return to gospel faith and practice. It includes interpretation of the religious, social, and missionary aspects of Christian life. It is semi-institutionalized in communities and groups. The Charismatic Renewal claims not to be just a style of prayer nor a certain spiritual gift, or even prayer itself. The heart of charismatic spirituality is the heart of Christian spirituality, that is, deeper conversion to Christ Jesus, continual openness to the power of the Spirit, and the spreading of the good news to all people. None of these is an optional interpretation or emphasis in Christian life.

In a very real sense, the goal of the Charismatic Renewal is to help revitalize the Church and then to disappear as a formal movement of renewal. That is already beginning to happen in personal ways as individuals who have been profoundly influenced by charismatic life slowly move from specific charismatic activities to work and serve in other ecclesial settings, especially the local parish.

Four Key Characteristics

There are four factors of the charismatic movement which are at the center of the Christian mystery and Christian life.

The first is the emphasis on faith and personal commitment to Christ. This is the essential basis of Christianity. Charismatics have discovered, or rediscovered, the necessity of a lively, personal commitment to Christ as the foundation of Christian life. The processes of formation in charismatic communities are essentially processes of conversion, leading one to repentance and new life in Christ.

Secondly, the Holy Spirit and the praise of God are also essential to Christian life. Praising God is a Christian act, not a charismatic specialty. Whether or not one's style of prayer includes raising hands in the air, Christians are all called to praise God, as the liturgy bears witness. The Charismatic Renewal is re-teaching the Church that truth.

Thirdly, Charismatic Renewal, standing within a larger movement in the Church, calls everyone back to community life as an environment for Christian growth and development. In this it is certainly not unique, for one of the major themes of Christian life in these last twenty years has been the call for deeper community life. Charismatic Renewal, in all its diversity, is developing a multitude of forms of community life — formal and informal, structured and loosely organized. Some demand long-term commitment, but most are suitable for adaptation to ordinary parish life.

Fourthly, the renewal has taught the Church the meaning of "grass-roots ecumenism" and how Christian unity is happening. Although formal dialogues and theological discussions are very important, they will never bear fruit unless ordinary people have learned that, in Christ Jesus, there are no barriers too big that cannot be broken through by the power of the Spirit. Learning to pray together, share Scripture (even argue about it), live community life — and bear the pain of the disunity shown by the lack of one Eucharist — are all preparing the soil and allowing the seeds of the full unity of all Christians to grow.

Critical Juncture

Charismatic Renewal as a movement is at a critical stage of its growth and evolution. The wildfire stage of incredible enthusiasm and spectacular growth in numbers is over. It has won a great measure of respectability in the Church, although there are still many people who react with a shiver to the news that a person is a "charismatic."

The challenge to charismatic life is twofold. The first challenge is not to settle for an exclusivity of language, lifestyle, and prayer which makes it difficult for its gifts to be recognized and shared. There is the danger of an "in" language developing similar to *Ultreyas* (Cursillo), and mystagogy and enlightenment (Neo-Catechumenate). These develop what Wayne Meeks calls "the language of belonging" which all too often can also become a language of exclusion.[67] The second challenge is to resist the temptation to be content with "having a good time praying" and to begin serious consideration of how its primary agenda of community-building can be translated into effective social action.

But there is a twofold challenge to the whole Church also. First, the Church must consistently and constantly refuse to

---

[67] Wayne Meeks, *The First Urban Christians* (Yale University Press, 1983), 85.

marginalize the movement as a renewal force and to see it only as an alternate spirituality. Continuation of this tendency to regard charismatics as simply experts in exuberant prayer could impoverish the Church. Second, it must refuse to settle for less than the full power, presence, and gifts of the Spirit, active and operative in the whole of Church life, its religious, social, and mission dimensions. The Spirit, whose presence urges the believer to be good news and to spread this good news, is a Spirit of unending generosity. The believing community must not refuse to ask for all that can be given.

Founders

Before leaving this section, I think it is important to say something about the founders of the various movements, especially the ones I have selected for closer examination, because in their founding charism lies a revelation of the truth not just for the movements but also for the Church. In Beyer's opinion, the charism of the founder possesses one fundamental characteristic, what he calls a "spiritual fruitfulness" and which he locates in the fatherhood or motherhood of the founder. This fruitfulness is expressed "mystically" within the group in so far as each member, in harmony and communion with the founder, lives out the original charismatic experience and enriches it with all their own gifts of nature and grace.[68]

Allow the Charism to Breathe

Beyer argues that a charism is a gift that is fundamentally ecclesial in character, not a gift made just to the founder but a gift to the entire Church, and a gift which can only be lost through

---

[68] Cf. J. Beyer, "La Règle des Moines: Sagesse et Institution," (1982): 124-129. See also Antonio Romano, *The Charism of the Founders* (St. Pauls, 1989).

infidelity or ignorance.[69] Even if it be born and brought to fruition only in a local Church, the ecclesial dimension of the charism
always retains its universal character, because the local Church is
the universal Church in miniature. The charism is specifically missionary because it builds up the body of Christ by that particular
witness of life and pastoral action signified by the movement.
Thus, any recognition and welcome of the gift demands not only
respect and gratitude from the immediate recipients but also from
the local Church.

Once accepted as such, a gift of the Spirit relies on the "trust
and care of the hierarchy, in collaboration with and in the Church"
yet without letting these familial bonds, this collaboration, deform
it in any way. To welcome a charism means to give it room to
breathe, room to bear witness so that it can give that very service
for which it was itself given. In order to do this, it must be received into the pastoral life of the Church but in such a way that
the charism is not modified, still less obstructed, by the projects
of a "shared pastoral plan." Rather, in order to receive the Lord's
gift, it may be necessary to modify the preconceived pastoral
project.[70]

Though they are historically bounded, the founders' experience of God tends to set up a unique mechanism for formation,
through which the later followers gain similar experience and identity. I used here the notion of the "experience of God" in which
the identity experience and the conversion experience merge together.

Cursillo

In the case of the Cursillo movement the founding charism
was given to a group which comprised a bishop, some priests and
laymen. In this sense it was a collective charism which called them
together to pray and discern. Out of this engagement, they expe-

---

[69] Romano, 99.
[70] Romano, 100.

rienced a conversion which called them to work together to renew the Church. Under the inspiration of the Holy Spirit they
devised a spiritual program that called millions to conversion and
to a deeper walk with God.

The leaders worked as a team that prayed together, shared
their Christian lives together, studied together, planned together,
acted together and evaluated what they had done together. Together they worked at the task of forming Christian life among
the young people in Mallorca. Out of their common efforts, something new in the life of the Church was born. Church renewal,
spiritual renewal, pastoral renewal, the pilgrim style, a pastoral
plan, teamwork among leaders; the Cursillo movement grew out
of all these things. It developed not by accident nor through a
clearly specified plan, but was an organic development of the efforts of a group of faithful who had dedicated themselves to the
work of God.

Neo-Catechumenate

The Neo-Catechumenate was founded by Kiko Argüello
who had a deep mystical experience that caused him to have a deep
love for the poor. His charism was enriched by that of Carmen
Hernàndez who came to join him in his work. Her expertise as a
trained theologian allied to his mystical experience saw the birth
of the Neo-Catechumenal Way.

Emmanuel, France

One of the largest ecclesial movements in Europe is the Emmanuel community whose headquarters are in Paris. It was
founded by an elderly lay celibate, Pierre Goursart, an eminent
film critic, and a young female doctor, Martine Catta.[71] Their lives

---

[71] Gérald Arbola, "Emmanuel Community: Testimony," *The Ecclesial Movements in the
Pastoral Concern of the Bishop: Laity Today* (2000), 141-147.

became enmeshed when they gathered together to pray and heard the call of God to found a community based on three simple principles. Adoration created Compassion which in turn enabled Evangelization.

Communion and Liberation

Communion and Liberation was founded by an individual, Luigi Giussani. Luigi Giussani was born in 1922 in Desio, a small town near Milan. His mother, Angela, gave him his earliest daily introduction to the faith. His father, Beniamino, a member of an artistically talented family, a carver and restorer of wood, spurred the young Luigi always to ask why, to seek the reason for things. At a very young age Luigi Giussani entered the diocesan seminary of Milan, continuing his studies and finally completing them at the theological school of Venegono under the guidance of masters like Gaetano Corti, Giovanni Colombo, Carlo Colombo, and Carlo Figini. There, the conviction grew in him in those years that the zenith of all human genius (however expressed) is the prophecy, even if unaware, of the coming of Christ. The guiding idea of the movement is that Christianity is an event that invests and tends to determine the whole of man's life. Christ the Redeemer is at the center of history and the cosmos. Faith is therefore the source, the criterion of judgment, and the only adequate motivation for action.

Giussani, by temperament, was an unlikely personality to begin a movement which young people find so attractive. Small in stature and with a rasping voice, he was an unlikely candidate in the eyes of the world. Yet his own prayer life and his desire to bring the Gospel to an increasingly pagan culture enabled him to find a language and a method of formation which met the needs of his time. Thousands of people from all over the world have responded to his charism and their dedication to lives of mission and charity are now enriching both the local and the universal Church.

Charismatic Renewal

Most unexpected and surprising of all the new movements has been the arrival of the Charismatic Renewal which has no human founder. It was an unexpected surprise of the Spirit, one that many attribute to the prayer of Pope John XXIII at the opening of the Second Vatican Council. At that moment, he prayed for a new outpouring of the Spirit, "Lord, renew your wonders in this our day as by a new Pentecost."[72] Shortly afterwards a young university student, Patti Mansfield, on a weekend retreat at Duquesne University, experienced an anointing by the Holy Spirit. It became known as "baptism in the Spirit" and the graces of the new movement spread at an electrifying pace throughout the Catholic Church, enabling the members to appropriate in a deeper way the graces of their sacraments of Baptism and Confirmation. The Bible became a living word, breathed by God and breathing God, as St. Ambrose said. Members of the renewal discovered themselves to be in the presence of God's holy action, God present and active in history. That was the miracle that filled the biblical prophets with awe and caused them to leap for joy: "Shout for joy, you heavens, for Yahweh has been at work! Shout aloud, you earth below!" (Is 44:23).

Founders can clearly be seen as essential historical mediators of a definite charismatic economy through which God continues to speak to his people. These founders, by the way they live, become prophetic signs, reminding the Church that at the heart of human destiny lies the riches of God.

Conclusion

I have chosen to examine in some detail three out of a host of new ecclesial movements that have sprung up all over the world

---

[72] Pope John XXIII, *Humanae Salutis* in *The Documents of Vatican II*, ed. W.M. Abbott, The America Press (1966), 709.

to create a flavor of this new reality sweeping the Church. Their brief history and overview indicates they bring energy, dynamism and excitement but they also engender suspicion, disturbance and hostility. As Pope John Paul II said:

> [Their] unexpected newness… has given rise to questions, uneasiness and tensions; at times it has led to presumptions and excesses on the one hand, and on the other, to numerous prejudices and reservations.[73]

One of the blessings and paradoxically one of the weaknesses of the new ecclesial movements is that they have been animated largely by lay people. This became possible largely due to the dramatic impact of the Second Vatican Council. The Church rediscovered herself as the People of God, all members equal by virtue of a common baptism. This opened the way for a new and dynamic ecclesiology that enabled the birth and the acceptance of the new ecclesial movements. Vatican II created an ecclesiological climate that fostered and nurtured the maturing of these fledgling new ecclesial communities. Clearly, the contemporary lay movements could hardly have arisen, let alone survived, in the Ultramontane Church of Pius IX. For they have obviously been nurtured by a new sense of the laity's role, which is enshrined in the Vatican II Constitution on the Church, *Lumen Gentium*. The new ecclesiology that emerged from Vatican II was crucial in creating a milieu that enabled the new ecclesial movements to find their voice and their identity. However the lay voice only emerged after a checkered history and it is revealing to see how it was shaped by certain historical moments and by prophetic people whose work foreshadowed much of what is embodied by the new movements today.

---

[73] Pope John Paul II, "Address to the delegates on the occasion of the Meeting with the Ecclesial Movements and the New Communities (Rome, 30 May, 1998)," *Laity Today* (1999): 222.

Appendix 1

To the Clergy and People of the Diocese:

In September 1979 I welcomed the commencement of the "Neo-Catechumenal Way" in this diocese out of sincere and fervent hope that it would be a fruitful and valuable addition to the work of evangelization and upbuilding of the local Church of Clifton. Since that time and recently I have received reports and information which have cast doubts on the efficacy and desirability of the "Neo-Catechumenal Way" in this diocese. These representations suggest that the methodology of catechesis and evangelization of the "Way" with its attendant spirituality has been and is a cause of disunity and spiritual harm. Consequently, as chief Pastor of the Diocese I established a panel of enquiry in January 1996 under the chairmanship of Mr. Thomas Millington with the Very Rev. Barnaby Dowling and Mrs. Valerie James to investigate the truth of those reports and misgivings.

After carefully considering the findings of this enquiry and extensive consultation with the Diocesan Council of Priests and other advisors, I have decided that the methodology and spirituality of the Neo-Catechumenate have been a cause of serious disunity and spiritual harm among certain of Christ's Faithful and therefore I decree as follows:

[1] that the catechetical and evangelization methods of the "Neo-Catechumenate" are neither beneficial nor appropriate for use in this diocese;

[2] that the "Neo-Catechumenate" is to be discontinued in the Diocese of Clifton, forthwith.

Given at Clifton, this twenty-eighth day of January in the year of Our Lord 1997 and the nineteenth year of the Supreme Pastorate of Our Holy Father Pope John Paul II.

Bishop of Clifton

THE FOUNDATIONS

CHAPTER THREE

The Emergence of the Laity

The arrival of charisms has always, inevitably, involved a certain upheaval. Change in any aspect of life can often be disturbing and the same is true within the life of the Church. For every one of those who embrace the new, one can readily find another who resists or objects to any change in the status quo. Skeptical voices currently raised against the liberty afforded to some of these new ecclesial movements is an inevitable part of their historical evolution. What follows is an attempt to reflect on some of the major movements for change and reform within the Church. An historical sweep of lay spirituality and the legacy of previous "movements" in the history of the Church is a necessary prerequisite to provide a backdrop which situates the new movements in the life of the Church.

Laity in the Embryonic Church

The word *laikos* is not found in the New Testament. The vocational distinctions that we take for granted today were virtually unknown in the first two centuries of Christianity. Their idea of different "spiritualities" for different members of the Christian Community would have been foreign to the early Christians. In the New Testament the Church is portrayed as a fellowship or community rooted in Jesus Christ. Christians were identified as disciples (Ac 6:1; 7:7; 9:1; 10:9), believers (Ac 10:45; Eph 1:2; Col 1:2), and saints (Rm 1:7; 16:16; 1 Cor 1:1; Eph 2:19).[1] Donna Orsuto asserts that "an encounter with Jesus often led to discipleship which meant that the followers of Jesus were set apart for God alone."[2] The concepts of holy priesthood, priestly kingship and spiritual temple (1 P 2:9ff.; 1 Cor 3:16ff.; 2 Cor 6:1-26ff.; Eph 2:19-23) were all used in this context of a special call.[3] St. Peter in his first letter stresses the call to holiness and the call to live the Christian vocation in the world.

> But you are a chosen race, a royal priesthood, a holy nation, God's own people, that you may declare the wonderful deeds of him who called you out of darkness into his marvelous light. Once you were no people but now you are God's people; once you had not received mercy but now you have received mercy (1 P 2:9-11).

St. Peter is pointing out the distinctive difference between those who are Christians and those who are not. The Christian call to a particular way of life makes them a sign of contradiction in the world. They are encouraged to live a life of faith that flows into their daily lives and relationships and particularly to hope in God in the midst of trials and difficulties. The call to perfection

---

[1] Cf. A Faivre, *The Emergence of the Laity in the Early Church* (Mahwah, NJ: Paulist Press, 1990). The original French version of this work was published in 1984 but in a later article published in 1986 in *Freiburger Zeitschrift fur Philosophie und Theologie*, the author modified some of his opinions.

[2] Donna Orsuto, "Spirituality of the Laity," *Compendium of Spirituality*, 22. Compiled by Emeterio de Cea, OP. Translated and adapted by Jordan Aumann, OP (New York: Alba House, 1992). See also K. Egan who argues that in the light of Vatican II teaching and the 1983 Code of Canon Law the best understanding of lay spirituality is to be found in the context of a call to discipleship. Cf. K. Egan, "The Call of Laity to a Spirituality of Discipleship," *The Jurist*, 47 (1987), 71-85. In a footnote Egan applauds the article "Call and Discipleship" by F. Segovia in the book, *Discipleship in the New Testament*, ed. F. Segovia (Philadelphia: Fortress Press, 1985).

[3] Cf. E. Niemann, "Laity," *Encyclopedia of Theology*, ed. K. Rahner (London: Burns and Oates, 1986), 814.

extends to each and every member of the community: "He who calls you is holy. Be holy yourselves in all your conduct" (1 P 1:15).[4]

Such a life of holiness did not involve a rejection of one's place in the world or in society. On the contrary, Christians are called to accept their particular situation in life (cf. 1 P 2:13). A life of holiness includes witnessing to the truth in word and deed (1 P 3:14), a life of purity, and a profound reverence for the Lord. Moreover, it required a mutual exchange of gifts for the common good (1 P 4:10). Although there were many roles and ministries in the early Church, all were called as members of the one royal priesthood.[5]

A. Faivre summarizes the situation of the laity in the early Church as follows:

> The laity as such were not recognized in the New Testament, which speaks only of people, a holy people, a chosen people, a people set apart, a *kleros* entirely responsible for carrying out a royal priesthood and calling on each one of its members to give to God true worship in spirit.... One searches the New Testament in vain for a theology of the laity.... The people experience their vocation as believers collectively.[6]

Yet it is important to note that in spite of this basic equality there were differences within this one people because of the various charisms and offices that contributed to the upbuilding of the Church.[7] As L. Bouyer points out, "the Church was an illegal, or

---

[4] Louis Bouyer, *The Spirituality of the New Testament and the Fathers* (London: Burns and Oates, 1960), 150-156. See also the following commentaries: B. Reike, *The Epistles of James, Peter and Jude* (New York: Doubleday, 1964), 85-95. E. Best, *1 Peter* (New Century Bible, London: Olifants, 1971), 109-131.

[5] Orsuto, "Spirituality of the Laity," 24.

[6] Faivre, *The Emergence of the Laity in the Early Church*, 7.

[7] E. Niemann, "Laity," *Encyclopedia of Theology*, ed. K. Rahner (London: Burns and Oates, 1986), 814. He notes that gifts differ according to charism (1 Cor 12:7; 14:26) and authority, including ministers (1 Cor 4:11; 2 Cor 3:5; 6:4), presidents (Rm 12:8; 1 Th 5:12; Heb 13:7, 17, 24), pastors (Eph 4:11), elders (Tt 1:5), and teachers (Ac 13:1; 1 Cor 12:28).

at least unrecognized, association and to adhere to it always meant accepting the ban of ordinary society, a ban which might go as far as a direct threat to life and possessions."[8] Personal discipleship, allied to a close knit community, characterized these early Christians. Although there was a variety of roles and functions, clergy and laity were united in a common effort to survive in a hostile world.

Laity in the Early Church to the Middle Ages

During the New Testament times, the Church was understood as the people of God, a community characterized by radical freedom, radical equality, radical sharing and radical service. According to St. Paul, it was a fellowship in which all racial, social and sexual differences were eliminated (cf. Gal 3:26-28). What Paul asserts here is that in the Church there is no place for the oppositions that prevail in the rest of society. Jesus is absolutely forthright in the rejection of domination (cf. Mk 10:42-45).

In this egalitarian Church there are varieties of charisms which blossom into diverse ministries. The Pauline and Deutero-Pauline letters deal with them at some length. Gradually, the ministry of leadership emerges. But it is clearly understood that the leadership ministry, like all other ministries, is for the building up of persons and communities. Paul speaks of the authority "which the Lord gave for building you up and not tearing you down" (2 Cor 10:8; see also 1 Cor 13:10).

The early Christian leaders thought of themselves as ministers of Christ in the service of the people (2 Cor 4:5; 1 Cor 9:19). There was no question of their lording it over the community (1 P 5:1-5; 2 Cor 1:24). Jesus, the servant, was the model for all Christian ministers (Mt 23:25-27; Mk 10:42-45; Jn 13:13-17). As E. Schillebeeckx has remarked:

---

[8]   Bouyer, *The Spirituality of the New Testament and the Fathers*, 190.

According to Paul and the whole of the New Testament, at least within the Christian communities of believers, relationships involving subjection are no longer to prevail. We find this principle throughout the New Testament, and it was also to determine strongly the New Testament view of ministry. This early Christian egalitarian ecclesiology in no way excludes leadership and authority; but in that case, authority must be filled with the Spirit, from which no Christian, man or woman, is excluded, in principle, on the basis of the baptism of the Spirit.[9]

As Yves Congar has pointed out, "there is no distinction between 'lay people' and 'clerics' in the vocabulary of the New Testament."[10] But such a distinction began to be made already at the end of the first century. According to A. Faivre,[11] the word *laikos* is first used in Clement of Rome's *Letter to the Corinthians* written circa 95 A.D. Clement of Rome spoke of "*laikos*" who are distinguished from the high priest, the priests and the Levites.[12] For Clement the distinction between the clergy and the laity was a functional one and in no way went against the *koinonia*, the communion, that existed among the members of the Corinthian Church.

Neither Justin nor Irenaeus used the word *laikos*,[13] but by the beginning of the third century, distinct categories between *kleros* and *laikos* gradually emerged. This can be seen in the writings of Tertullian, Clement of Alexandria, Origen and Cyprian. Although laymen like Origen (who later became a priest) were teachers in

---

[9] Edward Schillebeeckx, *The Church With a Human Face* (London: SCM, 1985), 39.

[10] Yves Congar, *Lay People in the Church* (London: Geoffrey Chapman, 1965), 4.

[11] A. Faivre, "The Laity in the First Centuries," *Lumen Vitae* 42 (1987), 129-139. See also J. Tracey Ellis, "The Catholic Laity: A View From History," *American Benedictine Review* 37 (1968), 256-268.

[12] Clement of Rome, *The Letter to the Corinthians*, Chapter 40.

[13] Faivre, *The Emergence of the Laity in the Early Church*, 25-40.

the catechetical schools of the third century, even these functions were eventually consigned to the clergy. Faivre states that by the end of the third century,

> the term lay was used to describe men — and not, it would seem, women — who belonged to the Church, but were not bishops, presbyters, or deacons and who were not in a general way members of the clergy. The layman was quite certainly regarded as inferior to the clergy at that time.... In principle, he could not reach the same level of perfection. From this period onward, the layman's function was to release the priest... from all his material concerns, thus enabling him to devote himself exclusively to the service of the altar.[14]

Yet this development set the tone for centuries to come. Some of the Fathers did offer positive approbation and support on lay spirituality,[15] but the dominant attitude of the early Church was one of *fuga mundi*. The martyr, the monk, and the virgin fled the world and these were extolled as models of lay sanctity. In a telling comment, F. Wulf states that

> Patristic theology is quite outspoken on the subject: "A mother will have a lower place in heaven, because she is married," says St. Augustine, "than her daughter because she is a virgin." Monastic exegesis normally understood the parable of the sower to mean the hundredfold fruit was the martyrs, the sixtyfold the virgins, and the thirtyfold the married people.[16]

---

[14] Ibid., 69.

[15] Clement of Alexandria and John Chrysostom speak positively about Christian perfection in the midst of the world, although Chrysostom does speak of married life as a concession to human weakness. See A. Auer, *Open to the World: An Analysis of Lay Spirituality* (Baltimore: Halcion Press, 1966), 32 ff.

[16] See F. Wulf, "Introductory Remarks" in Vorgrimler, *Commentary on the Documents of Vatican II* (New York: Herder and Herder, 1969, Vol. 1), 297.

However, since Christian perfection or holiness was always understood with reference to love of God and neighbor, it was conceded that a layperson whose life manifested exemplary charity could surpass the sanctity of a mediocre monk.[17] Thus, theoretically, the measure of perfection consisted not so much in a particular way of life, but in love of God and neighbor.[18] The martyr was the example *par excellence* of this perfect love.[19] Since virginity and the monastic life were eventually seen as a type of martyrdom or a substitute for martyrdom,[20] it was only a matter of time before the monastic ideal was seen as the perfect expression of love. Since detachment from the world was so greatly emphasized in the early Church, in practice, the model for Christians living in the world was an adapted version of monastic spirituality.[21] As L. Doohen has observed,

> Many laity abandoned civil society to enter the monastery, and others at least took up residence close to the monastery, where they could live a partial monastic penance. The latter were the lay elite of their day, but their life and spirituality were monastic, not lay.[22]

It was in the monasteries that the Roman virtues of *ordo* and *stabilitas* were baptized and promoted for the external good of the

---

[17] Y. Congar cites several examples in *"Laïc et Laïcat,"* in *Dictionnaire de Spiritualité*, IX, col. 82.

[18] This was the teaching of St. Augustine, who is quoted by A. Auer in *Open to the World: An Analysis of Lay Spirituality*, 24. "This is genuine worship of God, true religion, sound holiness, and that alone is the service to God."

[19] "He who dies for Christ," said St. Ignatius of Antioch, "has accomplished the work of perfect love" (cited by A. Auer in *Open to the World: An Analysis of Lay Spirituality*, 36).

[20] Cyprian urged the virgins to imitate the martyrs, but Origen and Methodius actually equated virginity with martyrdom. John Chrysostom considered virginity to be the highest virtue and Jerome asserted that it was the perfect sacrifice offered to God. Cf. A. Auer, *Open to the World: An Analysis of Lay Spirituality*, 37.

[21] Most of these comments are based on the article by D. Orsuto, "Spirituality of the Laity," 26-27.

[22] L. Doohen, *The Lay-Centered Church* (Wilmington, DE: Glazier, 1987), 97.

Church's gradual expansion throughout Western Europe and the spiritual welfare of those who entered her doors. From the viewpoint of some medieval monastic writers, life in the monastery was, indeed, the realization of Christian life. As Rupert of Deutz contended, being a Christian meant being a monk.[23]

In effect, this position suggested that the monastic life manifested what the Church should really be about: the holiness of God mediated to human beings, but a holiness separated from the world. "The monk leaves the world. Like every Christian, he detaches himself from it. But even more, because of special vocation, he separates himself from it."[24] However, what St. Augustine had envisaged as the necessary tension between the City of God and the City of Man gradually collapsed as the earthly city (the secular world) was either absorbed into, or forgotten by, the City of God (the monastery). In the sacralized world of the feudal monastery, paradise was restored, so that the monk, through prayer, could surrender himself to the delights of heavenly contemplation.[25] As Jean Leclerq has suggested, medieval monastic writings clearly nourished the desire and yearning for celestial life: "Everything [in monastic culture] is judged according to its relationship with the final consummation of the whole reality.... The present is a mere interlude."[26] Consequently, the apostolate among the laity was, for all practical purposes, pointless and unnecessary. If the monastic experience was, indeed, the locus of grace and the taste of paradise, what need remained for active ministry in secular society? If the *eschaton* were realized in the monastery, why the need to work with men and women for its fulfillment in the world?

One can see two main views which contributed to a negative approach to lay spirituality. There was a subtle dichotomy between clergy, who were concerned with sacred affairs, and laity,

---

[23] *De vita vere apostolica*, iv, 4 (*PL*, CLXX, 644).

[24] Jean Leclerq, *The Love of Learning and the Desire for God* (New York: Fordham University Press, 1960), 70.

[25] Ibid., 68.

[26] Ibid., 83.

whose competence was primarily with secular matters. Secondly, monasticism and virginity were espoused as the way to Christian perfection and this led to the view that the lay state, particularly the married state, was a concession to human weakness. Lay persons in search of perfection often tried to live a watered-down monastic life.

Laity in the Middle Ages

According to Samuel Torvend, the following socio-economic factors — increasing population, land reclamation, urban growth, expansion of education opportunities, new trade routes, an emerging merchant class — shaped a new consciousness in medieval culture which strongly influenced the religious spirit of medieval urban life, a spirit which prompted, as we have suggested, the expansion of the *vita christiana* from the monastery to the market place.[27]

Furthermore, as M.D. Chenu suggests, the emergence of scientific inquiry moved the medievals to contemplate and study "the harmony of the cosmos... the place of man in the universe... where he was himself a nature... where he tried to exercise his mastery in full consciousness of his own reason for being."[28] This scientific concern for the natural world of human existence found its counterparts in the growing naturalism of Western art and theological interest in creation as an instrumental manifestation of the Creator. Simply stated, the medievals of this period developed and encouraged a new sensitivity to the position of humanity, all men and women, in the universe.

It should not be surprising, then, to discover the skepticism which greeted such curiosity concerning human nature. While the

---

[27] Samuel Torvend, "Lay Spirituality in Medieval Christianity," *Summer* 3, no. 2 (1983), 117-126.

[28] M.D. Chenu, *Nature, Man and Society in the Twelfth Century* (Chicago: University of Chicago Press, 1968), 232.

monastic viewpoint tended to diminish the necessity, use, and enjoyment of things in the world (in the quest for the new Jerusalem, who needed to enjoy the created order?), the emerging interest in the "world-as-world" fostered an enthusiasm for the "laws of nature, an awareness of the demands of reason, and the value of social structures."[29]

In this environment, where new forms of scientific, theological, and commercial activity abounded, the identification of the *vita christiana* with the *vita monastica* gradually crumbled. As the secular world bubbled with unprecedented activity in thought, commerce, and art, monastic writers tended to be more puzzled and confused than tolerant or responsive to those new forms of cultural and religious vitality which were swirling around them.[30] And as European culture moved away from the stability of vassalage and monastic religion, the rigid cohesiveness of feudal life began to disintegrate.

Gratian (c. 1189) encapsulates the thinking of this period when he states,

> There are two kinds of Christians, clerics and lay people.... They (the laity) are allowed to marry, to till the earth, to pronounce judgment on men's disputes and to plead in court, to lay their offering on the altar, to pay their tithes; and so they can be saved, if they do good and avoid evil.[31]

At the end of the 13th century this view is again endorsed by Stephen of Tournai who declared, "in one city and under one

---

[29] Chenu, *Nature, Man and Society in the Twelfth Century*, 228.

[30] Anselm of Havelberg in *Dialogi: De unitate fidei et multiformitate vivendi ab Abel usque ad novissimum electum* (*PL*, CLXXXVIII, 1141) defends the evolution of "a Christian religion subjected to so many variations, altered by so many innovations, upset by so many new laws."

[31] *Corpus Iuris Canoni*, 12,1,7. Y. Congar notes that by the time of Gratian, cleric and monk were for all practical purposes assimilated under the one heading, *Lay People in the Church* (London: Chapman, 1985), 9.

king there are two peoples whose difference corresponds to two sorts of life…. The city is the Church; her king is Christ; the two peoples are the two orders of clergy and laity; the two sorts of life are the spiritual and the fleshly…."[32]

Most of the laity were uneducated and were classified as *illiterati* as opposed to the clerics who were the *literati*. Laity were the carnals in contrast to the clergy and monks who were spiritual.[33] With the exception of the rulers and princes who were usually well educated, the spirituality of the laity was reduced to moral teaching.

Enthusiasm for the *vita apostolica* as the primary model of the *vita christiana* did not diminish. Rather, its attractiveness as the best way of Christian life was grasped, at least intuitively if not consciously, by those men and women of the Church who, in desiring to live the gospel intently and experience Christ's life tangibly, became promoters of lay religious movements independent of the monastery and, at times, removed from ecclesiastical control.[34]

Characteristics

The inherent foundation of these lay movements was twofold. First, we discover in them a fervent belief in the universal nature of the call to live a Christian life, albeit in a variety of shadings which ran from lay confraternities to the blatantly heretical Cathari. All persons — lay as well as clerics, monks, and friars — were called to imitate Christ and his disciples, so the leaders of these movements suggested. Thus, Christian life in the secular

---

[32] Prologue to the *Summa super Decreta*, in Mirbt, *Quellen Zur Geschichte des Paptsums*, n. 318, as quoted by Congar, *Lay People in the Church*, 13.

[33] See Jean Leclerq, *The Spirituality of the Middle Ages* (London: Burns and Oates, 1986), 10. See also L. Doohen, *The Lay-Centred Church*, 96.

[34] Margaret Aston, "Popular Religious Movements in the Middle Ages," *Chr. World*, 157-170.

world could be lived as a full-fledged vocation and one in which the fullness of grace was potentially operative. As we are told by James of Vitry, all Christians, by virtue of their baptism and adherence to the rule of the Gospel, participate in the *vita christiana*.[35]

The second characteristic that marked many of the lay movements was a circumvention of the existing religious institutions. Through their pursuit of the *vita apostolica*, popular movements offered an alternative to the traditional dependency of the laity upon a diluted form of clerical or monastic spirituality. As participants in this ideal, emphasis was placed upon those aspects of Christian life which had been cherished in monastic culture but now were promoted in the secular world: fraternal charity, study of Scripture, voluntary poverty, active proclamation of the faith.[36]

Abuses

Of course the abuses of this "evangelical awakening" involved the occasional usurpation of the episcopal prerogative to preach the faith, a claim which, in the hands of the French and Italian Cathari, prompted papal preaching missions to correct their errors, a bloody crusade to eliminate their leaders, and an episcopal inquisition to silence their teachings and practice. By claiming the right to preach and teach Christian doctrine, the Cathari blurred the distinction between doctrinal preaching (*articuli fidei*) and public exhortation in the faith (*verbum exhortationis*), a distinction made quite clear by Innocent III in 1201.[37]

At the same time, a doctrine of spiritual dualism was being preached by certain groups, notably the Albigensians, which promoted a gross contempt of material goods, the body, and sexual-

---

[35] *Libri duo quorum prior orientalis… alter occidentalis historiae* (Douai, 1597), p. 357, as quoted in Chenu, *Nature, Man, and Society*, 357.

[36] Chenu, *Nature, Man, and Society*, 239-69.

[37] Ibid., 249.

ity — a contempt paralleled in the heretical teaching which denied the human nature of Christ, the value of the sacraments, and the established ministries of the Church. In essence those groups which were heretical taught in both theory and practice that divine truth was vouchsafed only to the simplest and poorest hearers, a teaching which tended to separate Gospel from theology, experience from learning, and spirit from matter.[38]

Yet, it is important for us to discern in these popular movements, whether orthodox or heretical, the fundamental yearnings of the spirit which they experienced. Margaret Aston suggests that popular religion "amounted to an endeavor to live with the inexplicable and intolerable."[39] In the face of the unknown, popular belief was, for the most part, attached to the concrete and the tangible, not because popular spirituality was necessarily materialistic, but because visible or literal forms could readily express the presence of the divine or personal commitment to an ideal.

It is not difficult, then, to recognize why such great popularity was accorded to St. Francis and his followers in their literal appreciation of the mystery of Christ, an appreciation which captured the spiritual imagination of thousands. By their devotion to the humanity of Christ, witnessed in the popularization of the *crêche* at Grecchio and a pronounced devotion to the historical life of Christ, the Franciscans channeled the popular preference for an affective spirituality in a direction both orthodox and meaningful.[40]

Concurrently, the Dominicans, prompted by their speculative bent, encouraged the literary-historical study of Scripture, an effort which had parallels in the vernacular translations of Scripture made by Valdes, a lay evangelist who also promoted active study of Scripture among his followers.[41] The two mendicant or-

---

[38] D. Knowles, and D. Obolensky, "The Middle Ages," in *The Christian Centuries* 2 (1969), 365-371.

[39] Aston, "Popular Religious Movements," 158.

[40] Chenu, *Nature, Man, and Society*, 254.

[41] As cited in Chenu, Ibid., 254-55.

ders, Franciscans and Dominicans, engaged the popular religious spirit which desired to experience the life of Christ and to understand the Christ of Scripture. Though born themselves in a new religious milieu, they served as midwives at the birth of a new understanding in spirituality, one which attempted to situate the activity of grace wherever men and women responded to it in faith, whether in the cloister or the city square.

The imitation of Christ and his disciples, the study of Scripture, the desire to communicate the faith, and a willingness to serve the needy — these were the ideals which shaped the evangelical project of many lay movements in the later Middle Ages. Once the break with monastic spirituality had begun, the *ministerium verbi inter gentes* ("the ministry of the Word among the people") could rightly become an experience and project in which a variety of persons could participate. Obviously, it would be wrong to assume that the laity emerged as prominent leaders in the organization of the Church. But it would not be incorrect to suggest that whenever the Church "seeks to find its proper theater of activity in the world, it has proper recourse to laymen, who are familiar with and inhabit this world, and not first to clerics who have more or less abandoned it."[42]

That the *vita christiana* was planted, nourished, and came to fruition in a variety of forms both bizarre and normal attests to the extraordinary hungers of the medieval spirit and the desire which many medievals experienced to translate those yearnings into some visible form of life or devotion. That these lay movements turned, not to the established *vita monastica*, but to the "rule of the Gospel" testifies to the perduring strength and ability of the word of God to serve as a source of spiritual renewal in every age. For we know that the spirituality of the laity which emerged in western Europe during the later Middle Ages heralded a new appreciation for the activity of grace present in every order and profession of the Catholic faith, an activity bound not by the so-

---

[42] Ibid., 220.

cial sluggishness of cloister or Church, but present in the encounter between grace and nature, Christ and culture, the Gospel and secular existence.

The Franciscan Movement

A notable example of an authentic movement of the Holy Spirit during this era was the Franciscan movement of the thirteenth century which helped to define a new lay spirituality and encouraged lay teaching and scholarship. Unlike the monastic orders who had withdrawn from the world to discover intimacy with Christ, the Franciscans were drawn to an apostolic ministry that brought them into constant contact with all sorts of people in the towns and villages whence their wanderings took them. Although small in number at the outset they were strengthened by the parable of the little yeast that transforms the dough (cf. Mt 13:33). The initial exodus whereby Francis left the security of one life to answer radically the call of Christ to live a totally different life is another feature of a movement which is as relevant today as it was in the time of Francis. Distancing and diversity were fundamental to the new call. They had to be removed from the lifestyle which they had known, to become distant from it in some way, to become other, so that their presence among the world could become a transforming one. Exponents of new expressions of faith are always disconcerting; they disturb the peace, they question our own way of being catholic, they may even provoke our anger or contempt.

> Sometimes they were pelted with mud; sometimes jesters put dice in their hands inviting them to play; others pulled at them from behind, dragging them along by their cowls. These and other similar pranks were played on them by people who considered them of no account and tormented them as they pleased.[43]

---

[43] Marion A. Habig, ed., *St. Francis of Assisi: Writings and Early Biographies*, 4th Rev. Ed. (Chicago: Franciscan Herald Press, 1983), 928.

Francis did not concern himself with pastoral plans nor did he develop an apostolic strategy or devise missionary activities. He had no intention of founding a religious order. He only wanted to share the lifestyle of Christ and be dedicated to Him.[44] Bonaventure reports that it was through a revelation from heaven that he "realized he was sent by God to win for Christ the souls which the devil was trying to snatch away. And so he chose to live for the benefit of his fellow man, rather than for himself alone, after the example of him who was so good as to die for all men."[45]

Francis conceived of the apostolate more as an irradiation of life wholly dedicated to God than as the assumption of an ecclesial service.

In so doing Francis raised an aspect of pastoral life that is of great importance, one that is especially provocative for our time: the entering into the redemptive action of Christ through progressive assimilation to Christ by his imitation. In this way the apostle becomes capable of making Christ transparent in his life and the Redeemer present in his action. The necessary diversity or otherness of the witness without which renewal cannot be achieved, is produced not by outward forms and conditions of life but by the apostle's greater closeness to Christ.[46]

The Parisian Controversy

A driving impetus for Francis and his followers was the call to be evangelists and this caused controversy between the mendicant and secular clergy as the conflict at the University of Paris highlighted. The outcome of this Parisian controversy between the secular clergy and the new movements is of "permanent sig-

---

[44] See the edition of the *Fonti Francescane* by the Movimento Francescano (Assisi, 1977), with helpful introductions. Also "Some Mendicant Views of the Origins of the Monastic Profession," *Cristianesimo nella storia* 19 (1998), 31-49. See also Marion A. Habig, ed., *St. Francis of Assisi: Writings and Early Biographies*.

[45] *Fonti Francescane*, 654.

[46] Cordes, *In the Midst of Our World*, 28.

nificance."[47] Supported by the Pope, protector of the universal mission of the Church, "the exponents of a restricted and impoverished idea of the Church, which absolutizes the structure of the local Church,"[48] were rejected.

Thomas Aquinas, in reviewing the dispute, defined the secular clergy as the representatives of a narrowly closed local Church structure, opposed to the evangelizing movement, comfortable with the Clunaic monastic tradition of separation from the local Church, asceticism and contemplation. Aquinas defended the approach of the new mendicant orders, Franciscans and Dominicans, citing Christ himself as the model and asserted the superiority of the apostolic life over purely contemplative forms.

> The active life that brings to others the truths attained through preaching and contemplation is more perfect than the exclusively contemplative life.[49]

Thomas was an heir of the monastic tradition, which, heretofore, had taken its mandate from the approach of the primitive Church. In harmony with this tradition, Augustine had focused his monastic rule on Acts 4:32: "The company of those who believed were of one heart and soul." Thomas Aquinas added a critical additional insight about the *vita apostolica,* namely Christ's instructions to the apostles in Matthew 10:5-15.

> The apostolic life consisted in the fact that the apostles, after they had abandoned everything, went through the world, proclaiming and preaching the Gospel, as shown by Matthew 10, where they had been given a rule.[50]

[47] Cf. Yves Congar, "Aspects ecclésiologiques de la querelle entre mendiants et séculiers dans la seconde moitie du XIIIe siècle et le début du XIVe," *Archives d'histoire doctrinale et littéraire du Moyen Age* 28 (1961), 35-151.

[48] Ratzinger, "The Ecclesial Movements: A Theological Reflection on Their Place in the Church," 43.

[49] St. Thomas Aquinas, *Summa Theologiae* 3.40.1.2.

[50] St. Thomas Aquinas as cited by P. Torrell, "St. Thomas Aquinas, Contra Impugnantes Dei Cultum et Religionem" in *St. Thomas Aquinas, The Person and His Work* 1 (1996), 90.

Ratzinger states that "the rule of life and mission that the Lord gave to the apostles is itself the permanent rule of the apostolic life, of which the Church has a perpetual need. It was on the basis of this rule that the new movement of evangelization was justified."[51]

Francis, Dominic and their followers lived this new lifestyle within a community and in so doing they reflected the medieval concept of man who was conceived not as an individual but as a social being. It is always in community that the Christian lives his relationship with God. The biblical and patristic concept of the Body of Christ or "Communio" was very real.[52]

Changing Perception of Priesthood

Another important change was the gradual acceptance of the idea that the clergy had Christ-given power to fulfill certain functions. Till the 12th century, the Church held a sacramental, iconological view of ministry.[53] But then this view was changed. And the change can be seen in the subtle transformation that took place in the understanding of the title "Vicar of Christ," which at that time was given to the Pope, the bishops and even the priests. Originally it meant that Christ was present and active in his minister. This view was based on the idea that God and the celestial powers were actively involved in the earthly sphere. But gradually a "possession-of-power theory" came to prevail. According to this theory, Christ at the beginning gave power to his vicar, that is, to "a representative who takes his place and who hands on to those

---

[51] Ratzinger, "The Ecclesial Movements: A Theological Reflection on Their Place in the Church," 43.

[52] Paul Josef Cordes, "Communio in the Church: Towards a Theocentric Understanding of Unity" (1996), 1-12 (a private document circulated to leaders within the Catholic Fraternity, circa 1996). See also by the same author, *In the Midst of Our World, Forces of Spiritual Renewal* (San Francisco: Ignatius Press, 1988).

[53] Yves Congar, *Power and Poverty* (London: Geoffrey Chapman, 1964), 62.

who came after him, in an historical sequence of transmission and succession, the power thus received."[54] In other words, Jesus Christ bestowed his power on the Apostles who transmitted it to the bishops, who in their turn share it with the priests and the deacons. Speaking of this new understanding of the ministry in the Church, Joseph Neuner says:

> Thus leadership in the Church is seen no longer as a participation in Christ's mission for the realization of God's reign, but as a power and competence given to a group of people, the hierarchy, to rule the community of the faithful in analogy to a secular government.... Luther's revolt is not primarily a theological challenge of traditional doctrines but a revolution against the domination of the Christian people through the clergy in a spirit totally alien to Jesus Christ.[55]

At the dawn of the modern period, Josse Clichtove (1472-1543) developed a theology and spirituality of the priesthood. The image of the priest he helped to shape was that of a man who by virtue of his state of life was "detached from the world, even from the world of the Christian laity."[56]

This is how E. Schillebeeckx sums up Clichtove's views:

> The idea of "being taken out of the world," i.e., escape from the world, completely determines this image of the priest.... Priesthood is essentially defined by its relation with the cult (and not with the community), though this is the cult of the community.... To be a priest is to be a "cultic priest." Precisely on the basis of this relation to the cult, the priest is the one who is set

---

[54] Ibid.

[55] J. Neuner, "Exploring Global Dimensions of Jesuit Priestly Apostolate," *Ignis Studies* 2 (1983), 12-13.

[56] Edward Schillebeeckx, *The Church With a Human Face* (London: SCM, 1985), 95-7.

apart from the people, and priestly celibacy is the only adequate expression of this essential separation.[57]

Summary

In summation, one can point to some positive developments in the Middle Ages which promoted lay spirituality, such as devotion to the humanity of Christ, profound reverence of the Blessed Sacrament, pilgrimages to Rome and other holy places, the emergence of quasi-religious associations such as the Knights Templar, a growing esteem for the Word of God, a deeper devotion to Mary and a greater appreciation of the sacraments.[58] However, genuine Christian conversion and perfection still tended to be irrevocably linked with monastic or clerical life. Such a reality was reinforced by the liturgy.

> The action is carried on by the clergy, while the ordinary faithful are reduced to a community of "hearers." A veil is drawn between them and the mystery — as by the liturgical language, the canon of the Mass pronounced inaudibly, the screen across the chancel, the decrease in the frequency of communion.[59]

From the years 1000 to 1600, the theme had been time and again reform, reform, reform. Yet still the Church struggled to come to terms with the new realities of emerging laymen and laywomen in a changing world. This new reality was not welcomed by Church leaders. In terms of structure it resisted. As Professor Chadwick says,

> If we seek a single theme running through the reforming endeavors of the Catholic Reformation, it would be the quest for more adequate clergy — better trained

---

[57] Ibid., 196.

[58] See Jean Leclerq, *The Spirituality of the Middle Ages* (London: Burns and Oates, 1986), 243-282; 344-372 ; also J. Gilchrist, "Laity in the Middle Ages," *New Catholic Encyclopedia* (1967), 33.

[59] Niemann, "Laity," 815.

and better instructed priests, priests resident in their parishes, bishops resident in their sees, pastors fervent and self-sacrificing and missionary minded, trained as confessors, celibate, mortified, able to teach in school, wearing canonical dress; a priesthood uncorrupted and incorruptible, educated and other-worldly.[60]

To be equal to the constant challenges by the royal courts of Europe, the papacy in its view could not allow itself to be weakened by lay influences. In the centuries to follow, the results of this irony would be cataclysmic.

The Council of Trent was greatly influenced by the theology of ministry prevalent at the time. While in its reform decrees, the Council dealt with such priestly tasks as preaching the word and pastoral care of the people, its doctrinal decrees define priesthood almost entirely in terms of presiding at the Eucharist (power of consecration) and administering the other sacraments.[61] This Council in many ways contributed to the widening of the gap between the clergy and the laity. As J. Neuner has remarked, "the Council of Trent has determined not only the theology but also the social image of the priest for the past centuries: priests form a secluded group with a social status of their own with their life and work centered round the altar."[62]

This is understandable since Trent had set itself the limited task of refuting the errors of the Reformers. As Schillebeeckx observes:

> Finally, the eight canons concerning the sacrament of ordination are a reaction against a view which reduces the priest to a preacher, spokesman and proclaimer

---

[60] Owen Chadwick, *The Reformation* (London: Penguin, 1964), 255.

[61] J. Neuner and J. Dupuis, *The Christian Faith*, 6th ed. (New York: ST PAULS/Alba House, 1996, n. 1714).

[62] J. Neuner, "Exploring Global Dimensions of Jesuit Priestly Apostolate," *Ignis Studies* 2 (1983), 13-14.

(with the result that at least in defining the functions of the priest the canons only stress his cultic activity and so do not say anything about the tasks of preaching and teaching, which were stressed so strongly by Scripture and the early Church as the task of ministers of the Church).[63]

Trent laid great stress on the hierarchical structure of the Church, while totally ignoring the universal priesthood of the believers.[64]

Laity in the Church from the Reformation to Modern Times

Because of its rigidity the Church would forever be altered by the Protestant Reformation and the Counter Reformation that followed. Undoubtedly, the role of the layperson was greatly enhanced by the Protestant reform movements. Luther's central issues of justification, good works, grace, as well as John Calvin's views on women in the Church and in society opened to thoughtful Catholics the prospect for new possible roles in the Church.[65] Discipleship could be seen as something broader than simply one's loyalty to the Church. It was once again seen as sharing in Christ's mission of salvation to the world. Like Paul, one could be a disciple by being a tent maker, a non-cleric. The message was that by baptism into Christ and sharing in the Eucharist of Christ we are disciples of Christ. We do not become disciples by virtue of ordination.

It cannot be said either that laypersons were a central focus of the Council of Trent (1545-1573), but they were affected. The

---

[63] Schillebeeckx, *The Church With a Human Face*, 200.

[64] Cf. J. Neuner and J. Dupuis, *The Christian Faith*, n. 1719.

[65] Thomas H. Greer, *A Brief History of the Western World*, Fifth Edition (New York: Harcourt Brace Jovanovich, 1987), 311 ff. See also Vivian Green, *The History of Christianity* (Leicester: Blitz Editions, 1968), 125 ff.

bishops of the Council hoped to enhance the layperson by focusing on better-trained and more deeply spiritual clergy, something of a holy trickle down theory. The results were mixed. The Council was further hampered by a continually defensive leadership and the fear of Protestant taint if a Gospel rather than an ecclesiastical approach to the issues of laymen and laywomen were adopted. Counter-Reformation Catholicism, resplendent in so many ways, seemed to regard the laity as an afterthought, a misplaced object in the magnificent baroque edifice of the Church. The more silent and docile the laity was, the better. Both the Reformation and the Counter Reformation impacted heavily on lay spirituality. The Tridentine ecclesiology of the "perfect society" conspired to keep laity at the bottom of the pyramidical structure yet many of the new spiritual developments with their emphasis on personal and affective prayer helped the laity to find God in the midst of the world.

One of the most important figures for lay spirituality during this period was St. Francis de Sales (1567-1622) who wrote perhaps the first treatise on lay spirituality. In his preface to the *Introduction to the Devout Life* he stated that he was writing for those who live in towns, within families, or at court.[66] He acknowledged the validity of the secular life but while he insisted that all Christians from every walk of life are called to the perfection of charity, this did not mean a watered-down monastic spirituality.

Laity in the Secular World

Yet if the laity were denied access to ecclesiastical power, laymen and laywomen advanced in the secular world. Through the American and French revolutions they redefined western civilization. The concepts of unalienable rights, freedom of speech, free-

---

[66] St. Francis de Sales, *Introduction to the Devout Life* (New York: ST PAULS/Alba House, 1992; Dublin: Gill, 1944).

dom of assembly, government of the people, even freedom of religion, empowered every citizen. The divine right of kings had given way to the divine right of the common man. From now on it is the citizen who is the foundation of civil power, not the king or the emperor. Still the Church remained negative and defensive. This was true for many reasons. For one, there were strong anti-clerical sentiments in the revolutionary movements. Also the Church was still connected to the falling nobility, not the emerging citizen. The Protestant theologian Jose Miguel Bonino spoke of "tensions of a Catholicism pulled in one direction by its ancient alliances with centers of powers, in another by its concern to be in touch with the people."[67]

But now the old order was fading, albeit slowly. Even Leo XIII, who ushered the Church into the modern world, was hardly modern on the subject of the laity. In a letter to the archbishop of Tours, he defined the layman as "he who, in the Church, obeys and honors the clergy."[68] Not all agreed with this assessment and one of the great protagonists who challenged the prevailing mentality was John Henry Newman (+1890).

Newman (1801-1890) — A Prophetic Voice

Newman was ahead of his time in advocating a much greater degree of lay participation in the life of the Church than was common in the nineteenth century. In this outlook, he anticipated the teaching of the Second Vatican Council. It was Newman's sense of frustration at the hierarchical Church's refusal to allow the laity their proper role in the life of the Church that in fact led to his first theological writing as a Catholic. After his return from Ire-

[67] Quoted in W. Dayton Roberts, *Strachem of Costa Rica* (Grand Rapids: Eerdmans, 1971), 130.

[68] Cf. Geoffrey Robinson, "Signposts for an Emerging Church," *The Mix* (1996): 96. See also Xavier Rynne, *Letters From Vatican City: Vatican Council II, the Third Session* (New York: Farrar, Straus & Giroux, 1965), 50.

land following his resignation as rector of the University, Newman became more and more involved in the affairs of the organ of the liberal Catholics in England, the *Rambler*. Although Newman disapproved of the tone and the more extreme views put forward in the magazine, he nevertheless very much approved of its aims and objectives, and not least its championing of the rights of the laity.

On May 13, 1859 Newman received a letter from a priest, John Gillow, a professor of theology at Ushaw College, Durham, the leading seminary in England. He protested against a passage in the May issue of the *Rambler* (the first issue which Newman himself had edited) about the bishops' recent pastorals on the Royal Commission on education. Newman acknowledged that the passage, which Gillow described as "objectionable," was written by himself. In the passage objected to, Newman, while apologizing for any offense the *Rambler* had inadvertently caused the hierarchy, stated boldly and uncompromisingly his view that the bishops must really desire to know the opinion of the laity on subjects in which the laity are especially concerned. "If even in the preparation of a dogmatic definition the faithful are consulted, as lately in the instance of the Immaculate Conception, it is at least as natural to anticipate such an act of kind feeling and sympathy in great practical questions...."[69] And he concluded with a general warning against the misery of any division between the rulers of the Church and the educated laity, coupled with a strong plea to the bishops:

> Let them pardon, then, the accidental hastiness of manner or want of ceremony of the rude Jack-tars of their vessel, as far as it occurred, in consideration of the zeal and energy with which they haul to the ropes and man the yards.[70]

---

[69] *The Letters and Diaries of John Henry Newman*, ed. Charles Stephen Dessain et al. (London: Nelson; Oxford: Clarendon Press, 1978-84), vol. xvii, p. 514. Hereafter abbreviated as LD.

[70] LD, xix, 129-30.

Newman immediately wrote back to Gillow, tersely enquiring what the grounds of the objection were. He also informed his own bishop, Dr. Ullathorne, of the complaint, explaining that in the reference to the definition of the Immaculate Conception, to which Gillow had taken especial exception, he had only been pointing out that "the Christian people at large were consulted on the fact of the tradition of the Immaculate Conception in every part of the Catholic world."[71]

Gillow wrote to explain that Newman's words seemed to mean that the infallibility of the Church lay with the laity rather than the hierarchy. Newman replied that Gillow had misunderstood the word "consult": "To the unlearned reader the idea conveyed by 'consulting' is not necessarily that of asking an opinion. For instance, we speak of consulting a barometer about the weather. The barometer does not give us its opinion, but ascertains for us a fact.... I had not a dream of understanding the word... in the sense of asking an opinion."[72]

Gillow accepted the explanation without demur: it had never even occurred to him as a theologian to use the word "consult" in such an un-theological sense. However, Dr. Ullathorne, Newman's bishop was not so accommodating. "Our laity were a peaceable set, the Church was at peace. They had a deep faith — they did not like to hear that anyone doubted."[73] Newman pointed out that he knew from experience that the laity in Ireland, for example, was "docile" but "unsettled." In the course of their talk, the bishop said something like, "Who are the laity?" Newman answered that the Church would look foolish without them.[74]

Yet, Bishop Ullathorne's view was not an isolated one, as Monsignor Talbot's remarks to Cardinal Manning bear witness:

---

[71] Ian Ker, "Newman and the Idea of Lay Movements," Seton Hall University: the Archbishop Gerety Lectures, January 1990. Available at www.shu.edu/programs/treasury/Spirit/Gerety/010090.html. Accessed on 21 November 2001.

[72] LD, xix, 131, 133, 135.

[73] LD, xix, 140-1.

[74] Ibid.

What is the province of the laity? To hunt, to shoot, to entertain. These matters they understand, but to meddle with ecclesiastical matters they have no right at all.[75]

Newman was determined to deal more fully with the place of the laity in the Church. The famous article "On Consulting the Faithful in Matters of Doctrine"[76] was completed in time for the July issue. Newman begins by defending his use of the word "consult," which he says in ordinary English "includes the idea of inquiring into a matter of fact, as well as making a judgment." Thus, for example, a "physician consults the pulse of his patient; but not in the same sense in which his patient consults him." It is in the former sense that the Church "consults" or "regards" the faith of the laity before defining a doctrine. The *Rambler* was written for lay people, not for scholastic theologians, to whom the word "consult" would naturally "signify its Latin sense of consult with."[77] Having defended his use of the word consult, Newman now turned to consider the question, why consult the laity? The answer is plain, "because the body of the faithful is one of the witnesses to the fact of the tradition of revealed doctrine, and because their consensus through Christendom is the voice of the Infallible Church."[78]

There are channels of tradition through which "the tradition of the Apostles, committed to the whole Church… manifests itself variously at various times," none of which "may be treated with disrespect," even though the hierarchy has sole responsibility for "discerning and discriminating, defining, promulgating and enforcing any portion of that tradition."[79] He himself, he explained, is "accustomed to lay great stress on the *consensus*

---

[75] E.S. Purcell, *Life of Cardinal Manning* (London: Macmillan, 1895), 318.

[76] John Coulson, ed., *On Consulting the Faithful in Matters of Doctrine* (London: Geoffrey Chapman, 1961). Hereafter abbreviated as *Cons.*

[77] *Cons.*, 75-77, 106.

[78] *Cons.*, 63-72.

[79] *Cons.*, 63.

fidelium"[80] in order to compensate for the lack of testimony from bishops and theologians in favor of defined points of doctrine. He then used his celebrated historical example drawn from that period of the early Church's history which he had studied so deeply and intensely as an Anglican.

In spite of the fact that the fourth century was the age of great doctors and saints, who were also bishops, like Athanasius, Ambrose, Chrysostom and Augustine, "nevertheless in that very day the divine tradition committed to the infallible Church was proclaimed and maintained far more by the faithful than by the Episcopate."[81] During the Arian heresy of that era, in that time of immense confusion, the divine dogma of our Lord's divinity was proclaimed, enforced, maintained and (humanly speaking) preserved, far more by the "*Ecclesia docta*" than by the "*Ecclesia docens*"... the body of the episcopate was unfaithful to its commission, while the body of the laity was faithful to its baptism.[82]

The importance of the illustration is shown by the fact that it occurred so early in the history of the Church and involved the very identity of Christ. Newman boldly concludes by saying that "there was a temporary suspense of the functions of the teaching Church, the unpalatable truth being that the body of bishops failed in their confession of the faith."[83] For him the danger in his era, when the hierarchy was so faithful and orthodox, was that the role of the laity would be neglected but "each constituent portion of the Church has its proper functions, and no portion can safely be neglected."[84] The article ends with an almost defiant challenge, in the well-known words:

> I think certainly that the *Ecclesia docens* is more happy
> when she has enthusiastic partisans about her than
> when she cuts off the faithful from the study of her

---

[80] *Cons.*, 72.

[81] *Cons.*, 75-77.

[82] *Cons.*, 106.

[83] *Cons.*, 75-77.

[84] Ibid.

divine doctrines and requires from them a *fides implicita* in her word, which in the educated classes will terminate in indifference, and the poorer in superstitions.[85]

According to Newman the bishops were simply terrified of "the natural influence"[86] an educated laity could exercise. Newman also thought that the hierarchy had good reason, in the circumstances, to be afraid of the laity, who, he believed, "could do anything if they chose." As for those clergy like himself who were not enamored of the prevailing authoritarianism and clericalism, "our only hope," he remarked, "is in the laity knowing their own strength and exerting themselves."[87] Indeed, there appeared to be "ecclesiastics all over Europe, whose policy it is to keep the laity at arms length; and hence the laity have been disgusted and become infidel, and only two parties exist, both ultras in opposite directions."[88]

As a Catholic, Newman was not only anxious for recognition of the laity, but he was also keenly aware of the need to make the Church more "popular." He had already as an Anglican readily agreed (in a review article) with the French Catholic thinker de Lamennais that the Latin Church rose to power, not by the favor of princes, but of people. Clearly one can see that his thought and practice anticipate the rise in the twentieth century of the phenomenon of the ecclesial movements with a dominant lay spirituality.

Newman and Movements

In looking for anticipations in Newman of this banding together of lay people into movements, one cannot help but recall

---

[85] *Cons.*, 106.
[86] LD, xxi, 384.
[87] LD, xxi, 398.
[88] LD, xxi, 394.

in the first place that Newman himself as an Anglican headed a "movement" consisting of both clergy and laity, a movement we call the Oxford or Tractarian Movement. In the beginning it was very much a clerical movement, the initial idea being to form a society of clergy centered on Oxford, but with branches spreading all over the country. However, Newman much preferred the less structured idea of a loosely knit movement to a formally organized society or association. He was strongly opposed, in particular, to any kind of formal authorization of the Tracts for the Times (which he initiated) by a committee or board. Instead, he wanted the Tracts to be circulated by personal contact and to be personally written by individuals.[89] As he put it in the *Apologia*, his principle was that "Living movements do not come of committees."[90]

Today the various flourishing ecclesial movements differ greatly in the extent of their organization and structure, with some highly organized and closely knit communities at one extreme, and at the other extreme a multitude of loosely affiliated and more or less unstructured prayer groups and communities belonging to the Charismatic Renewal movement. Newman's own connection with, or interest in, lay movements to some extent reflects this variety. For on the one hand he deplored attempts to organize the Tractarian Movement into an organized association or society with rules and officers, while on the other hand his own vocation as an Oratorian priest involved him closely in a lay group with a definite framework and link with a priestly community itself bound, albeit loosely, by a canonical rule.

Perhaps in conclusion we may say that not only was Cardinal Newman's theology of the laity a brave and brilliant anticipation of *Lumen Gentium* and *Apostolicam Actuositatem*, but his concern that the Church should once again become a Church of the

---

[89] See Ian Ker, *John Henry Newman: A Biography* (Oxford: Clarendon Press, 1988), 81, 84-85.

[90] *Apologia pro Vita Sua*, ed. Martin J. Svaglic (Oxford: Clarendon Press, 1967), 46.

people and his acute insight into the apostolic potential of lay people banding together foreshadows both the base communities and the new ecclesial movements of the Church of the twentieth century.

Modern Times

Particularly within twentieth century Europe, various factors began influencing the genesis and direction of a new theology of the laity. First, the incongruence of masses of inactive Catholics in democratic countries, where participation was expected in the political process, became increasingly evident. Secondly, Protestant Churches had already reformed the ideology and theology, if not fully the reality, of lay participation. As Catholics and Protestants increased their interaction, especially in northern Europe and the United States, the Protestant model exerted an influence on Catholics, clerical and lay. Finally, theological, biblical, patristic, and liturgical movements all pointed to the necessity of active involvement of the laity in the Church. Historical and systematic scholarship began drawing the main outlines of a theology of the laity. Major theologians such as Congar (+1995), Rahner (+1984), von Balthasar (+1988), and de Lubac (+1991) were attracted to the question because of their concern to rethink the nature of the Church.[91] As early as 1952, Hans Urs von Balthasar had written that the hour of the laity was sounding in the Church. From that point onwards he saw the passivity of the laity, not only as an untapped resource, but as an impoverishment. "One who is merely passive does not really receive: to possess, one

---

[91] Yves Congar, *Lay People in the Church* (Geoffrey Chapman, 1965) and *Priests and People* (London: Chapman, 1966); Karl Rahner, "Notes on the Lay Apostolate," *Theological Investigations* 2 (1963), 319-352, and *Christians in the Market Place* (New York: Sheed and Ward, 1966); Henri de Lubac, *The Splendor of the Church* (San Francisco: Ignatius Press, 1986); Hans Urs von Balthasar, *The Christian States of Life* (San Francisco: Ignatius Press, 1983).

must accept; and the more spiritual the gift, the more gratefully and happily it should be accepted. Thus the reception of grace becomes automatically an action — an action that accepts, takes hold of, understands, executes, and transmits."[92]

He saw the urgency of equipping the laity to take up their role in the life of the Church and this point was taken up by Jacques Leclerq shortly before Vatican II.

> The laity, formed to the divine life of the Church, have to transform the world. And they will transform it, if they are genuinely Christian. One of the fundamental tragedies of Christianity as it has developed in history is that the laity have not carried out their task. And perhaps this tragedy simply follows from another, equally fundamental, namely, that the clergy have not fulfilled theirs. The clergy were to form the laity, and they have not done so to a sufficient degree. Then, for lack of properly formed laymen, they have tried to take the place of the laity and have done so badly.[93]

Conclusion

The diversity and plurality of reform movements has been a constant feature of the life of the Church since its inception. Lay people have been to the fore in the promotion of many of these reform movements. One can readily see that a creative tension has always existed within the Church, a tension which some scholars have defined as a pull between tradition and progress.[94] The legacy of past reform movements illustrates how a dynamic sense of tradition can be grounded in the past as it moves forward into the

---

[92] von Balthasar, *The Christian State of Life*, 337.

[93] Jacques Leclerq, *Christians in the World* (London: Geoffrey Chapman, 1971), 71.

[94] Cf. Chenu, *Nature, Man, and Society*, 310-330.

future. The image of the Roman god Janus presents itself as a useful image of ecclesiastical reform, in that the Church continually looks to the past and the future at the same time.

A dynamic sense of tradition, demonstrated by the innovative mendicant orders, was grounded in obedience to the Church's authority but it also complemented a more static sense of tradition, illustrated by the Cistercian and Carthusian return to monasticism's original *contempus mundi*. We can discern in many of the reform movements a marriage, albeit somewhat rocky, between conservation and innovation. Pope Gregory VII (1073-1085) stressed that in his reforms he was not adding anything new to the Church but only reiterating her traditions. Peter of Blois (c. 1135-1211) described such efforts as the renewal of forgotten treasures.

> We are like dwarfs standing on the shoulders of giants; thanks to them, we see farther than they: busying ourselves with the treatises written by the ancients, we take their choice thoughts, buried by age and the neglect of men, and raise them, as it were, from death to renewed life.[95]

This brief overview of the emergence of lay spirituality is important because one can recognize that the new ecclesial movements have emerged out of this historical evolution of the Church. Who the laity are is as important as what the laity do. There had been a tendency to ignore or to dismiss or to downgrade the involvement of laity in the Church and to define them by task and function rather than by identity. During the nineteenth century it became quite clear how the idea that priests possessed sacred power aggravated the clergy-laity divide. In a schema on the Church prepared for Vatican I we find this statement:

---

[95] Quoted in Chenu, *Nature, Man, and Society*, 326.

But the Church of Christ is not a community of equals in which all the faithful have the same rights. It is a society of unequals, not only because among the faithful some are clerics and some are laymen, but particularly because there is in the Church the power from God whereby to some it is given to sanctify, teach, and govern, and to others not.[96]

Although this draft was disregarded, nevertheless it expresses a significant theology prevalent at that time. Pope Leo XIII who made Newman a cardinal and championed social Catholicism was the same Leo XIII who declared error in the Bible an impossibility, criticized socialism and was no friend of the modernists. A much earlier predecessor, Pope Innocent III who personified how canon law had become the engine of the papal monarchy and bureaucracy, allowed the Franciscans and Dominicans to flourish and at Lateran IV directed monastic orders to meet frequently in general chapters to reform themselves. Contradictions and tensions have always been at the heart of change in the Church because God's Spirit works through people.

What should be evident from this examination of the laity's evolution within the Church and their necessary role in its ongoing reform is that change is an inevitable feature of life and the Church cannot be immune to that. Its call is to build on Christ's dictum that one must take from the old and the new (Mt 13:52). Slowly but surely over the centuries, with the invaluable help of prophetic voices, the laity have reclaimed their proper position. This renewed awareness of their baptismal dignity and call has in turn led to an eruption of new communities of faith, founded and led by lay people, alive with the power of the Holy Spirit. Within the tradition of the Church, one can see that they are building on a firm legacy from the past.

---

[96] As quoted by Avery Dulles in *Models of the Church* (Garden City, NY: Doubleday, 1974), 35.

CHAPTER FOUR

Vatican II: A Watershed

With the passage and promulgation on November 11, 1964, of the Dogmatic Constitution on the Church (*Lumen Gentium*) the Church as an institution and (as that document itself uses the expression) "as the People of God," would never be the same.[1]

A new and comprehensive ecclesiology was needed to complete and to develop the work begun in Vatican I. Indeed, it had been the Reformation that challenged the Church to define her own nature, to clarify her role and to vindicate her exercise of authority in purely religious matters. In response to the threat of Protestantism, the theology of the Church tended to emphasize the hierarchical and institutional dimensions; it emphasized structure, authority, the sacred power of the Pope, bishops and clergy. This theology prevailed for over 400 years until a truer definition of the Church, her nature and her mission was reclaimed.

At Vatican I, ecclesiology had been deeply influenced by the concept of a perfect society. This concept had been adopted from the State and "gave priority to the institution over the mystery. This encouraged the development of an extrinsic ecclesiology cen-

---

[1] Aloysius Wycislo, *Vatican II Revisited, Reflections By One Who Was There* (New York: Alba House, 1987), 49.

tered upon the visible and hierarchic aspects of the institution of the Church."[2] In the light of this hierarchical and reductive idea of the Church, it is clear how "the element of personal charism would not only fail to receive much attention but would, on the contrary, attract a good deal of resistance. It was considered dangerous for the institution as such, and far too allied to the ecclesiology of the Protestant Reformation."[3]

Broadly speaking, one could say that Vatican I concentrated mainly on the institutional Church whereas Vatican II focused on the Church as a movement, as something that must grow in history, as basically eschatological in purpose. In §8 of *Lumen Gentium* it is pointed out that the movement and the institution are not two separate realities, but form one complex reality. By the same token the distinction is real enough, and forcefully implies that the whole value of the institution depends on how much it supports the movement, and that it should not obstruct the movement. In the opening paragraph of *Lumen Gentium* the Church is described as a sacrament or a sign and instrument of "intimate union with God" and of that union which Christians have with one another.[4] The rediscovery of this truth was summed up by the liturgist, Benedictine Father Godfrey Diekmann, OSB (1908-2002),

> The bishops of the world discovered at Vatican II the catholicity of the Church. They experienced the living, existential Church, with its staggeringly diversified problems and needs and hopes. Ecclesiology could never again be for them a schoolbook abstraction, described in neat categories. The living Church, in the person of its bishop, had, as never before in its history, become fully aware of itself, its nature and mission, and

---

[2]   A. Franzini, "Carismi e istituzione nella Chiesa," *AA.VV. La Legge per l'uomo. Una Chiesa al servizio* [Rome] (1980), 27.

[3]   Franzini, 27.

[4]   Cf. *Lumen Gentium*, §1.

each succeeding week of common effort and personal
contacts (during the Council) brought new disclosures.
The Council itself was, in effect, the most potent cata-
lyst for a truly contemporary ecclesiology.[5]

The People of God

This contemporary ecclesiology led to a deeper reflection on
the laity and on their mission in the Church. The emphasis was
changed from a legal-institutional definition of the Church towards a theological conception and definition. The critical cat-
egory of this new definition became characterized as the "People
of God": the Church is the new people of God called by faith in
the Risen Lord and sealed by baptism in Jesus Christ. All the baptized participate with full rights in this vocation and mission. All
are people of God, active and responsible members of the Church
for its mission. This new mindset is well summarized by the words
of Arthur Elchinger, Coadjutor Bishop of Strasbourg who stated
memorably:

> Yesterday the Church was considered above all as an
> institution; today it is experienced as a community. Yes-
> terday, it was the Pope who was mainly in view; today
> the Pope is thought of as united to the bishops. Yes-
> terday the bishop alone was considered; today all the
> bishops together. Yesterday theology stressed the im-
> portance of the hierarchy; today it is discovering the
> People of God. Yesterday it was chiefly concerned with
> what divided; today it voices all that unites. Yesterday
> the theology of the Church was mainly preoccupied

---

[5] Cf. Vincent A. Yzermans, *American Participation in the Second Vatican Council* (New York:
Sheed and Ward, 1967), 74-75.

with the inward life of the Church; today it sees the Church as orientated to the outside world.[6]

In the midst of this mindset, the Council began to articulate a new role for the laity in the Church, by virtue of their "common priesthood." As *Lumen Gentium*, §10 states,

> The baptized, by regeneration and the anointing of the Holy Spirit, are consecrated into a spiritual house and a holy priesthood.... Though they differ from one another in essence and not only in degree, the common priesthood of the faithful and the ministerial priesthood are nonetheless interrelated. Each of them in its own special way is a participation in the priesthood of Christ.[7]

In §33, it is even more specific, "The lay apostolate, however, is a participation in the saving mission of the Church itself." In *Lumen Gentium*, §12 the Council clearly states that the Holy Spirit not only works through the Sacraments and the hierarchy, but also bestows gifts upon all members of the Church, including special charisms for the reform and more extensive growth of the Church; it urges that the charisms should be welcomed with gratitude and a feeling of consolation for the growth of the Church; that decisions regarding the authenticity and good use of the charisms belong to those who govern the Church; and that the pastors have the responsibility not to extinguish the fire of the Holy Spirit but discern everything and keep what is good.[8] The same teaching is included in §3 of *Apostolicam Actuositatem*.[9]

---

[6]   Herbert Vorgrimler, ed., *Commentary on the Documents of Vatican II* (New York: Herder and Herder, 1967-69), 108.

[7]   Cf. *Lumen Gentium*, §10; Austin Flannery, ed., *Vatican Council II: The Conciliar and Post-Conciliar Documents* (Boston, MA: St. Paul Revised Edition, 1988).

[8]   Cf. Ibid., §12.

[9]   Cf. *Apostolicam Actuositatem*, §3.

Lumen Gentium

Although the Council Fathers did not provide a systematic definition of the laity, we do find in *Lumen Gentium* the essential elements for formulating an accurate definition, namely the *genus* and the specific difference. After describing the priestly and prophetic functions of the People of God, which is the Church, *Lumen Gentium* discusses the hierarchy of the Church in Chapter III and the laity in Chapter IV.

> Everything that has been said of the People of God is addressed equally to laity, Religious and clergy.... The term "laity" is here understood to mean all the faithful except those in Holy Orders and those who belong to a religious state approved by the Church. That is, the faithful who by baptism are incorporated into Christ, are placed in the People of God, and in their own way share the priestly, prophetic and kingly office of Christ, and to the best of their ability carry on the mission of the whole Christian people in the Church and in the world. Their secular character is proper and peculiar to the laity.... By reason of their special vocation it belongs to the laity to seek the Kingdom of God by engaging in temporal affairs and directing them according to God's will.[10]

Later we read that the laity has, as their special vocation, "to make the Church present and fruitful in those places where it is only through them that she can become the salt of the earth."[11] Thus the distinguishing note of the laity is their secularity or, as stated in the Revised Code of Canon Law, "to permeate and perfect the temporal order of things with the spirit of the Gospel."[12]

---

[10] *Lumen Gentium,* §30-31.

[11] Ibid., §35.

[12] *The Canon Law, Letter & Spirit* (Veritas, 1995), Canon 225, §2.

The same canon reminds the laity not only of their rights, but also their duties in spreading the faith by virtue of their baptism and confirmation.

This canon removes two possible misunderstandings: (a) the error of thinking that spiritual tasks within the Church belong only to clergy; and (b) that of thinking that the renewed role of the laity is simply to undertake tasks which hitherto were done by the clergy. Instead it states in a general way the form of apostolate that is proper to the laity as such, wherever they may be throughout the world. Moreover, this canon concludes with the further illuminating prescription that this obligation of the laity actively to engage in the Church's apostolate is all the more insistent in circumstances in which only through them are people able to hear the Gospel and to know Christ.[13]

Renewed Understanding of Ministry

This ecclesial conception of the Council leads to a new conception of ministry and ministries in the Church. All ministries and charisms are God's gifts through the community. Although the term charism appears fourteen times in the documents of Vatican II, its import is not fully developed. In *Lumen Gentium*, §4 we read, "(The Spirit) furnishes and directs (the Church) with various gifts both hierarchical and charismatic..." but this is not expanded. In §12 of the same constitution we see the uncertainty as to how and where the charisms fit into the Church's ecclesiology.

> (The Spirit) distributes special graces among the faithful of every rank. By these gifts he makes them fit and ready to undertake the various tasks or offices advantageous for the renewal and up-building of the Church.... These charismatic gifts, whether they be the most outstanding or the more simple and widely dif-

---

[13] Ibid., 127, note 473.

fused, are to be received with thanksgiving and consolation for they are exceedingly suitable and useful for the needs of the Church.[14]

As Haughey points out in his commentary on this passage, it "isn't at all clear about the relationship between graces, gifts, offices and charisms; they are all smudged together. What, for example, does it mean in practice for 'the faithful of every rank' to be receiving gifts to 'undertake the various tasks and offices for the up-building of the Church?'"[15]

Again, Haughey posits the question, "How has the right to use these charisms in the Church been made operational?"[16] Moreover, in *Presbyterorum Ordinis*, §9, priests are encouraged to discover, "with the instinct of faith, acknowledge with joy and foster with diligence the various humble and exalted charisms of the laity."[17]

In a real sense the Council was unprepared to deal with the issue of charisms. They entered into the agenda almost by a backdoor, unexpectedly. There was a real danger that they would be excluded. Cardinal Ruffini spoke for many present when he argued that the charisms had ceased after the first years of the Church. Rampant clericalism was revealed in his assertion that,

> we cannot stably and firmly rely on charismatic lay persons for the advancement of the Church and the apostolate, for charisms — contrary to the opinion of many separated brethren who freely speak of the ministry of charismatics in the Church — are today very rare and entirely singular.[18]

---

[14] Cf. *Lumen Gentium*, §4.

[15] John C. Haughey, "Charisms: An Ecclesiological Exploration" in *Retrieving Charisms for the Twenty-First Century*, ed. Doris Donnelly, Liturgical Press, 1999.

[16] Haughey, 4.

[17] *Acts of the Second Vatican Council*, v. 10, pars 2 (Vatican City, 1972): 629-30.

[18] Haughey, 5.

Yet the prophetic impulse was also present as exemplified by Cardinal Suenens who objected insisting that "one should not think that the gifts of the Spirit consist exclusively of extraordinary and astonishing phenomena.... Do not all of us know, each in his own diocese, lay people, men and women, who are truly called by God... and given special gifts?"[19] In the same speech, he underlines the point that "Each and every Christian, whether lettered or unlettered, has his charism in daily life."[20]

Later, the Decree on the Apostolate of the Laity widens the subject of charisms to see them and their exercise for the good of the Church and the world: "From the reception of these charisms or gifts, there arise for each believer the right and the duty to use them in the Church and in the world for the good of mankind and the up-building of the Church."[21]

Baptism and Ministry

Each of the baptized shares in the dimension of ministry. The diversification of ministries is the expression of the ministerial dimension in the community. The ecclesiastical distinction between "laity" and "priests" ought not be based upon the fact that the priest has care of the kingdom of God, while the layman is characterized by his task in the world. Laity are defined not by their task in the world, but rather by their task in the Church, consequently, by an ecclesial-sacred mission. The theological and ecclesiastical definition of the laity is based, therefore, upon ecclesiastical membership (with an ecclesial call) in the kingdom of God, which is not the world.

---

[19] Léon Josef Suenens, "The Charismatic Dimension of the Church." *Council Speeches of Vatican II* (Glen Rock, NJ, 1964), 29-30.

[20] Ibid., 30.

[21] *Christifideles laici*, §3.

Baptism and Life

This ecclesial mission which the laity receive by their baptism is to integrate their vocation in earthly life with their communion of grace with God in Christ. In this way, the earthly mission becomes for the laity a portion of their total religiously oriented way of life. The baptized must thus integrate secular life with their faith and ecclesial being, which naturally means that apostolate in the world shall be typical of the Christian layman. In order to delineate what it means to be a layman, at least as an ecclesial phenomenon, we ought continually to bear in mind that baptism is the sacrament of our incorporation into the Church and so into Christ. Because incorporation into this tangible community of grace is the first and immediate effect of baptism, the believer receives in and with the grace of baptism the mission to take part in the essential function of the Church; he receives the mission to make his communion of grace with God into a visible form — in and through his own life.

Every baptized person, each Christian layman, thus carries with him a responsibility for the Church and for her function as a sign in the midst of the world. Wherever he stands as a citizen in the dimension of earthly life, the layman has the mission to be the *Church* in this dimension; that is to say, wherever these Christians stand in this world, the Church has to receive from them a visible form or stature, in their normal vocation, in their social intercourse with the rest of mankind, in their families, or in the resultant bonds with society and the community of all men.

A Feature of our Time

The new emerging lay apostolate has irrevocably become one of the features of our time and it marks a significant moment in the laity undertaking their proper role in the life of the Church. This was recognized at the Second Vatican Council which reflected on a new ecclesial sign, namely, the awakening of the laity to a new period of co-responsibility and sense of community. The words of the Council recognized this new period in the Church and at the same time invited the whole Church to continue along this way. The historical significance of the Dogmatic Constitution on the Church is that it is built on the idea of a People to whom God communicates Himself in love by sharing His Son with the world.

Rahner contends that "the Church is a sheepfold where the one and the necessary door is Christ...." In his view this demands an individual relationship with Christ, where the person "will need to be related to Christ the Crucified and Risen, in whose presence there is the ultimate, victorious and irreversible promise of God historically manifested to the world."[22]

Theological and Ecclesiological Implications

From a theological, ecclesial and pastoral point of view, the fact that an increasing leadership is being assumed by the laity is extremely significant. It is not simply leadership that substitutes for the absence of a priest or pushes him aside, rather it is the leadership of lay people, who by special charism and grace feel themselves called to become the animators of their Christian communities in prayer, in the sharing of the Word, in social and political engagements and in the works of charity and justice. These lay leaders point to a new period both in the conception and the function of authority in the Christian Community. There is a growing acceptance that such a charismatic element belongs to the nature of the Church. As Rahner said:

> there are things in the Church which cannot be planned, which cannot be institutionalized and which are unexpected.... There is a charismatic element in the Church, as part of the Church, and only complete with

---

[22] Karl Rahner, "Concern for the Church," *Theological Investigations*, 20 (1981), 145.

this element is the Church what God wants her to be and what she also always will be through His Spirit.[23]

Avery Dulles contends that the Church would "not be truly Church without… the charismatic feature, whereby God transforms the interiority of concrete persons and institutions."[24]

More Vatican II Documents on the Role of the Laity

Dei Verbum states that easy access to Sacred Scripture should be provided for all the faithful. The study of Scripture is the soul of theology.[25] It nourishes the people of God by enlightening their minds and setting them on fire with the love of God. From the table of God's Word and Christ's Body the faithful receive the bread of life. The ministry of the breaking of the Word includes preaching, catechesis and prayerful reading and study in order that the treasure of revelation entrusted to the Church may fill human hearts ever more and more.[26]

On the same day as *Dei Verbum* (18 November 1965) the Council published its decree on the laity, *Apostolicam Actuositatem*. This document asserts the right and the duty of the laity to fulfill their mission in the world, to promote the common good, to educate their children as Christians and to engage in catechetical work.[27] The apostolate, or mission, of the laity, to which all are called by virtue of baptism[28] "can attain maximum effectiveness only through a diversified and thorough formation."[29] The docu-

---

[23] Karl Rahner, "Observations on the Factor of the Charismatic in the Church," *Theological Investigations*, 12 (1974), 253.

[24] Avery Dulles, "A Church to Believe In," *Crossroads* (1992), 31.

[25] *Dei Verbum*, §24.

[26] Ibid., §21.

[27] *Apostolicam Actuositatem*, §11.

[28] Ibid., §2.

[29] Ibid., §28.

ment calls for a certain human and well-rounded formation which would include sensitivity to the movement of the Holy Spirit, solid doctrinal formation, knowledge of the social teaching of the Church, communication skills and a firm grasp of the principles of see, judge and act. Lay groups and associations are seen to have a key role in promoting formation for mission. The need to learn how to bear witness to Christ in the context of materialism is acknowledged.

Three further documents of the Council make specific reference to lay formation.

Christus Dominus states the bishop's responsibility for catechesis which should also extend to adults, adapting it according to the age, natural ability and circumstances of the listener. In the same paragraph we find, "Bishops should also strive to re-establish and better adapt the instruction of adult catechumens."[30]

Presbyterorum Ordinis places the priest's responsibility for education in the faith in the context of his pastoral responsibilities. As head and shepherd in union with the bishop, "he will gather God's family together in unity and lead it through Christ and in the Spirit to God the Father."[31] In seeking to support the layperson's vocation to charity and freedom the priest must recognize that "ceremonies however beautiful, or associations however flourishing, will be of little value if they are not directed toward educating adults in the attainment of Christian maturity."[32]

The decree on the Missions, *Ad Gentes,* called for the revival of the adult catechumenate which is the responsibility of all the faithful. It was to lead people in stages, celebrated in liturgical rites, into "the life of faith, liturgy and love."[33] This document described the role of the catechist as co-worker with the priest and as of maximum importance, calling for due professional formation and remuneration for full time catechists.

---

[30] *Christus Dominus*, §13-14.
[31] *Presbyterorum Ordinis*, §6.
[32] Ibid., §6.
[33] *Ad Gentes*, §14.

Vatican II's Impact

Hence we can see that Vatican II laid significant groundwork for a rediscovery of the role of laity in the Church. It recognized the need for all the faithful to have access to the inspiration of Scripture; it saw the emerging importance of catechesis for adults towards ecclesial maturity and missionary awareness; it recognized the shared responsibility of priests, bishops and laity for adult formation; it fostered the revival of the adult catechumenate. It constituted a new era for the Church and inaugurated a process which, in Rahner's words "will never allow the Church to return to the way she was."[34] Its theology enabled the arrival of the new ecclesial movements to impact in a meaningful way on the Church.

Vatican II and Ecclesial Movements

As Coda has pointed out, there is in fact a providential relation, aroused and sustained by the Holy Spirit, between the ecclesial movements and Vatican II.[35] Just as the reforms of Trent were subsumed into the life of the Church through the inspirational lifestyle of saints such as Charles Borromeo or Ignatius Loyola, today the witness of the movements is giving flesh to the renewal which Vatican II articulated. Moreover, "the identity and mission of those gifts that lie at the origin of and that animate the ecclesial movements"[36] should be placed in the context of the modern world at the end of modernity. This is a *kairos* moment, one which Balthasar called "the century of the reawakening of the Church in souls... to witness in the Church, such a flourishing and a multiplicity of lay movements, of which... the majority have arisen from the new impulses of the Spirit."[37]

---

[34] Karl Rahner, *I Remember*, SCM (1984): 90.
[35] Coda, "The Ecclesial Movements. Gifts of the Spirit," 90.
[36] Ibid., 92.
[37] Cordes, *In the Midst of Our World, Forces of Spiritual Renewal*, 14.

Role of Women

In the awakening of the laity to their role in the Church and in society, the presence of women after centuries of silence and marginality, acquires singular importance and attention. The natural talents and special charism of women infuses a new vitality in the Christian community and reveals a new face of Christian experience. Their sense of the concrete, their feminine sensitivity, their motherhood, their persistence in facing difficulties reveal hidden aspects of the Word of God, of Christian communion, of the experience of the Reign of God. Women have found a central place in the emergence of the new ecclesial movements which have sprung up all over the world; notwithstanding the dominance of the male role in many of these new movements, many women have been accorded leadership roles which have enabled them to exercise their giftedness in a host of ministries.

Church as *Communio* (*Koinonia*)

Vatican II rediscovered the Church as mystery and the Church as communion. Dulles provided six well-known models of Church: institutional; community; sacramental; herald; service; community of disciples.[38] He argued that the Church is a mixture of all six and to overemphasize any one can distort the reality of the Church. Nevertheless, he expressed the clearest preference for the community of disciples model and a least preference for the institutional model. This reflects an important Vatican II preference for a model of Church as "people of God," an Old Testament term which affirmed the personal, human and communal nature of the Church.[39] Such a community dimension of Catholic Christianity had been obscured for centuries by layers of triumphalism, clericalism and juridicism, that characterized an

---

[38] Avery Dulles, *Models of the Church* (Garden City, NY: Doubleday, 1974).
[39] *Lumen Gentium,* §9 & §10.

institutional view of Church.[40] As Gallagher stated, "religious anaemia is produced when the receiver encounters only the conventional or complacent externals of an institution, and when the communicators of faith fail to enter respectfully into the culture of the receiver."[41]

This predominant image of Church had distorted the essential nature of the Church of the New Testament.[42] In Bernier's view, "it seems relatively obvious that the formation of human community, through shared community with Christ is a key aspect of Christianity's early existence and activity."[43] Ludwig contends that with the Council, "Pope John XXIII initiated a revolution against ecclesiastical institutionalism (in order) to return the Church to the dynamic virtues of Christ-centered love, justice and service to a changing world."[44] Vatican II attempted to return to a more balanced, more authentic perspective of Church with the adoption of the biblical image of a wounded, unsure, sometimes unfaithful, pilgrim "People of God," led by imperfect and vulnerable human beings. This community dimension is perhaps one result of the new awareness of the Church's nature as developed by the Council. As one bishop prophetically put it, "I feel that the notion and practice of an evermore participatory Church, will be the most revolutionary idea coming from Vatican II and hence the yardstick to use in assessing developments — anywhere — in the post conciliar Church."[45]

In the Council the Church recognized that its fundamental perspective needed to be the renewal of its spiritual dimension, namely, the dimension of mystery. This involves true communion, not only with God, but with one another, a communion that

---

[40] G. Arbuckle, *Refounding the Church* (New York: Orbis Books, 1990).

[41] M. Gallagher, "Gospel and Culture, Conflict or Challenge," *Conference* 13 (1996), 21ff.

[41] B. Cooke, *Ministry to Word and Sacrament: History and Theology* (Philadelphia: Fortress, 1976), 356.

[43] P. Bernier, *Ministry in the Church* (Mystic, CT: Twenty-Third Publications, 1992), 16.

[44] R. Ludwig, "Restructuring Catholicism for a New Generation," *Crossroads* (1995), 33ff. See also Arbuckle, 91.

[45] P. Claver, "Participation," *The Far East* 68: 18-19.

recognizes our giftedness and our vocation both lay and religious, male and female, and our complementariness. Out of this unity we can recognize the need to "bring the full tithe into the storehouse" and as the Lord says, "then try me in this. Will I not shower down blessings upon you from the heavens?" (Malachi 3:8-11).

The Council rediscovered a fundamental concept of the early Church with its understanding of the Church as a fellowship of local congregations, founded on the Eucharist. Furthermore, the universal Church and the local Church are both mutually inclusive.

However, true *communio* ecclesiology means that there cannot be active members on the one side and passive on the other. This ecclesiology puts an end to the pattern of a welfare Church for looking after people. This has incredible implications for both the local and the global Church. The concept of communion is without doubt the key concept for interpreting the ecclesiology of Vatican II. *Koinonia* is the transcendent innovation of the Council. The etymology of the Greek word, *koinonia*, is more vividly symbolic than its Latin translation *communio*, having its roots in Greek philosophy, especially in Plato, who understood it as a life-giving participation in the eternal realities. It denotes both unity in the holy and eternal persons of the Trinity but also unity in the holy gifts/things which emanate from the Trinity. The New Testament understands it in this way, especially in the person and letters of St. Paul and in the Second Letter of Peter (2 P 1:4), which reflects the Greek meaning in the phrase "sharers in the divine nature." Paul's use of *koinonia* ranges from the idea of shared holiness (2 Cor 6:14) to a participating in Christ's sufferings, to the unity of equity and justice demanded by participation in the Lord's Supper (1 Cor 10-11). He also brings under its umbrella the social duty to "share in the needs of the saints" (Rm 12-13), culminating in the practical injunction to the Corinthians to contribute money for the impoverished community in Jerusalem (2 Cor 9:13).[46]

---

[46] Friedrich Hauck, "Koinonia," in the *Theological Dictionary of the New Testament*, 3 (1965), 797-809.

Dennis Doyle, reflecting on the work of de Lubac, emphasizes that the Church, whatever juridical structures it may maintain, "finds its ultimate basis in relationships among human beings with God through Jesus Christ and the Holy Spirit."[47] Doyle
develops de Lubac's argument that to call the Church a communion is "to recognize both its historical and spiritual dimensions in
the face of the challenges of the modern world."[48] This gift enables the Church better to understand the human heart: "Catholicity, then, for de Lubac, implies not only an encompassing of
various dimensions of truth held in tension, and not only a so-
cially conscious embrace of all that is good and worthy, but also a
radical inclusion of all human beings in all of their depth and mystery."[49] Doyle sees de Lubac as combining, in his thought, the divine, mystical, sacramental, historical and social dimensions of the
Church. The latter quality, especially, renders the Church ever an
enemy of both individualism and exclusivism; it is a community
that "affirms and elevates whatever is good in human culture."[50]

J. Robert Dionne, in a small section of his *The Papacy and
the Church*, elaborates on "the Church as *Koinonia* on the level of
the Word."[51] Dionne is most concerned here with the development of doctrine, and ways in which it might take place
"*eiscyclically*" (from the Church into the center) and "*eccyclically*"
(from the papacy outward). He employs the text of 1 John 1:1-3
to illustrate how the Word of Life, when authentically proclaimed
and received, creates life-giving *koinonia*.[52]

J.M.R. Tillard, in his *Église d'églises*, elaborates on the conception of communion, and calls upon the Church to become what
Jesus meant it to be — a life-giving communion composed of dis-

---

[47] See Denis M. Doyle, "Henri de Lubac and the Roots of Communion Ecclesiology,"
Theological Studies 60 no. 2 (June 1999), 211ff.

[48] Ibid., 214.

[49] Ibid., 217.

[50] Ibid., 225.

[51] J. Robert Dionne, *The Papacy and the Church: a Study of Praxis and Reception in Ecumenical Perspective* (New York: Philosophical Library, 1987), 285-297.

[52] Dionne, 295.

tinct members, and of the divided nations of the world, to seek a shared life amid all their diversity. For Tillard, "humanity is truly itself only in communion."[53] This communion is symbolized by the Church of Pentecost as it responds to the call of the Prophet Isaiah to unite all peoples. But the Church itself has symbolized communion as much by its failures as by its achievements of communion. To the question, "Why do Christians lack the solidarity of the Body of Christ?" Tillard responds that they have failed to "discern about the Body"[54] (1 Cor 11:17-34). Christians forget the inseparable connection between the Eucharistic body and the ecclesial body with its unity and diversity. Tillard comments further: "It is the question of the Lord of Glory making his power present through his body. Thus the mission of the Church transcends any collapse into individualism."[55]

Most significant here is the argument that the Church is the communion of local Churches, each one contributing to the catholicity of the whole Body. The fact that these local Churches are set within different cultural contexts gives the universal Church its richness and variety. "Theology today speaks here of acculturation, of the translation of the one faith into the compost of peoples, of human traditions, of the old religious sources."[56] In this context, Tillard is especially concerned with the significance of "reception," which is accomplished, not primarily by canons or liturgical forms, but by finding an accord with the soul of a people.[57]

---

[53] J.M.R. Tillard, *Église d'églises: L'ecclésiologie de Communion* (Paris: Éditions du Cerf, 1987), 27.

[54] Ibid., 40-41.

[55] Ibid., 46.

[56] Ibid., 169. It is worth pointing out that at the time of this writing, not enough clarification had been made among theologians between the related words "acculturation," "enculturation" and "inculturation." Tillard will later, in the same book, employ the word "inculturation" in a more accurate expression of his meaning. For a fine brief summary of current usage of terminology on inculturation, see J. Peter Schineller, S.J., *A Handbook on Inculturation* (New York: Paulist, 1990). The difference between the cultural anthropology usage of "acculturation" (adapting to a foreign culture) and the theological usage of "inculturation" (the incarnation of the Gospel in a culture) is of vital importance.

[57] Ibid., 169.

This is how the Church carried out its mission of growth in the early centuries, developing a catholicity that was a "symbiosis" of diversity and unity, a communion of the infinite multitude of human forms in the unity of faith.[58]

Speaking theologically, the Church can serve as a model because it is a sacrament — the "fundamental sacrament" (*Ursakrament*). In a famous article, written before the Second Vatican Council, Karl Rahner stated, "The Church is the continuance, the contemporary presence, of that real, eschatologically triumphant and irrevocably established presence in the world, in Christ, of God's salvific will."[59]

This basic definition of sacramentality came into its own at the Second Vatican Council, especially in the Constitution on the Sacred Liturgy (*Sacrosanctum Concilium*), where the decree states: "The purpose of the sacraments is to sanctify [men], to build up the Body of Christ, and, finally, to give worship to God. Because they are signs, they also instruct."[60] According to Rahner, one aspect of this transcendent change, wrought by the Council, was that it officially actualized itself as the Universal Church. Heretofore, the Church had a limited understanding of its universality, in that it mainly exported its European dimension and made no effort to adapt its merchandise. Rahner characterizes this new aspect as being as earth shattering as St. Paul's leading the early Church away from a merely Jewish circle to a Church of the pagans. Rahner maintains that the de-judaisation of Christianity is a key to understanding what is about to happen: "The difference between western cultures and the present cultures of the whole of Africa and Asia, relative to which the Christianity of today must become inculturated so as to be finally a universal Church as it has already begun to be...."[61]

---

[58] Ibid., 181-182.

[59] Karl Rahner, "The Church and the Sacraments," *Inquiries* (1964), 189-199.

[60] *Sacrosanctum Concilium*, §2.

[61] Karl Rahner, "Towards a Fundamental Theological Interpretation of Vatican II," *Theological Studies* 40 (1979), 7ff.

Writing about the universal communion of the Churches, Tillard argues that, while the universal communion of bishops is of absolute importance for effecting the union of the Churches, these Churches have different customs, traditions and problems, different organizations, even different souls. "Yet, since the beginning, the Church has spread by taking on characteristics which have come from the territories where they were born."[62] In the Church of Churches, there is no question of a fragmentation, but rather of the union of all in one communion and indivisible community of salvation. Writing specifically about the local Churches, Tillard applies his final remarks to the diversity of cultures: the remarks could equally be applied to the new ecclesial communities and movements which reveal a diversity of spiritualities.

> Uniformity suffocates *communion*, while certain divergencies on fundamental points render it non-viable. Unity without diversity makes the Church a dead body; pluralism without unity makes of it a dismembered body. Shall we not grasp how, with the Spirit of God, they are to get along with each other in the healthy equilibrium that "communion of communions" implies?[63]

Summary

In this chapter I have looked at the impact of the Second Vatican Council which radically overhauled the prevailing vision of the laity's role within the Church. One of the direct fruits of the Council was a new impetus to embryonic lay groups some of which had come into existence prior to Vatican II. The reclamation of the concept of the Church as *communio* was pivotal. This

---

[62] Tillard, 326.
[63] Ibid., 401.

renewed ecclesiology of the Council encouraged and fostered the emergence of a host of vibrant and innovative forms of apostolate within the laity, most of which have subsequently been grouped under the term, "new ecclesial movements." Their emergence, both at global and local level, demanded a change of attitude so that a new methodology could be implemented. The dynamics of the opposition of the socio-juridical abstract and apologetic ecclesiology in vogue since the Counter Reformation and that of the new ecclesiology rooted in Scripture and the Fathers, historical and concerned with communion, which prevailed in the Council, is the milieu within which the new movements are evolving.

One of the significant features of the new movements is that they reveal the Church as a sacrament of Christ, the Christ who is present, not only by the Word, the Sacraments and the Ministry but also by a community of disciples who live the new commandment "to love one another as I have loved you" (Jn 15:17). The new ecclesial movements make Christ present through their communion with one another and with all men and women.[64] However, as the work of Tillard would suggest, it is important to see the new ecclesial movements, not as a threat or as a deviation from the norm, but as an exciting new expression of inculturation. The Church today continues to seek new ways to insert the Gospel truths into a variety of cultural contexts and in a host of authentic expressions. The ecclesial movements impregnate culture and society by their committed and faithful lifestyles, rooted in Gospel values.

In an interesting essay, "Religion as a Cultural System," Clifford Geertz outlines a methodology for interpreting culture as semiotic, focusing on cultural symbols, and, in turn, symbols as models. He has created a valuable distinction in articulating two types of models, models *of* and models *for*. The model *of* symbolizes what a reality already is, as in the case of a diagram of an existing dam, while the model *for* is like a blueprint for a new con-

---

[64] Ibid., 94.

struction.[65] Geertz's understanding of how a model *for* enables agents to manipulate external systems of symbolically expressed relationships — that is, to create new symbolic processes — is very apt in considering the impact of the new ecclesial movements and their varied, lived expressions of *communio*. The Church is not only a model *of* communion, but a model *for* a richer historical development of that communion. The new ecclesial communities may indeed be a model or a blueprint *for* the shape of the Church of tomorrow.

Almost inevitably, acceptance of these new groups into the mainstream of the Church has not always been straightforward. Caution, suspicion and skepticism in some quarters vied with acceptance, support and encouragement in others. However, history teaches us that to some extent such has always been the lot of the charismatic element of the life of the Church. I would like to review this aspect in the next chapter, in order to shed more light on the current place of these new movements within the Church.

---

[65] Clifford Geertz, *Religion as a Cultural System. The Interpretation of Cultures: Selected Essays* (New York: Basic Books, 1973), 87-125.

CHAPTER FIVE

Ecclesial Movements within the History of Charisms

Any study of the new movements inevitably leads to an examination of charisms. Movements claim implicitly or explicitly that they have been called into being by the Holy Spirit, gifted by him for mission and ministry. For example, if one looks at the Jesuits one can see that they have a clear belief that God anointed their founder, Ignatius, with a compelling call to mission.[1] There is a history of charism that is indissolubly intertwined with the history of the Church itself, not as an alternative to the exercise of the government of the Church and the Apostolic-Petrine ministry, but in providential synergy with it.[2] Balthasar contends that each of these charisms is like a bolt of lightning destined to illuminate a single and original point of God's will for the Church in a given time, by highlighting a specific point in divine revelation.[3] However, before pursuing this issue further it is important to examine how the Church past and present has used and understood the word "charism."

---

[1]   Cf. W.J. Barry and R.G. Doherty, *Contemplatives in Action, the Jesuit Way* (Mahwah, NJ: Paulist Press, 2002).

[2]   Coda, 77-104.

[3]   Cf. Hans Urs von Balthasar, *Two Sisters in the Spirit: Thérèse of Lisieux and Elizabeth of the Trinity* (San Francisco: Ignatius Press, 1992), 25.

Etymology

The etymology of the word, as it is generally used, signifies the object and the result of *charis* or grace. It means a kind of freely given divine favor, a present or a gift from God.[4] It is derived from the Greek root *char* and all words that share this root indicate something in the nature of well-being. The term *char* is translated by "to condescend, to grant grace, to give, to lavish," and it accepts the suffixes -ism, -isma, to give us the word charism or charisma. Nouns ending in -ma almost always carry overtones of activity. In our case, this would be a concrete result of being given grace.[5]

The term *charisma* was apparently not known in classical Greece nor in the world of Hellenic mystery religions nor in the Greco-biblical world with the sole exception of 1 Peter 4:10 and of course Paul. Wambacq postulates that the word was probably coined by St. Paul by linking the verb *charizomai* (= to please) with *charis* (= grace).[6] The word charisma is cognate with the word *charis*, grace, and could be defined as divine grace becoming concrete. Käsemann describes it as "the manifestation and concretion of the gracious power of God." The concept of charisma in Paul is closely related to the Holy Spirit. Thus in 1 Cor 12:4, the Spirit is represented as the source of the *charismata* (cf. Rm 1:11; 1 Cor 2:12 where the cognate verb is linked with the Spirit). A charism could therefore be defined as a gift of the Spirit.

New Testament Usage

The word appears seventeen times in the New Testament, fourteen times in Romans and 1-2 Corinthians, the other three times in texts written under Pauline influence (1 Tm 4:14; 2 Tm

---

[4] Cf. X. Ducross, "Charismes," DS, II (1953), 504.

[5] Antonio Romano, *The Charism of the Founders*, St. Pauls, 1989, 73.

[6] B.N. Wambacq, "Le Mot Charisme," *Nouvelle revue théologique* 97 (1975), 345-355.

1:6; 1 P 4:10). The word is used in a general way to designate gifts bestowed by God gratuitously (Rm 1:11; 5:15; 6:23; 11:29; 2 Cor 1:11). More often it is used in a more specific sense to designate those gifts which are used for the building up of the Christian community (Rm 12:6; 1 Cor 12:4, 9, 28, 30, 31 with which one could link 1:7; 1 Tm 4:14; 2 Tm 1:6 and 1 P 4:10). It is in this second sense that the word has become a permanent part of the Christian vocabulary.

In 1 Corinthians chapters 12-14, Paul gives us "a richer insight into community life than in any other passage in the New Testament." So spoke H. Conzelmann as he argued that these chapters together with 10 and 11 give one a theological compendium of community, community worship and practice — almost a miniature ecclesiology. Conzelmann calls this "the ongoing uniformity of the theological criticism of Paul."[7]

Charisms of the Corinthian Church

In the case of the Corinthians the *charismata* they received were individuated gifts, or personalized graces. The grace of Jesus Christ is that he died for us all. Each individual believer accepts this gift and appropriates the gift of salvation in a unique way, which depends on the individual's background, talents, temperament and constitutional makeup: "Each one has his own special gift (charisma) from God, one of one kind and one of another" (1 Cor 7:7b).

It is precisely this infinite and limitless variety of charisms that constitutes a community: "If all were a single organ, where would the body be? As it is, there are many parts, yet one body. The eye cannot say to the hand, I have no need of you, nor again the head to the feet, I have no need of you" (1 Cor 12:19-21). Such diversity is essential to any society. Clones do not make a

---

[7] H. Conzelmann, *I Corinthians* (Philadelphia: Fortress Press, 1975), 258.

community. However, what is required is not only diversity and multiplicity but also the hierarchy of charisms. The Corinthians failed to appreciate that the charisms were a gift not just for the individual but for the community.

Pneumatika versus *Charismata*

There was an obvious term available to Paul to convey the idea of the Spirit, viz. the word *pneumatikon*. He does use the term in 1 Cor 1 but in vs. 4, 9, 28, 30, and 31 he uses *charisma*. In v. 1, where he is referring to the letter he received from the Corinthians, undoubtedly he uses the word they had used themselves, but it appears *charisma* is his preferred term. Paul chose the word *charismata* in order to replace the word *pneumatika* used by the Corinthians (12:1). They were stressing inspiration, while Paul's choice of the word *charismata* helped him put the accent back on the gratuitousness on God's part and the usefulness for the Church.

Käsemann contends that such a preference infers a starting point for a theological critique.[8] It appears that the word *pneumatikon* had become so loaded with misleading associations that Paul found it necessary to replace it with a word of his own choosing which he could define in his own way. This hypothesis appears reasonable when we examine Paul's teaching against what we know or can realistically infer about Corinthian assumptions about the manifestations of the Spirit.

By inference, we can deduce that the Corinthians assumed that the Spirit was given to them for their own benefit and enrichment. Paul's correction of them highlights that they were conspicuously deficient in any sense of mutual responsibility. They were torn apart by competing factions (chapter 1-4). They were taking one another to court (chapter 6). They delighted in parad-

---

8   Ernst Käsemann, *Essays on New Testament Themes, Ministry and Community in the New Testament* (Philadelphia: Fortress Press, 1982), 136.

ing their Christian freedom, reckless of the effect it might have on their weaker brothers and sisters (chapter 8). They were failing to wait for latecomers at the Eucharistic meal (11:17-34). And yet they had the Spirit. Clearly for them the Spirit had nothing to do with the neighbor; it had only to do with me, my enrichment. One can also infer that the Corinthians took it for granted that the Spirit made its presence felt chiefly in spectacular manifestations. The care and tact with which Paul disparages any exaggeration of the value of tongue speaking in chapter 14 shows unmistakably how highly the Corinthians must have prized this particular gift. If so, we may surely infer that they thought of the gifts of the Spirit primarily in terms of things that were abnormal, spectacular, extraordinary.

Furthermore, one can conclude that they saw the Spirit as the special possession of a privileged few, a spiritual elite. They placed great store on tongue speaking, yet Paul asks in 12:30, "Do all speak in tongues of ecstasy?" By the form of this question in Greek, the negative reply is expected. If not all of them had it, then those who did, must have been seen as especially favored.

The Importance of *Diakonia*

In opposition to these assumptions, Paul affirms that every *charisma* that the Spirit bestows upon the Church consists of some sort of capacity to perform a service for the good of others.

Throughout chapters 12-14 Paul keeps insisting that this is the yardstick by which what is claimed to be a gift of the Spirit must always be measured. All gifts are related to the corporate body, the Church, and are assessed in the light of their contribution to that body's proper functioning, especially the up-building in *agapé*. The Corinthians are urged to aspire above all to excel in those gifts which build up the Church (14:12; cf. v. 26).

In contrast to the second assumption of the Corinthians, Paul makes it clear that the gracious gifts of the Spirit need in no way be strikingly spectacular. In several places he gives a list of the *cha-*

rismata, in vv. 8-10 and 28 and also in Romans 12:6-8. It is especially striking how he places them beside the apostolate and ability to help others; gifts of healing and gifts of administration (1 Cor 12:28). Likewise, in Rm 12:6-8 he speaks of works of mercy, almsgiving and helping others in distress. It is safe to say that these were things that never entered the Corinthians' heads to regard as signs of the working of the Spirit. Clearly for Paul, extraordinariness is irrelevant as a criterion of the Spirit's presence. This conviction of his is also reflected in his considered depreciation of speaking in tongues in chapter 14. Again in contrast to their approach, Paul insists that the Spirit leaves no believer ungifted. There is a stereotyped repetition of the fact that God gives to everyone. "In each of us the Spirit is seen to be at work" (v. 7). The Spirit distributes gifts "to each individual at will" (v. 11: cf. Rm 12:3).

Paul's argument was a shocking one for the faction in the Corinthian Church who placed such an emphasis on the dramatic gift of tongues. As Murphy-O'Connor points out, Paul is sometimes very hard on the spirit people. The savagely rhetorical questions of Paul in 1 Cor 2:6-16, 3:3-4 and 4:7 stress contemptuously that they are recipients not creators.[9]

Pauline Commonsense

Paul lays down three commonsensical principles to deal with these issues. The first one clearly is fidelity of these charisms to the truth of the Gospel message. Are the ecstatic exclamations orthodox? The words and tongues of the ecstatic are not to be judged by their novelty and power of attraction but by their fidelity to the Gospel. Secondly, Paul stresses the principle of unity, "a variety of gifts but the same Spirit" (1 Cor 12:4-6). If the first principle provides the criterion for judging the validity of the enthu-

---

[9]   Jerome Murphy-O'Connor, *Paul, A Critical Life* (Oxford: Clarendon House, 1996), 273-278.

siasts' outbursts, the second offers the antidote to that perennial conflict which has aptly been described as the conflict between charism and institution. All the charisms, the humblest and the most exalted, the flashiest and most conspicuous, as well as the hidden and most unremarkable, have their origin in the one and the same Spirit, Lord and God. It is because of this unity of origin that all the charisms can and should work together for the same end. Finally, Paul asserts the principle of the common good: "To each is given the manifestation of the Spirit for the common good" (1 Cor 12:7). The end of every gift is "the common good" (*sympheron*) which is whatever builds up the community, "so that the Church may be edified" (1 Cor 14:26). Weiss calls this

> the basic rule for the *charismata* granted to the whole community. *Sympheron* is that which edifies the community. The profit of the individual is far less important than this. This ranks first for Paul himself and his apostolic ministry, "…not seeking my own advantage but that of many, that they may be saved" (1 Cor 10:33).[10]

Hans Küng put it very succinctly: "The charism relates to the community. The revelation of the Spirit is given to individuals with a view to the common good."[11]

Where Paul speaks negatively of the gifts, particularly tongues, he is not railing against the gifts as such but against the Corinthians' misunderstanding and abuse of them. If these gifts are to be truly for the up-building of the community and not a cause of fragmentation and division they must be seen in their proper context. They are for the "common good" not as personal adornments; their variety and diversity is a reflection of the various and diverse needs of the community, not carefully graded prizes in a contest of personal accomplishments.

---

[10] K. Weiss, *Theological Dictionary of the New Testament*, 976-77.

[11] Hans Küng, *The Church* (London: DLT, 1967), 131-132.

Agapé

To harness them for the good of the community and the service of the Lord, all of them, without exception, need to be subject to a love that is not jealous or boastful, not arrogant and rude, not insistent on its own way, not irritable or resentful or gloating at another's wrong, but a love that is patient and kind, rejoicing in the right, bearing all things, believing all things, hoping all things, enduring all things. This love never ends, "As for prophecies, they will pass away; as for tongues they will cease; as for knowledge, it will pass away" (1 Cor 13:8).

Agapé is the greatest of the virtues, the characteristic virtue of the Christian faith. It has to do with the mind and the will: it is not simply an emotion which rises unbidden in our hearts: it is a principle by which we deliberately live. *Agapé* has supremely to do with the will. It is a conquest, a victory, an achievement. It is, in fact, the power to love the unlovable.[12] The ideal of "Christian charity is not to treat others as if they were one's best friend but to be to them as life-giving as God is to us in Christ."[13]

Corinthian Abuse of the Gifts

Clearly Paul's Letter to the Corinthians is an assertive pastoral letter sent to correct abuses in a Church founded some six years earlier. The community or at least a sizable section of it had developed a distorted doctrine of Christianized human nature. Basic morality had been neglected with implications of fornication and incest being arrogantly tolerated in the community. A charismatic leadership had developed which extolled *glossolalia* as a superior spiritual gift and this in turn entitled such *afficionados* to extra respect and gave them an elite position within the commu-

---

[12] William Barclay, *New Testament Words*, SCM (1964), 21-22.
[13] Jerome Murphy-O'Connor, *1 Corinthians: New Testament Message*, Veritas (1980), 124.

nity. As Paul said in the Greek phrase, *pros to sympheron*, the gifts are given for the common good. We find several lists of these gifts of the Spirit.

In 1 Corinthians 12 we find utterances of wisdom, and knowledge, faith, healings, miracles, prophecy, discernment of spirits, tongues and the interpretation of tongues. In Ephesians 4 we can note apostles, prophets, evangelists, pastors, teachers in roles of service. Romans 12 gives prophecy, ministry, teaching, exhortation, almsgiving, ruling and doing works of mercy. Other lists occur in the New Testament but it is clear that there is never an attempt to give an exhaustive list of the gifts of the Spirit, who, quite simply, breathes where he will (John 3:8). Everything we receive from God is a gift.

Emergence of Hierarchy

However, this early understanding as articulated in 1 Cor 7:17, 'The general rule is that each one should lead the life the Lord has assigned to him or her," was soon bypassed. The letters to Timothy refer specifically to the office of presbyter (such as Timothy) who received his charism through the laying on of hands. Timothy was exhorted not to "neglect the gift" (charism) he received at that time (1 Tm 4:14) and this message was reinforced with a call to "fan into a flame the gift (charism) of God bestowed when my hands were laid on you" (2 Tm 1:6). The Corinthian ministry of charisms seems to have been superseded by a ministry exclusive to presbyters and bishops. Moreover, their ministry derives its legitimacy not specifically from a charism, but to their being in a continuum with the apostles. This change took place within forty years, if we accept the Corinthian letters as being around the 50's and the letters to Timothy around the 90's. Paul's experience with the excesses of the Corinthian Church may have accelerated this development.

Bishop and Charism of Leadership

Whatever the exact historical development, the bishop now became responsible for discerning the validity of the charisms and in Balthasar's view this was a charism of leadership attached to the office. For Balthasar, the existence of these offices began with the call and subsequent training of the twelve by Christ himself. He describes the role of office in the Church as "crystallized love," one that takes its *raison d'être* from this font and source.[14] As overseers, the *episkopoi* held offices so that the bearers of charisms could function through the structures which they, the officeholders, supervised.[15] This concept of a charism of office has been traditional in the Church since the days of Irenaeus of Lyons, who spoke of the "sure charism of truth" (*charisma veritatis certum*) bestowed on the presbyter/bishop ordained in the apostolic Churches.[16] Vatican I had already taught that Peter and his successors possessed the charism of unfailing truth and faith (*veritatis et fidei numquam deficientis charisma*).[17] Vatican II picked up the term declaring that all bishops "have received through episcopal succession the sure charism of truth."[18]

Charisms and New Ecclesial Movements

Today the gifts associated with the explosion of new movements are akin to those distributed to various members of the Church at Corinth (1 Cor 12:11). They are particular gifts and not necessarily ones required for salvation or personal holiness (unlike faith, hope and love). These charisms are given for works within the body.

---

[14] Hans Urs von Balthasar, *Charis and Charism* (San Francisco: Ignatius Press, 1991), 313.

[15] Ibid., 330.

[16] Irenaeus, *Adversus Haereses*, IV.26.2.

[17] Vatican I, *Pastor Aeternus*, in H. Denzinger, C. Bannwart, and et al, eds., *Manual of Creeds, Definitions and Declarations on Matters of Faith and Morals 1854 - to the present*, §3071.

[18] *Dei Verbum*, §8.

Given that it is the bishop's task to bring unity, the plethora of charisms could be seen as an obstacle rather than a help. At a human level, it is easy to see how a bishop would find the emergence of special charismatic gifts problematic, yet tradition suggests that these gifts are vital for the Church's well being. Historically, when there has been power without order there has been chaos and turmoil. Likewise when there has been order without power there has been indifference, lifelessness and conformism. Power can overwhelm order and order can suffocate power. An institution that neither expects nor makes room for the Spirit to blow where he wills (Jn 3:8) will inevitably make its own order and structure dominate. Charisms remind the Church how dependent it is on the unpredictable wind of the Spirit. As we read in 2 Cor 3:17, "Where the Spirit of the Lord is, there is freedom."

Charism Does Not Equal Sanctity

Today we have rediscovered the truth that a charism is a free gift that equips a person to perform some function in the assembly. Clearly in the New Testament there is a definite refusal to equate holiness and charism. In Corinth, as I have outlined earlier, there were many who had charisms but were "puffed up" with pride (1 Cor 4:18-19; 5:2; 8:1); in contrast "love is not puffed up" (1 Cor 13:4). The fact that the charisms do not necessarily sanctify, re-echoes the warning given by Jesus in Matthew's Gospel, "On that day many will say to me, 'Lord, Lord, did we not prophesy in your name, and cast out demons in your name, and do mighty works in your name?' And I will declare to them, 'I never knew you; depart from me, you evildoers'" (7:22-23).

Renewed Appreciation of Charism

It is important to remember that this renewed appreciation of charism is a somewhat recent phenomenon and it was only in the latter part of the twentieth century that the issue of charism and its place in the Church became a focal issue.

Prophetically, Ernst Käsemann, the Lutheran exegete, wrote in 1949 what was then regarded as a highly provocative article in which he describes charisms as something which is an integral part of being a Christian.[19] He argued that, as was normative in the early Church, the Spirit individuates and concretizes the grace that each Christian receives in becoming a member of the body of Christ by the distinct charism with which each is endowed. The distinctiveness of each one's charism creates a call to live and serve in a distinctive way within the community. The Second Vatican Council in its final text of the Constitution on the Church eventually confirmed the place of charisms in the Church.

> It is not only through the sacraments and the ministrations of the Church that the Holy Spirit makes holy the people, leads them and enriches them with his virtues. Allotting his gifts, according as he wills (1 Cor 12:11), he also distributes special graces among the faithful of every rank. By these gifts he makes them fit and ready to undertake various tasks and offices for the renewal and building up of the Church; as it is written, "the manifestation of the Spirit is given to everyone for profit" (1 Cor 12:7).[20]

In the same document the Council stated, "Whether these charisms be very remarkable or more simply and widely diffused, they are to be received with thanksgiving and consolation since they are fitting and useful for the needs of the Church."[21]

---

[19] Ernst Käsemann, *Essays on New Testament Themes*, SCM Press (1964). See especially the chapter on "Ministry and Community in the New Testament," 63-94.

[20] *Lumen Gentium*, §9.

[21] Ibid., §12.

Council Debate over Charisms

However, this decision only emerged after a turbulent debate. Many at that Council shared the view illustrated by Cardinal Ernesto Ruffini in his intervention at the Second Vatican Council, that the *charismata* outside the official office holders were only for a brief period in the Church's history, pending the establishment of Church order.[22] These held that charisms were rare and extraordinary gifts that had become virtually extinct after the apostolic age, a view represented on the council floor by Cardinal Ruffini.

These divergent views were reflected in two varying notions of charism as outlined in Catholic encyclopedias. According to X. Ducross in *Dictionnaire de Spiritualité*, charisms are extraordinary gifts of grace, such as one might find in the lives of saints and mystics.[23] Yet A. Lemonnyer sees charisms as gifts of grace to equip people for the roles and ministries which they are to hold in the body of Christ. Some of these gifts are extraordinary, many are not.[24]

A Flawed Perspective

Louis Bouyer in a review of charismatic movements in the history of the Church argues that "the comparatively modern view that charism and regular organization in the Church would normally be in a state of nervous tension, if not of war, is not based on fact but on prejudice."[25] He attributes the emergence of this view to Gottfried Arnold, an eighteenth century pietistic teacher, whose work he brands as "brilliant but very superficial and overly

---

[22] Haughey, 46.

[23] *Dictionnaire de Spiritualité: Ascétique et Mystique*, II, 503-507.

[24] A. Lemonnyer, *Dictionnaire de la Bible*, supplement II, 1233-1243.

[25] Louis Bouyer, "Some Charismatic Movements in the History of the Church," *Perspectives on Charismatic Renewal*, Edward D. O'Connor, ed. (1975), 114.

systematic...." He believes that any objective study shows that Church authorities have been at pains to avoid condemnation wherever possible and have been disposed "to integrate these movements into the life of the Church so as fully to exploit for the whole Christian body the riches of their experience."[26]

Historically the first Pentecostal movement to turn to heresy was Montanism,[27] so called after the founder, Montanus. They came to hold that their extraordinary gifts were the only authentic gifts of the Spirit and they rejected the regular hierarchy as not sufficiently spiritual, in stark contrast to their own radical asceticism. Their theology was certainly underpinned by a perspective of martyrdom which was influenced by the teaching of Ignatius of Antioch, and by such works as *The Martyrdom of Polycarp*[28] and the *Passion of Felicity and Perpetua.*[29]

The Monastic Movement

A more authentic charismatic expression of the Spirit at work was the later emergence of the monastic movement. Bouyer defines

---

[26] Ibid.

[27] Cf. John Finney, *Fading Splendour, a New Model of Renewal*, DLT, 2000:65. Montanus gave his name to the "New Prophecy" which began in Asia Minor but soon spread rapidly. It preached an earthenware gospel in comparison with the carefully crafted bone china of contemporary theology. The Age of the Son had now given way to the Age of the Spirit; the millennial rule of Christ was soon to begin with the descent of the Heavenly Jerusalem near Pepuzza in Phrygia; the prophets and prophetesses were the messengers of God; tongues and other charismatic gifts were to be exercised. The movement demanded a life lived according to strict rules — purity in sexual relationships, much penitential fasting, steadfastness in times of persecution. They saw themselves as superior to other Christians; they were the "pneumatikos pneumatike" — spiritual Christians for other spiritual Christians. About 200 A.D. they won their most famous convert when Tertullian joined them and their most famous martyrs were Perpetua and Felicity. They were condemned as heretics by a number of Church Councils and at the Council of Iconium in 287 it was decreed that they had to be rebaptized if they were to join a Catholic Church.

[28] Text and translation in *The Apostolic Fathers*, II, ed. by G.R. Canke (Harvard: 1913), 307-345.

[29] A. Robinson, *Passio: Texts and Studies*, Cambridge University Press (1891), §2.

monastic asceticism as "a victorious struggle of the Spirit with the powers of the world, taking place in the believer."[30] This is clearly evident in the oldest document on monasticism, *The Life of St. Antony*[31] written by St. Athanasius circa 360. Here the true monk is presented as a man in whom the presence of the Spirit and its dominion are shown through the gifts of prophecy and miraculous powers especially healing, both spiritual and physical. This gives the monk a spiritual calling power, a spiritual authority which enables him to call forth a life of the Spirit in others.

From its inception the monastic movement was essentially a lay movement, one that had sprung up spontaneously. Significantly the Church authorities, beginning with Athanasius, far from opposing the movement or casting an unduly critical eye upon it, tended very early to seize the opportunities it provided to recruit a better clergy and a better episcopacy. Athanasius's letter to the monk Draconitus bears testimony to this fact.[32] Moreover, St. Basil, the great leader of the Cappadocian Church, made strenuous efforts to make monasticism the principle and focus of a renewal of the whole Church life. Likewise, the first monks such as Antony were among the supporters of the bishops in their struggle with heretics such as Arius.

Bouyer's research into later spiritual writers such as Evagrius Ponticus (346-399), Pseudo-Dionysius, Diadochos of Photike and St. Symeon (949-1022) led him to conclude that, in the view of these scholars, only those bishops and priests who had experienced a "conscious outpouring of the Spirit in us making us aware of our actual union with Christ and of our adoption by the Father through a joyful surrender of our whole being to divine love" could be "true spiritual leaders." Bouyer contends that "throughout the monastic tradition of the East (and a good part of the West)…

---

[30] Bouyer, 120.

[31] English translation by Robert Meyer, St. Athanasius, *The Life of St. Antony*, Newman Press (1950), §107.

[32] Athanasius to Draconitus, IV. Migne PG: 521-534; The Nicene and Post Nicene Fathers, Second Series, Vol. IV, Letter 49, 557.

the true monk is not he who merely conforms to an external rule, but only he who has attained a personal experience of the inner light... even if he is a layman, such a one has more right to be a spiritual father than any priest or bishop who knows nothing of this experience."[33]

The Advocacy of Cardinal Suenens

In more modern times it was Cardinal Suenens who played a crucial role in securing due recognition for the charismatic gifts in the Dogmatic Constitution on the Church (*Lumen Gentium*). He maintained that the charisms need not be extraordinary; they were still given and disseminated among the faithful for the tasks and ministries of the Church. It was he who proposed that the chapter on the hierarchy should be placed after the chapter on the People of God. Furthermore, he eloquently argued that "at baptism we all receive the fullness of the Holy Spirit, the layperson as well as the priest, bishop, or pope. The Holy Spirit cannot be received more or less, any more than a host is more or less consecrated."[34]

Pneumatology and Ecclesiology

The application of the theology of the Holy Spirit to ecclesiology was a significant development of the Council and it led to Congar's assertion that "one of the Council's greatest restorations to the role of the Holy Spirit in ecclesiology has been that of the *charismata*."[35] O'Sullivan too believes that the Council "accomplished a renewal of Catholic theory about charisms."[36] As

---

[33] Bouyer, "Some Charismatic Movements in the History of the Church," 123.

[34] Suenens, *A New Pentecost?*, 86.

[35] Congar, *I Believe in the Holy Spirit*, 191.

[36] Francis J. Sullivan, *Charisms and Charismatic Renewal*, Gill and McMillan (1982), 79.

a fruit of this re-evaluation, the realization grew that the Church is "inconceivable if it is marginal to or without the Holy Spirit."[37] In fact, the *charismata* cannot be thought of as if they were "purely peripheral phenomena or mere accidentals to the life of the Church.... Their purpose is to build up the mystical body.... This era of the Church, which is a Church journeying towards the last age and the *parousia* of the Lord, is the era of the Holy Spirit."[38]

At the same time it must be acknowledged that in *Lumen Gentium*, in particular, and in the conciliar documents in general, the link between the *charismata* and the Holy Spirit is not as close as some theologians would have hoped. Tillard, for example, considered the Holy Spirit had been presented as a secondary dimension.

> Certainly it (*LG*) speaks about the Holy Spirit, while (how could it have been possible?) the 1964 draft makes no reference to this Divine Person. And this when dealing with a key matter... the Decree is still too much focused on the power of man and insufficiently focused on the primordial fact that religious life comes from God. Every day, in his economy of love, God gives religious life to the Church through the Holy Spirit. The institutions of religious life actually represent an original flowering of the life of the Spirit, a permanent charism given by God to his people.[39]

Rahner claims that "the institutional factor in the Church... remains encompassed by the charismatic movement of the Spirit in the Church, the Spirit who again and again ushers the Church

---

[37] Gonzales Hernandez, "La Nuova Coscienza Della Chiesa e I Suoi Presupposti Storoco – Teologici," *La Chiesa del Vaticano II*, AA.VV (1965), 250.

[38] Léon Josef Suenens, "La Dimension Charismatique de L'Église," *Discours au Concile Vatican II*, AA.VV (1964), 31.

[39] Jean Marie Tillard, "Les Grands Lois de la Rénovation de la Vie Religieuse," *Vatican II Revisited*. AA.V (1964), 94. Cf. *Unam Sanctam*, §62.

as an open system into a future which God alone, and no one else has arranged."[40] Rahner further asserts that the charismatic element in the Church simply isn't on the same plane as the institutional but is "the first and the most ultimate among the formal characteristics inherent in the very nature of the Church as such."[41] He saw "the institutional element in the Church simply as one of the regulating factors (albeit a necessary one) for this charismatic element."[42] He regrets that the Council did not state that the charisms belong to the constitution of the Church but merely noted that "they are exceedingly suitable and useful for the needs of the Church." He concludes his reflection by lamenting that in Vatican II "the Church of officialdom still continues constantly to occupy the center of the ecclesiological stage" even after the Council itself had prophetically placed the People of God chapter ahead of the one concerned with "the Church's official functionaries."[43] Likewise, Balthasar in speaking of the Church as a visible society said

> It is grace itself that assumes hierarchical and institutional forms in the Church in order the better to lay hold on man, who is of course a being bound by nature, structure and law.... but it is also grace itself that takes shape in the most personal aspects of a believer's life through the charismatic mission of vocation in order to transform the unique talents and traits of the individual into what grace alone can envisage.[44]

---

[40] Karl Rahner, "Observations on the Factor of the Charismatic in the Church," *Theological Investigations*, 12 (1974), 86-97.

[41] Rahner, "Observations on the Factor of the Charismatic in the Church," 97.

[42] Ibid., 88.

[43] Ibid., 97.

[44] Hans Urs von Balthasar, *The Theology of Karl Barth* (San Francisco: Ignatius Press, 1992), 387.

Deeper Appreciation of Baptism

Although not fully developed in any one document, a renewed appreciation of the meaning of Christian baptism is at the center of Vatican II's theology of Church and ministry. Previously, theology had spoken of the lay apostolate as a share in the ministry of the ordained but now the Council proclaimed that by virtue of their baptism and confirmation the laity shares in the priestly, prophetic and royal mission of Christ (*LG* 31; *AA*, 23.) With this mission comes a shared responsibility to witness to the Gospel and to announce the good news.[45] Both the blessing of the water and the consecration of the chrism in the Easter Vigil confirm that the baptized are not passive hearers of the word. Form C, in the Blessing of the Water, proclaims: "You call those who have been baptized to announce the Good News of Jesus Christ to the people everywhere." Likewise, in consecrating the chrism the minister proclaims: "Through that anointing you transform them into the likeness of Christ, your Son, and give them a share in his royal, priestly and prophetic work."[46]

Ministry of the Baptized

This is not to deny that there is a distinct role for the ordained, an office of discernment and a responsibility for ordering charisms specifically entrusted to the bishop. However, this is cast in a new light by the more fundamental emphasis of the Council that all the baptized share in the mission of the Church by virtue of their baptism and that the word of God is entrusted to the entire Church, not solely to the *magisterium*.[47] This assertion by the Council finds support not only in the liturgical tradition of the

---

[45] *Ad Gentes*, §35.
[46] *Lectionary*, Easter 1, Preface 1.
[47] *Dei Verbum*, §10.

Church[48] but also in the theology of Thomas Aquinas.[49] The Council of Florence (1438-1445), quoting a minor work of St. Thomas, taught that baptism is "the gateway to the spiritual life; by it we are made members of Christ and belong to his body, the Church."[50] St. Thomas maintained that the one who had been baptized and confirmed "receives the power publicly, and as it were *ex officio*, to profess faith in Christ in speech." Those gifted with charisms have a responsibility to find ways to exercise these gifts for the building up of the Church.

> From the reception of these charisms or gifts... there arises for each believer the right and the duty to use them in the Church and in the world for the good of all and for the up-building of the Church.[51]

The bestowal of charisms depends on God's good pleasure, not on the ordinance of man. St. Paul in 1 Cor 12:11 says that the Spirit apportions the gifts to each one as he wills — a passage quoted by *Lumen Gentium* when it acknowledges that they are given "to the faithful of every rank."[52] The Dominican theologian, Christian Duquoc, expresses the matter succinctly:

---

[48] Cf. Mary Collins, *The Baptismal Roots of the Preaching Ministry* (Washington DC: The Pastoral Press, 1987), 175-195. Collins argues that the Church's liturgical tradition illustrates that the language of "anointing by the Holy Spirit" so as to be formed for a share in the mission of Christ was primarily the language of Christian Baptism in the early Church, but in later practice was transferred to refer primarily to the ordained.

[49] ST 3a, q.69, aa.3-6; q.68, a.1 ad3.

[50] Cf. the article on Baptism in *Ecclesia*, "A Theological Encyclopedia of the Church" by Christopher O'Donnell, Liturgical Press, 1996, 40-41. See also DS 1313-1314/ND 1308, 1412.

[51] *Apostolicam Actuositatem*, §3. See the new Code of Canon Law (1983), Canon 759: "In virtue of their baptism and confirmation lay members of the Christian faithful are witnesses of the Gospel message by word and example of a Christian life." See also Canon 255 in which the baptized are not only encouraged to proclaim the Gospel but also told that it is their responsibility to so do.

[52] *Lumen Gentium*, §12.

The charisms bear witness at the core of the institution to the fact that it is necessary for its very survival not to lock itself up in a legal order or a rationally planned institution. The charism constitutes a bridge between the Church as event and the Church as institution, or the gratuitous and the legal, or the unpredictable and what is planned, or the Spirit and the structure.[53]

Charisms Given for Service and Mission

Congar understands charisms as gifts of a public nature given by the Holy Spirit to the baptized faithful for the service and the mission of the Church. "The great rule is that the purpose of these gifts is to edify and to be useful to others and to the community as such."[54] St. Paul lists the "discernment of the spirits" (1 Cor 12:10) as one of the charisms, without referring to any connection between discernment and office. In the Pastoral Constitution on the Church in the Modern World, Vatican II teaches that the whole people of God, clergy and laity together, have the task of discerning the signs of the times (*GS* §44; cf. §4 and §11).[55] However, the Dogmatic Constitution on the Church asserts that the judgment about the genuineness of charisms rests with those who preside over the Church, i.e., with the Pope and the bishops (*LG* §12, referring to 1 Th 5:12, 19-21). Congar asserts that the ordained ministry exists to serve the whole community of the faithful.[56] The clergy and the hierarchy must relate to the baptized

---

[53] Christian Duquoc, "Charisms as the Social Expression of the Unpredictable Nature of Grace," *Charisms in the Church* (New York, 1978), 93ff.

[54] Yves Congar, *The Word and the Spirit*, 35; *Called to Life*, 91; *Renewed Actuality*, 15; *Pneumatology Today*, 448; *Esprit de l'homme*, 58; *Holy Spirit*, 129.

[55] *Gaudium et Spes*, §44; cf. §4 & §11.

[56] Congar, *Power and Poverty*, 17, 25, 54; *The Word and the Spirit*, 115; *Institutionalised Religion*, 146; *Mother Church*, 43; *Autorité et liberté*, 25; *Autorité, Initiative*, 38,75; *Lay People*, 31; *Priest and Layman*, 99.

faithful not in a dominating or superior manner but in a way that encourages and fosters discipleship in Jesus Christ.[57]

Congar is critical of the mystique of authority that has been cultivated in the Church and is characterized by the complete identification of God's will with the institutional form of authority.[58] The authority of the hierarchy is not identical with God's.[59] Yet Congar rightly maintains that episcopacy has authority, as underlined by the Fathers of the Church (Ignatius of Antioch, Cyprian, Irenaeus, Hippolytus and Origen) from the very beginning.[60]

General and Ministerial Priesthood

Cardinal Suenens, speaking at a symposium of European bishops in Chur, Switzerland in 1969 spoke about the impact the rediscovered primacy of the Church as the People of God would have on the ministerial priesthood. Stressing that the proper ministries of the hierarchy can be discovered only in the larger context of the Church as the ensemble of the baptized, he remarked that "the ministerial priesthood is distinct from the general priesthood, though directed toward the latter." Fundamentally, he insisted that the ministerial priesthood, for the bishop as well as the priest, is secondary to the status and mission of these people as baptized.[61]

---

[57] Congar, *Power and Poverty*, 98.

[58] Congar, *Power and Poverty*, 71-73; *The Word and the Spirit*, 54.

[59] Congar, *Tradition*, 337-338.

[60] Cf. Congar, *Tradition*, 106; *Autorité, Initiative* and especially *Power and Poverty*, 69, where Congar criticizes the Reformation for refusing the right of any human authority to enter into the field of man's religious relationship with God.

[61] *The Suenens Dossier*, 107. In his Pastoral Letter on Pentecost, 1970, Suenens commented, "We cannot enhance the priesthood of the faithful without looking with new eyes at the ministerial priesthood — which although irreplaceable — must be lived differently." See also L.J. Cardinal Suenens, *Memories and Hopes*, trans. Elena French (Dublin: Veritas, 1992), 153.

Proclamation of the Gospel

As Vatican II emphasized, the proclamation of the Gospel is pre-eminent among the tasks of the bishop as pastor of a local Church[62] and the primary duty of priests as co-workers with their bishops.[63] As overseer of the community charged with preserving both the authentic tradition and the unity of the body of Christ, the bishop is entrusted with the responsibility for recognizing and ordering the many diverse charisms of all the baptized within the local Church. In *A New Pentecost?*, Suenens makes reference to the episcopal office as "the charism of discerning charisms."[64] In a unique way the bishop bears the responsibility of Paul's exhortation in the First Letter to the Thessalonians: "Test everything, hold fast to what is good" (5:21). Yet, full cognizance must also be given to the preceding verse which reminds the bishop: "Do not stifle the Spirit. Do not despise prophecies" (5:19-20).

Cardinal Suenens

In *A New Pentecost?* Suenens envisioned a renewal which included an "institutional overhaul at every level," and at the same time, "a spiritual renewal of exceptional richness." However, in 1987 he stated quite openly, "If you were to ask me whether Vatican II was indeed a new Pentecost, I would say 'yes' — in terms of grace that was offered — and 'yes and no' in terms of grace received."[65] Nevertheless, when asked his hopes for the year 2000 he replied that "we should rediscover the secret of Pentecost, which is a mystery of conversion (*ad intra*) and of the apostolate (*ad extra*). And that we should not be afraid of the symbols of the wind

---

[62] *Lumen Gentium*, §25.

[63] *Presbyterorum Ordinis*, §4.

[64] Suenens, *A New Pentecost?*, 191.

[65] Suenens, *Memories and Hopes*, 392.

which shakes the house — without uprooting it! — and of the flames which kindle from a spark."[66]

Definition of Charism

The contemporary Catholic concept of charism is authoritatively set forth in the Dogmatic Constitution on the Church (§12) which speaks of "special graces by which God renders (the faithful) able and willing to undertake the various tasks and offices that help the renewal and up-building of the Church."

Vatican Council II, clearly echoes this doctrine of the apostle Paul, when we are told,

> Whether these charisms be extraordinary or more simple and widespread, they are to be received with thanksgiving and consolation since they are fitting and useful for the needs of the Church. Extraordinary gifts are not to be rashly desired, nor is it from them that the fruits of apostolic works are to be presumptuously expected. Those who have charge over the Church should judge the genuineness and proper use of these gifts. Their office is not to extinguish the Spirit, but to test everything and retain what is good.[67]

John Paul II takes up and amplifies this teaching from the Council:

> The Holy Spirit, in entrusting the different ministries to the Church Communion, enriches it with other gifts and particular impulses, called charisms. These can take the most diverse forms, either as expressions of the absolute freedom of the Spirit who grants them, or as re-

---

[66] Ibid.
[67] *Lumen Gentium*, §12; Cf. *Ad Gentes*, §28, *Apostolicam Actuositatem*, §3.

sponses to the multiple exigencies of Church history....[68]

New Ecclesial Movements as Charisms?

Whether extraordinary or simple and humble, charisms are graces of the Holy Spirit which have, directly or indirectly, an ecclesial usefulness, for the edification of the Church, for the good of human persons and for the needs of the world. On more than one occasion, John Paul II has referred the conciliar expressions of *Lumen Gentium* to the charisms of the new ecclesial movements.[69] The Pope has affirmed that:

> if realized in a genuine way, the new movements of spirituality are based on these charismatic gifts which together with the hierarchic gifts (i.e. ordained ministries) form part of those gifts of the Holy Spirit with which the Church, Spouse of Christ, is adorned. Charismatic gifts and hierarchic gifts are distinct but also mutually complementary.... In the Church, both the institutional aspect and the charismatic aspect, both the hierarchy and the associations and movements of the faithful, are co-essential and concur to the life, renewal and sanctification [of the Church], albeit in a different way and such as to ensure reciprocal exchange and communion.[70]

---

[68] *Christifideles laici,* §25.

[69] *Lumen Gentium,* §4 & §12.

[70] John Paul II, "Address to the Ecclesial Movements gathered for the International Colloquium," *Insegnamenti* II, X/1 (1987): 446-478.

Charism and Mission

Worldwide, we can see the expansion of various charisms among the lay faithful, men and women. They are given to a determined person, but they can be shared by others so that they are maintained through time as a living and precious heritage which engenders a particular spiritual affinity among many persons.

When we were baptized and confirmed, we were consecrated by the Holy Spirit for a mission in the Church through the charisms which the same Spirit granted us. This charismatic aptitude for mission takes different forms:

(i) A personal and non-transferable charismatic gift: the case of individual gifts such as that of religious founders.

(ii) A double charismatic gift: the case of gifts shared in marriage.

(iii) A collective charismatic gift: the case of institutes of consecrated life, of spiritual movements in the Church and other types of Christian associations.

This collective or shared charism implies a specific mode of being, a specific mission and spirituality, a style of life and structure at the service of ecclesial communion and mission. Participation in a collective charism facilitates the formation of the members of a determined group, produces a better cohesion of this same group, forms a more solid identity, gives the sense of belonging to a spiritual family, is a source of creativity and strength for responding eagerly to the signs of the times.

New Ecclesial Movements as Collective Charisms

The new ecclesial movements are an example of a collective charism at work in our midst. Collective charisms, as gifts of the Spirit, are a dynamic impulse that continually develops in harmony with the Body of Christ which is in constant growth. They are entrusted to human groups to be lived and interpreted, to be made fruitful and witnessed to in the service of ecclesial communion in the different cultural contexts of today's world. Some of these collective charisms can be shared as a gift of the Spirit by persons belonging to different states of life.

> Every institute of consecrated life, priestly association, missionary regrouping, ecclesial movement in the Church... has at its foundation a collective charism, which is an experience of the Father, by a free gift of the Spirit, to build up and serve the Body of Christ.[71]

This collective charism, as a founding charism or charism of the founders, is called to be constantly lived, conserved, deepened and developed in harmony with the Body of Christ which is in constant growth. Collective charisms, besides being shared, can be lived and considered as charisms open to new forms of presence and expression in different historical circumstances.

Finally, it should be understood that it is not the founder who communicates the charism to those who associate themselves with him or her. Only the Holy Spirit is the author of charisms in the Church and it is the Spirit alone who communicates them. The group around the founder is born when a certain number of persons become aware of their own vocational grace upon meeting the founder. They join him or her in order to fulfill their particular call. It can be said that the founder mediates the charism through the spiritual harmony that is established between the founder and the others. All the charisms, as numerous and varied as they are, are united in the single mission of the group. The different charisms find their identity in their mutual relationship within the center of communion and mission of the group.

---

[71] Paul VI, *Evangelica Testificatio*, 11-12; SCRIS, *Mutuae Relationes*, 12.

Conclusion

I would suggest that a studied reflection of charism requires a revision of the traditional theologies of ministry. I refer to criteria of validation and organization of them. The very sacred character of the liturgical actions and the strong association between priestly ministry and authority in the Church have conditioned us to adapt a sacred and liturgical point of view to give preference to these ministries. In this way the functions and ministries associated with cult occupy the first place in our theological value system, while more secular ministries are relegated to a secondary place. I suggest this should change. Remembering St. Paul's advice to the Corinthians, it is necessary to recover the communitarian criteria to validate and give preference to charism and ministry. Charisms and ministries take on more importance for the Christian in the measure that they build up the Christian community. As already cited, Rahner claims that "the institutional factor in the Church… remains encompassed by the charismatic movement of the Spirit in the Church, the Spirit who again and again ushers the Church as an open system into a future which he himself, and no one else, has arranged."[72]

It is worth recalling the words of Yves Congar on this matter:

> The Church is not built up merely by acts of the official ministers of the presbytery but many kinds of services, more or less stable or occasional, more or less spontaneous or recognized, some consecrated by sacramental ordination. These services exist — they exist even if they are not called by their real name, ministries, even if they do not yet have their true place and status in ecclesiology…. Eventually one sees that the decisive pair is not "priesthood-laity"… but much more that of ministries or services and community.[73]

---

[72] Karl Rahner, "Observations on the Factor of the Charismatic in the Church," *Theological Investigations* 12 (1974), 97.

[73] Yves Congar, *Ministères et Communion Ecclésiale*, Paris (1979), 17 & 19.

It also helps us to understand the diversification and the distributions of charisms and ministries among all the members of the community, ordained and lay, male and female. Finally and perhaps more importantly, it helps us to accept the deep Christian meaning of the ministries done by the baptized in the search of a more human, more loving and more just society: promotion, assistance, defense of human rights, etc. These theological keys must stimulate reflection and theological discernment rooted in our apostolic and ecclesial practices. Schillebeeckx proposed that,

> Above all, these new forms of prayer should be conceived by the laity themselves and not from behind theological "round table" conferences, which are already surrounded by the "good aroma" of conceptions from cloistered brains; these concepts will be batted about for the worse because the "brains" will tend to read their own priestly or religious training into the situation of the laymen's life. The "without incense" and "between the concrete and the asphalt" mystique will prove this to be true![74]

The reason for the present abundance of charisms lies primarily in the sovereign will of God. Fr. Francis Martin calls it "a sovereign work of God's mercy."[75] A condition that makes the reception of the charisms possible is expectancy. As René Laurentin has observed, there is much in our present age that corresponds to the world and faith of the first generation of Christians.

> In the New Testament period as today, crisis and change provoked creativity. The New Testament is an example of the predominance of movement over sys-

---

[74] Edward Schillebeeckx, "The Dominican Third Order: Old and New Style," *Dutch Tertiary Magazine* (Aug-Sept 1960). Before it was published, it was delivered as an address to the regional directors and administrators of the Third Order, first at Louvain on June 6, 1960, and then at Utrecht on June 29, 1960.

[75] Cf. Fr. Francis Martin, "Charismatic Renewal: A Sovereign Work of God's Mercy" (1981). Recorded by CRS Services, Dublin.

tem which is a widely proclaimed goal today. The period of the New Testament had also undergone the most radical experience of declericalization ever seen; this was characteristic of the transition from the Old Testament and pointed the way to a purification and a transcendence, which would not be a negation of the sacred but a sacralization of life itself within the loving body of Christ. The first and most important lesson is that the ministries of the New Testament are functional; their goals are determined by the service of the community and not by the bureaucratic apparatus.... Another important aspect found in the New Testament is that ministries are fundamentally missionary.[76]

At the present time there is a new eagerness to receive charisms. A widespread openness to charisms has been lacking in the Church for many centuries, perhaps due to the persistent influence of the Montanist heresy of the third century which led to a subsequent distrust of the unusual, of emotion and of enthusiasm. Some charisms were always expected, such as the grace to hold a particular office, but, on the whole, the faithful tended to associate remarkable charisms with saints. The advent of the new ecclesial movements in this century has seen a remarkable outpouring of charisms and it is marked by an expectant faith with regard to such charisms. They are presumed to be part of the normal life of the Christian community.[77] The sudden and unexpected arrival of these new charisms into the Church brings into focus the relationship between the institutional Church and the charismatic Church. Fundamentally, they are a witness to the perennial fertility and life-renewing power of the Marian dimension of the Church, that dynamic life force which continues to give life and causes us to focus on the call of Christ.

---

[76] René Laurentin, "The New Testament and the Present Crisis in Ministry" (1971), 14.

[77] Cf. Killian McDonnell and George Montague, *Fanning the Flame: What Does Baptism in the Holy Spirit Have to Do With Christian Initiation?* (Collegeville, MN: Liturgical Press, 1991).

IMPACT ON THE CHURCH

CHAPTER SIX

The Marian Profile of the Church

Solving Charismatic and Institutional Tension?

The horizon of the Spirit is always challenging. The first Christians were slow to comprehend existentially the universality of their mission and why the Spirit went ahead of them into Samaria, Antioch and the Graeco-Roman world (Ac 9:31; 10:44). The action of the Spirit not only shook culture but drew the disciples away from the traditions and institutions which could not incarnate the omnipresent *Pneuma*. "Where the Spirit of the Lord is, there is freedom" (2 Cor 3:17).

Life in the Spirit is just that, a life, but one that is transformed by grace. This enables a free giving of the self for service and this enables ministry. As Paul's writings indicate, the effect and the gifts of new life in the Spirit are closely related to ministries. Although Paul is aware of some extraordinary effects of the Spirit, he always leads *pneumatika* and *charismata* back to ministry for the community on behalf of the good news, always back to the ordinary, to daily life and love. Inward maturity, holiness and outward growth are the goals of the Church, not flamboyant miracles. In Paul's ecclesiology, charism is not the alternative or rival to daily ministry but its very source.

Charism and Institution: The Protestant Perspective

There has been a tendency in modern exegesis and theology to separate charism and official ministry, to pit pneumatic power against community. This was particularly true of Protestant scholars who sought to find in the origins of Christianity "a tension between liberty and order, between humanity and grace."[1]

Adolf Harnack rejected connections between charisms and the lasting central, traditional ecclesiastical offices,[2] while E. Schweizer proposes a dual structure in the early Churches, one of which was charismatic, more or less unrelated to ministry.[3] R. Sohn concluded that the tension between office and charism illustrated a primal opposition between institution and spirit.[4] Exegetes such as Bultmann interpreted the prophets as ecstatic, independent preachers whose teaching about Jesus, the later Church decided, was not dependable.[5] Even Käsemann who tempered much of this approach contends that the first Christians knew no ecclesial order and that charism is present in the existential act of ministry.[6] In all of this we discover a negative dialectic between law and the Gospel, a hostility between the individual and social nature (both sinful) and grace. Structure is mistaken for authoritarianism. This takes attention away from the real counterpart of charism; not the threat of ministry but the fulfillment of ministry.

---

[1]   Thomas F. O'Meara, *Theology of Ministry* (Mahwah, NJ: Paulist Press, 1983), 62.

[2]   A. Harnack, *The Constitution and Law of the Church* (New York, 1910), 236.

[3]   E. Schweizer, *Church Order in the New Testament* (London, 1961), 183.

[4]   Cf. Yves Congar and Rudolph Sohm, "Nous Interroge Encore," *Revue des sciences philosophiques et théologiques*, 57 (1973), 263ff.

[5]   Cf. *Geschichte Der Synoptischen Tradition* (Gottingen, 1964), 135.

[6]   Ernst Käsemann, *Essays on New Testament Themes* (SCM Press, 1964). See especially the chapter on "Ministry and Community in the New Testament," 63-94.

The Catholic View

Within the Roman Catholic tradition there is a tendency to see harmony between grace and creation, between spirit and structure. Sullivan encapsulates the essence of Catholic thought in his excellent book on *Charisms and Charismatic Renewal.* As he puts it,

> There are two distinct, but equally important, ways that the Holy Spirit breathes life into the body of Christ: on the one hand, by his covenant relationship with the Church, guaranteeing the effectiveness of its sacraments and official ministries, and on the other, by his unpredictable and often surprising charismatic interventions. For the purpose of safeguarding and handing on tradition, a system with established offices of leadership is needed. But it is equally true that for the purpose of shaking the Church out of the complacency and mediocrity that inevitably creeps into any institution, the Church needs the charismatic interventions of the Spirit.[7]

However, this tradition also became infected with the virus of clericalism and medieval and baroque theologies sought to sever any harmony between the charismatic and the institutional. O'Meara states that,

> The emphasis upon hierarchical ministry constituted by legal code was so strong that the charismatic had to flee to the edge of Church life, to the monastery and spiritual life where from an esoteric world women and lay persons were permitted occasionally to utter a prophetic word.[8]

---

[7]   Francis J. Sullivan, *Charisms and Charismatic Renewal: a Biblical and Theological Study* (Gill and MacMillan, 1982), 47.

[8]   O'Meara, 64.

Persistent Temptation

The history of ecclesiology and mysticism is fraught with this temptation to separate or to draw a line between the charismatic and the priestly. Montanists threatened the Church in the third century and this may have accelerated priestly control over charismatic ministry.[9] Likewise, Joachim of Fiore (1135-1202) left his Cistercian Order to proclaim the beginning of an age of the Spirit, a time of freedom of the Spirit which was to replace the time of the letter.[10]

> He announced the coming of the last age of the world, the imminent end of the time of the Word Incarnate, of the New Testament, and of the clerical Church: they were soon to be replaced by the time of the Spirit, the revelation of the Eternal Gospel and the monastic Church.[11]

Yet the charismatic kept reappearing as outlined in chapters I and II. It was dealt with by asserting the superiority of stable sacramental power over transient charisms. Freedom and spirit were in the charisms but obedience and Church were in the priesthood. The Church may have needed the charismatic for inspiration but ultimately the charismatic must yield to the authority of the Church. Teresa of Avila is the charismatic, Bañez, her confessor, is the Dominican priest. Francis of Assisi is the charismatic, Innocent III is the ecclesial center. Thomas Aquinas summed up

---

[9] Finney, 65.

[10] For a discussion of the various aspects of the thought of Joachim of Fiore, see Yves Congar, *I Believe in the Holy Spirit* (London: Geoffrey Chapman, 1983); Yves Congar, *The Holy Spirit in the "Economy"* (New York, London: Seabury Press, Chapman, 1983), 126-137. See also Marjorie Reeves, *The Influence of Prophecy in the Later Middle Ages, a Study in Joachimism* (Notre Dame, IN: Notre Dame Press, 1993).

[11] George Tavard, *The Church, Community of Salvation* (Collegeville, MN: Liturgical Press, 1992), 233.

the salient difference by distinguishing between charism (*gratia gratis data*) and public ministry (*officium*). While offices lead people to justification and holiness, because of their particular intensity and because of their inspiration of people in the world, these *freely given graces* (*charisma*) are transitory and clearly distinct from the official ministries of the Church.[12] Catholic ecclesiology, albeit recently, has since distanced itself from this medieval construction. As Küng wrote:

> We have seen that charisms… are found throughout the Church rather than being restricted to a particular group of people…. Hence one can speak of a charismatic structure of the Church which includes but goes far beyond the hierarchical structure of the Church…. It (charism) signifies the call of God, addressed to an individual, to a particular ministry in the community, which brings with it the ability to fulfill that ministry.[13]

Bernard Cooke accepts the fundamentally charismatic nature of the Church but opposes the conflict between charism and institution.

> Ministerial role is the expression of charism. Not only such manifestly "charismatic" activities as prophecy are rooted in this empowering by the Spirit, but also regularized teaching and structured governing. This means that one cannot simply contrast "charism" and "institution" in the life of the Church. Institutions themselves are meant to be the organs through which the Spirit-animated community expresses its life.[14]

---

[12] ST II-II, q. 171, intro; I-II, q. III aa. 1, 4, 5.

[13] Hans Küng, *The Church* (London: DLT, 1967), 188.

[14] B. Cooke, *Ministry in Word and Sacrament: History and Theology* (Philadelphia: Fortress, 1976), 198.

Church Structure Is Fundamentally Sacramental

With the emergence of the movements in the Church some have tried to set up a dialectic between institution and event, or institution and charism.[15] As Ratzinger points out, such a concept is flawed. The fundamental institutional reality that characterizes the Church is her sacramental ministry in its varying degrees. Ultimately the sacrament, that significantly bears the name *Ordo*, is, in the final analysis, the sole permanent and binding structure that forms so to say the fixed order of the Church.[16]

> As it is a sacrament, it must be perpetually created anew by God and it is primarily called into existence by Him, at the charismatic and pneumatological level. The Church is not our institution, but the irruption of something else, that it is intrinsically *iuris divini*, has as its consequence that we can never apply institutional criteria to her and that the Church is entirely herself only where the criteria and methods of human institutions are transcended.[17]

Christological versus Pneumatological

Of necessity, the Church has institutions of purely human right to enable administration and organization but there is always the danger that if they become too powerful they can jeopardize the order and the vitality of her spiritual reality.

Another dialectical pairing proposed is that between a christological and pneumatological view of the Church. It is argued that the sacrament of Church belongs to the christological-incarnational aspect which then needs to be supplanted by the

---

[15] Ratzinger, "The Ecclesial Movements; a Theological Reflection on Their Place in the Church," 25.

[16] Ibid.

[17] Ibid., 26.

pneumatological-charismatic element. Undoubtedly, a distinction needs to be drawn between Christ and the Holy Spirit but they are also united as a *communio* with the Father and with one another. Christ and the Spirit can only be rightly understood together. "The Lord is the Spirit," says Paul in the Second Letter to the Corinthians (3:17). The ever new presence of Christ in the Spirit is the essential condition for the existence of sacrament and for the sacramental presence of the Lord.[18]

Law versus Gospel

A third model suggested is the relation between the permanent order of ecclesial life and new irruptions of the Spirit on the other, sometimes characterized in terms of Luther's dialectic between Law and Gospel which leads to a tension between the cultic-sacerdotal aspect and the prophetic aspect of salvation history. In this outlook the movements would be ranged on the side of prophecy.[19]

Schindler suggests that "initially, the Church in her institutional dimension originates in the Son of God who, as Word, becomes the visible image of the invisible God, in the womb of Mary";[20] and that the Church "in her charismatic dimension begins with the Holy Spirit who, as breath of the Father, remains unseen, while nonetheless revealing the Son and causing the Son's conception in Mary."[21] Yet Schindler is at pains to avoid any kind

---

[18] Ibid., 30.

[19] Ibid., 31.

[20] Cf. Joseph Cardinal Ratzinger, "Der Heilige Geist als Communio: Zum Verhältnis von Pneumatologie und Spiritualität bei Augustinus" in *Erfahrung und Theologie des Heiligen Geistes*, ed. C. Heitmann and H. Muhlen (Munich: Kösel-Verlag, 1974), 235. "The Church in Christ as the one who descended, a continuation of the humanity of Jesus Christ"; cf. also Balthasar's tracing of "the institutional form of the Church back to the form of Christ," in Hans Urs von Balthasar, *The Glory of the Lord: Seeing the Form* (San Francisco: Ignatius Press, 1982), 570-604.

[21] David Schindler, "The Ecclesial Movements: Institution and Charism," *Laity Today* (1999), 59. Cf. also *Catechism of the Catholic Church*, nos. 485, 724.

of dualism in this attempt at differentiation. Such a distinction is properly understood only in light of the Tri-unity of God and the circumincessive relations among the Three Persons.

> Failure to see that both the Son and the Spirit are both "objective" and "subjective" (albeit in a different order) will leave us in the end with a dualism — or relation of mere juxtaposition between institution and charism in the Church, which is exactly the source of the problems of Joachimism and clericalism.[22]

A Certain Freedom Needed

The different spiritual awakenings and renewal movements are also today largely a wholesome disturbance of the traditional order. However, in practice it is difficult for the institutional authorities to completely absorb and integrate the spiritual impulses. Therefore, it is legitimate and necessary that these different aspects of intensive Christian life be able to develop within the Church but not necessarily in already existing structures. The Holy Spirit, who guarantees the unique solidarity of the Church with her Lord, grants unity and multiplicity at the same time. He guarantees much more freedom of spiritual effects, of ways of life and also of knowledge than we would allow ourselves. But, in the end, this multiplicity serves a new form of unity. This does not consist in the abolition of plurality, but rather in its free collaboration toward a whole, as St. Paul expressed in his First Letter to the Corinthians. For this collaboration, it is decisive that spiritual renewal is consciously done and credibly practiced as an enduring mission of all Christians.[23]

The acceptance of this perspective has gained increasing sup-

---

22   Schindler, "The Ecclesial Movements: Institution and Charism," 60.

23   Cf. *Christifideles laici,* §18 ff., especially §24, the remarks concerning charisms.

port within the Church, notably from Pope John Paul II who was in the forefront in championing the ecclesiality of the new movements. I will return in some detail in the next chapter to the huge contribution he made to the acceptance of the new ecclesial movements within the Church. However, before examining the pope's unique and invaluable interventions one must acknowledge the leading exponent of a fusion between the charismatic and the institutional in this century, namely, the great Swiss theologian, Hans Urs von Balthasar.

Balthasar's Contribution

He saw their relationship not as adversarial but as complementary and he explained it as the ongoing creative tension between the Marian and the Petrine within the Church. His contribution to the present reality is worthy of some focused attention. In particular, he advocated a return to asserting the primacy of the Marian principle of the Church. Brendan Leahy has looked at this dimension in the work of Balthasar and his perceptive analysis sheds significant light on this dimension.[24]

Leahy concedes from the outset that the task he has set himself is a daunting one, given the encyclopedic range of Balthasar's work and the inclusive methodology that characterizes his work. To select one key aspect and concentrate exclusively on it is almost to run counter to the all-embracing approach adopted by Balthasar himself. Yet the Marian principle is a dominant feature in the work of Balthasar, as numerous eminent commentators on his work have pointed out. Kehl depicts it as the nodal point of his thought.[25] Hembrock sees it as a central viewing point in his

---

[24] Brendan Leahy, *The Marian Profile in the Ecclesiology of Hans Urs Von Balthasar* (New City, 2000). Much of the material that follows is elicited from the scholarly treatment of this subject by Leahy.

[25] Medard Kehl, "Kirche als Institution: Zur Theologischen Begründung des institutionellen Charakters der Kirche in der neuren deutschsprachigen katholischen Ekklesiologie" (1976), 248.

ecclesiology,[26] while Louth endorses the fundamentally Marian structure of his work.[27]

Leahy asserts that Balthasar's purpose is not just to consider Mary as a personal model for discipleship but to grasp the profound reality of the Marian principle animating every aspect of the life of the Church from generation to generation. Balthasar sees the acceptance of this as the beginning of "a breathtaking adventure." His work seeks to deepen our understanding of the dynamic relationship between the Marian and the Petrine profiles within the Church, both of which are agents of unity. Leahy articulates his task as extracting and presenting both "the explicit references as well as the fragmentary intuitions and hints found hidden in the galaxy of his theological work."[28]

Enriched Understanding

Leahy reviews the historical development of the awareness of the Marian profile within the Church which Balthasar chronicles in his work. Like Cardinal John Henry Newman, Balthasar asserts that Marian doctrine has remained the same from the every beginning but our understanding of it has deepened with time and ongoing meditation. As all of his work is rooted in the school of the Church Fathers, Leahy conducts us briefly but skillfully through the writings of a number of key mentors who influenced Balthasar in his theology. Clement's *Letter to the Corinthians*, c. 96 A.D., and *The Shepherd of Hermas*, c. 140 A.D., reveal that the Church was seen as paradise restored and this realm of new life is expressed in terms of feminine imagery. The bride

---

[26] Matthias Hembrock, "Die Ekklesiologie Hans Urs von Balthasar: Das Marianische Prinzip in der Kirche," Unpublished doctoral thesis, 1986, 2.

[27] John Riches, "The Place of Heart of the World in the Theology of Hans Urs von Balthasar's Theology," *The Analogy of Beauty* (Edinburgh, 1986), 147-163, especially 150.

[28] Leahy, 13.

motif in Scripture, notably Ephesians 5, contributed to the ecclesial realm being depicted as a subject on her own, with feminine beauty and characteristics. The Church, the Bride of Christ, came to be seen as a mother who birthed us into new life with Christ and nurtured and sustained us through the sacraments. Mary was similarly depicted as the new Eve in the writings of Irenaeus and Justin. Virgin-mother-Church and virgin-mother-Mary become almost inseparable. Yet this intertwining did not, as yet, project Mary as mother of the faithful. The emphasis was on the Church's motherhood of the faithful and in this sense the patristic period subordinates Mary's role to that of the Church. Hence Balthasar describes her role in the theology of the early Church as discreet and anonymous.

Mary as *Theotokos*

However, after the Nicene confirmation of Christ's divinity, at Ephesus in 431 A.D. Mary was declared *Theotokos* and out of this emerged further reflection on Mary as the archetype or model of the Church. Mary not only gave birth to Christ, but she continues to birth other Christ-like figures, namely the members of Christ's body.

Ephesus is for Balthasar a pivotal moment in the understanding that Mary implicitly contains all the properties of the Church. Ambrose, Methodius and Origen alluded to the *anima eclesiastica*, an idea that each soul penetrated with the love of Christ inevitably expands to seek a Church consciousness. This notion fitted perfectly with the developing appreciation of Mary in the Church. Yet Mary's role was by no means secure. Even the great Augustine, whom Balthasar lauds on so many occasions, adopts a minimalist approach to identifying Mary with the Church, seeing her only as a parallel rather than identification.

The Carolingian epoch gave rise to an acceptance that the Church was not spotless but in fact quite stained with the sin of its members. The nuptial imagery of Christ and the Church faded into the background and the beauty of the inner radiance of the Church was temporarily lost. However, simultaneously devotional practice increased around the person of Mary, the one described as *Theotokos*. Mary now came to be viewed as the bride of Christ, the one who perfectly represents the Church. No longer is she seen as subordinate to the Church but identical with it. Furthermore, her role as mother also comes to the forefront. Her yes to God to become the mother of Christ bears an eternal fruitful harvest in the life of the Church. Unfortunately, errors crept in to this understanding of Mary and at times she was elevated to a position of divinity that is at variance with Catholic tradition and doctrine.

Mary in Recent Councils

At the First Vatican Council, on the defensive against the philosophies of the Enlightenment and the Protestant reformers, the Church adopted a siege mentality that caused it to focus its energies on its hierarchical structure and its laws and dogmas. The feminine dimension that had called forth the Church's mystical reality dimmed and waned, although private Marian devotion continued, albeit often sullied by distortion and excess. Not until the Second Vatican Council, under the inspiration of the Holy Spirit and after a major internal struggle within the Council, was Mary finally inserted into the Constitution on the Church. Balthasar saw this as the natural progression of the Church finding herself.

The Petrine role had been articulated in the face of countless attacks over the centuries by a host of opponents such as the Jansenists, Conciliarists, Protestants, etc. that led to the First Vatican Council's declaration of the pope's infallibility. Likewise, Mary's role emerged in the midst of similar struggles over the centuries. Balthasar refers to the interesting historical fact that the two definitions concerning her, namely her Immaculate Conception and her Bodily Assumption frame, "not by chance" the papal dogma of infallibility. In this fragment of history Balthasar sees the motherhood of the Marian embracing and containing the Petrine. His review of the documents of Vatican I caused him to state that they speak of both a Marian and a Petrine unity in the Church.[29]

Post Vatican I saw a spate of theological speculation about Mary and a number of encyclicals but these were not integrated into the other theological disciplines and did not bear fruit until a renewed interest in patristic thought and biblical study prepared the way for Vatican II.

Vatican II

In essence, Vatican II highlights the role of the Church as the sacrament of unity with God and of unity between all mankind. The Petrine unity is the key hierarchical principle which is a manifestation of its exterior unity but the Marian element, Mary's spousal maternal presence at the heart of the Church uniting heaven and earth, manifests the interior unity of the Church.[30] Although Balthasar rejoices in this affirmation by the Second Vatican Council, he regrets the diminution of the nuptial bridal imagery between Christ and Mary. Leahy refers to *Mulieris Dignitatem* wherein Pope John Paul II acknowledges Balthasar's insights when he teaches that the Marian profile is "as fundamental and characteristic for the Church as the Petrine — perhaps even more so...."[31] As Balthasar tirelessly proclaims, *Love Alone: the Way of Revelation.*[32] To discover this love is to be converted and to enter into the mystery. Mary is the paradigm. She surrenders to the will

---

[29] Hans Urs von Balthasar, "Spouse of the Word," *Explorations in Theology* 2 (1991), 23-24.

[30] Leahy, 36.

[31] *Mulieris Dignitatem* (1988), 27, fn.55.

[32] Hans Urs von Balthasar, *Love Alone: the Way of Revelation* (London: Burns & Oates, 1998).

of God, gives herself completely, yet remains free and discovers the truth in her ongoing *Yes*.

Balthasar's Four Principles

Balthasar refers to four principles that operate in the Church. The Petrine is clearly visible within the hierarchy, recalling the person of Peter and his responsibility to proclaim the *kerygma*. The Pauline is linked to Paul and his missionary zeal and the ongoing eruption of charisms in the Church, although obedience to Peter is stressed. The Johannine dimension is the search for unity in seeking to synthesizes the first two and it respects the apocalyptic-prophetic dimension. The Jacobin reflects the continuity of the Old and the New Testaments and reflects the historical reality evidenced in law and tradition and dogma. All are closely connected with the Marian which is the meeting point for all of them.[33] Mary is a woman whose origin is within the mystery, who makes communion possible and is on an eternal mission as mother and bride of Christ.

The ontology of the Church is such that there is a mutual indwelling (*circumincession*) in Mary of these four principles and if any of these are absent the Marian profile of the Church suffers. Office, love, tradition and newness are difficult to unite but this is Mary's role and the Petrine is to manifest its function in the heart of the Marian *communio* and the *collegium* of bishops.

The Primacy of the Marian

Perhaps shocking for some, in Balthasar's ecclesiology, the Marian is primary and the Petrine occupies a subordinate role. The Catechism states that the Marian dimension of the Church, even

---

[33] Hans Urs von Balthasar, *Theo-Drama III: Theological Dramatic Theory* (San Francisco: Ignatius Press), 352.

if it is intrinsically ordered to the Petrine, precedes it in order of holiness.[34] Yet the two are not in opposition but in dynamic tension. This is a life-giving force for the Church, one which enables the proper functioning of charisms and institution. As Ratzinger has pointed out in an article on the emergence of lay communities, the existence of the institution and the *ordo* is of itself a charism for the Church and it is a false premise to set the institutional and the charismatic in opposition to each other.[35]

The perennial surprises of the Spirit as charisms are showered on the Church to vivify and inspire fruitfulness in the Church and this is at the heart of the Marian dimension. The Petrine role is to hold fast and to test and to bring together and to keep order and to protect, to preserve tradition, to preach the Word; it has an objective reality. The Marian principle is the subjective holiness of the Church, not only in terms of being formed by the institutional, but also in the existential freedom of the Spirit. The Spirit is normative and is the agent of freedom to foster and to inspire, to give life and to let be. Balthasar understands that the Holy Spirit exists in the Church as both institution and charism. The Marian and the Petrine move towards one another in reciprocity in order to become one Church of Christ. Leahy highlights five key points of this relationship that are ever at play together.

Important Elements Interwoven

Firstly, the incarnational dimension of the Church, as bride of Christ demands a structure and this is provided in the form of sacraments and ministry founded by the bridegroom, Christ be-

---

[34] Cf. *Catechism of the Catholic Church*, no. 773.

[35] Joseph Cardinal Ratzinger, "The Ecclesial Movements: a Theological Reflection on Their Place in the Church," *Laity Today* (1999), 25-29.

cause "Life and form are inseparable elements in the whole life of the Church."[36]

Secondly, the institution enables the ongoing possibility of the nuptial dialogue between "Mary — Church and Christ throughout history."[37] The Petrine gives to the Church in Eucharist and the sacrament of Reconciliation life-giving substance and the Marian dimension is the response of gratitude and faith which is expressed in new forms of ecclesial life and spirituality that emerge in various historical eras.

Thirdly, the institution provides a necessary order or governance, a rule of life that protects us in our weakness, and guides us deeper into Marian holiness.

Fourthly, both are involved in educating us in our call to love according to the mind of Christ. The institution provides not only a rule but also forms within us an *anima ecclesiastica*[38] which leads us deeper into the wisdom of Mary, who is Seat of Wisdom and the *Anima ecclesiastica* par excellence.

Fifthly, both play a pivotal role in protecting and cherishing the prophetic dimension of the believing community and in making this aspect explicit in the Church. This is an area of tension but it is one of great promise and of great hope. As Newman pointed out, the Petrine has to guard the prophetic but it must also listen to it, to keep itself pure and holy as well as to protect the purity of the Church.

Papal Role

Some would contend that the role of our late Holy Father bears testimony to this in a powerful manner. His endorsement and encouragement of the emerging new ecclesial communities at a time when skeptical voices were raised, made explicit this new

---

[36] Leahy, 13.
[37] Leahy, 130.
[38] Leahy, 186.

prophetic gifting by the Spirit. The emergence of these groups and their enthusiasm for evangelization and love of the Church has enlivened and enriched the Petrine. This bipolar character of the Church's life is the great drama wherein the believer's experiential knowledge which comes from the fullness of Christ and authority's official knowledge which is imparted by Christ directly, interact with one another.

The Petrine Lives in the Marian

Yet Balthasar is convinced that the logical development of the ecclesiology of Vatican II is that the Petrine find its home within the Marian principle. As Leahy articulates it, "…the Marian Principle is the liberating embrace of this Petrine ministry."[39] Ratzinger confirms that the Church "is not merely institution… but person… woman… Mother." He asserts that

> The Marian understanding of the Church is the most decisive contrast to a merely organizational or bureaucratic concept of Church…. It is only in the Marian that we become Church. In her origins the Church was not made, but born. She was born when the *fiat* was aroused in Mary's soul.[40]

Rediscovery of the Feminine

Leahy notes Balthasar's sense of urgency about recapturing the treasure of the Marian dimension of the Church. There is the abiding danger of male functionalism dominating the Church leading to a potentially inhuman and soulless reality. The redis-

---

[39] Leahy, 139.

[40] Leahy, 198. See also, "Die Ekklesiologie Des Zweiten Vatikanums," *Internationale katholische Zeitschrift Communio* 15 (1986): 41-52, especially 52.

covery of the feminine is critical because without it the Church is less than whole. Marian spirituality is not an option but a vital necessity for all believers because she is the model of letting Christ be formed in us according to the work of the Holy Spirit.

The first and last significance of the Church as an event is the birth of Christ, who is "all, and in all" (Col 3:11). As St. Louis Marie Grignion de Montfort recognized, "Two alone are capable of giving birth together, in synergy, to the Son of God in the flesh and, in him, to us as sons of the Father — namely, the Holy Spirit and Mary."[41]

Coda points out in his review of the movements that, as a gift of the Spirit, they must be linked with Mary. History teaches us that at times of the outpouring of the Spirit, the Church is reminded of three fundamental attitudes it should maintain: virginal submission, spousal love, maternal fruitfulness. In his view these attributes are mirrored in the ecclesiology of Vatican II which spoke of mystery, communion and mission. As he puts it, "Is this not just another way of referring to the same reality?... In other words, do not these three fundamental attitudes refer to the presence and action of Mary, Virgin, Spouse and Mother in the mystery of Christ and of the Church?"[42]

The lives of the saints are witnesses as part of "Mary's train" to the ongoing yes of the Church to God, the Father, and they are necessary models to inspire the people of today. They also remind us of the mystical element of the Church and again this is part of the Marian principle because as the one "full of grace," she is full of all charisms and points us to the eschatological dimension of faith. Finally, Balthasar sees this as the hour of the laity with the burgeoning explosion of a host of lay communities and world communities who have a profound sense of the Marian

---

[41] Coda, "The Ecclesial Movements. Gifts of the Spirit," 103. Cf. Piero Coda, "La Ss.Ma Trinità e Maria nel 'Trattato della vera devozione' di S.Luigi M. Grignion de Montfort," *Nuova Umanità* 15, no. 86 (1993), 13-45.

[42] Coda, "The Ecclesial Movements. Gifts of the Spirit," 103.

principle in their communitarian life and love of the Church. Coda applauds Balthasar for calling forth "a sense of reawakening in the whole people of God" to "the Marian form of their ecclesial identity."[43] Balthasar recognized in the movements "a stimulus and a providential chance in this direction."[44]

New Ecclesial Movements as Marian

Their charismatic origins, the primacy of spirituality which characterizes them, their mainly lay profile, their ecclesial loyalty, their heightened awareness of communion and evangelization, their authentic ecumenism, all underline their Marian character and their mission. Balthasar invites not only ecclesial movements but the whole Church to look to Mary, "as the prototype of the Church, on whose figure we should model ourselves." He issues a salutary warning that in the midst of all our reforms and renewals that "we do not lose sight of the one perfect measure, indeed the prototype itself...." We need to "keep our gaze permanently fixed on Mary... simply to understand what the Church, ecclesial spirit and ecclesial conduct are."[45]

Conclusion

Mary is a pivotal figure in our understanding of Church. St. Luke in the book of Acts, immediately after listing the names of the twelve apostles, speaks of the women, including Mary, being gathered together as *ekklesia*.[46] This picture is so vivid that it was repeatedly painted in later centuries in connection with the Pen-

---

[43] Ibid., 104.
[44] Ibid.
[45] Ibid.
[46] Cf. Ac 1:12-14.

tecost event and has brought forth an impressive iconographic tradition. Usually, Mary is seated in the center of the assembly with the twelve apostles to her left and right.[47] In this way Mary herself becomes an image of the *ekklesia*, the *real symbol* of faithful listening and receiving.

Schindler refers to the *Catechism* where it states that, "the mission of the Holy Spirit is always conjoined and ordered to that of the Son. The Holy Spirit, 'the Lord, the giver of Life,' is sent to sanctify the womb of the Virgin Mary and divinely fecundate it, causing her to conceive the eternal Son of the Father in a humanity drawn from her own."[48] As Schindler points out, we can say that the distinct but united missions of the Spirit and the Word, and hence the original meaning of charism and institution, are disclosed in an archetypal way in terms of Mary's relation to Christ.[49] Schindler proposes that Mary's *fiat* and *magnificat*, under the power of the Holy Spirit, disclose the original meaning of the charismatic Church: the Church is authentically charismatic-spiritual only insofar as her creative activity (*magnificat*) is anteriorly receptive and *communio* building (*fiat*).

Papacy Did Not Create Movements

Ratzinger, in his historical overview of apostolic movements in the Church, stresses that the papacy "did not create the movements but it did become their most important backer in the structure of the Church."[50] He cites this as an example to illustrate the deepest meaning and the true nature of the Petrine office. The Pope's ministry is not merely that of the bishop of a local Church

---

[47] This picture is found as early as the *Rabbula Gospel Book*, a Syriac manuscript from the year 586 (Florence, Biblioteca Laurenziana). Cf. P. Sevrugian, "Pfingsten V. Ikonographisch," *TRE*, 26, 395-398.

[48] Schindler, 63. See also *Catechism of the Catholic Church*, no. 485.

[49] Schindler, 64.

[50] Ratzinger, *Movements in the Church*, 39.

but it is always referred to the universal Church and thus it has in a specific sense an apostolic character. The Petrine has to keep alive the "dynamism of the Church's mission *ad extra* and *ad intra*."[51]

Ministries and missions that are not tied to the local Church alone, but serve the universal mission and the spread of the Gospel, must always exist in the Church. The Pope has to rely on these ministries and they on him; and in the harmonious interaction between the two kinds of mission the symphony of ecclesial life is realized. As Ratzinger points out,

> The apostolic age, which has normative value for the Church, clearly emphasized these two components as indispensable for the Church's life…. In sum, we could even say that the primacy of the successor of Peter exists precisely to guarantee these essential components of the Church's life and to connect them harmoniously with the structures of the local Churches.[52]

In recent papal statements we find the pope reaffirming and in one sense reclaiming the Marian dimension of the Church, not in any narrow sense but as the true arbiter and guide, to chart the course between the institutional and charismatic tensions within the Church. The movements are a prime example of the Marian principle of the Church, and their emergence and acceptance bear testimony to the Petrine role of the Pope who has validated their ministry and encouraged their acceptance and dispersal throughout the Church. It is this aspect that I now wish to address.

---

[51] Ibid.
[52] Ibid., 46.

CHAPTER SEVEN

The Petrine Role

The role of the Pope is crucial in examining the emergence of the movements in the latter part of the twentieth century. When Jesus gave Peter a share in his power he strengthened him so that he could strengthen his brothers (cf. Lk 22:32). He established him as the rock on which he would build his Church, and handed him the Keys of the Kingdom (cf. Mt 16:18f.). However, he also asked him to imitate his weakness and embrace the triumph of the Cross.

> Truly, truly I say to you, when you were young, you girded yourself and walked where you would; but when you are old, you will stretch out your hands and another will gird you and carry you where you do not wish to go (Jn 21:18).

St. Paul describes Peter's destiny as the "one who is first is made the last of all, a spectacle to the world, a fool for Christ's sake" (cf. 1 Cor 4:9). Peter is strong despite his crucified weakness.[1] In the office of Peter there is the permanent coincidence of authority and abasement. It is when he is weak that he is strong.

---

[1] John Saward, *Christ is the Answer: The Christ-Centered Teachings of Pope John Paul II* (New York: Alba House, 1995), xix.

"My grace is sufficient for you, for my power is made perfect in weakness" (2 Cor 12:9).

Balthasar sets forth the paradox as follows:

> When He conferred His office on Peter, Christ exhorted Peter to follow Him to the Cross, so that in the institutional Church the mission laid on the believer should be one with his surrender of his life; such identity would not have been Peter's ethical achievement, but rather an incomprehensible grace from the Lord.... Christ establishes the Petrine form upon this simultaneity, which is peculiar to institutional authority, of humiliation and elevation to office. This simultaneity is the mode in which the Lord's identity can (subsequently) still take hold of the guilty Peter. It is an imitation beyond and despite failure which is marvelously represented in Peter's crucifixion with feet uppermost: it is the Cross, but in mirror image, which is the definitive symbol of the hierarchical situation.[2]

Papal Intuition

Pope John Paul II undoubtedly suffered a great deal because of his unflinching determination to proclaim the Gospel. Castigated as both a liberal and a conservative by disaffected elements, his understanding of the Church as both Marian and Petrine often brought him into conflict but such is almost inevitable. The Pope intuited that the movements are a flowering of true Marian spirituality and he came to recognize that they are gifts of the Spirit given for the enrichment of the Church. His affirmation of their

---

[2] Hans Urs von Balthasar, *The Glory of the Lord: Seeing the Form* (San Francisco: Ignatius Press, 1982), 566f. St. Peter is conformed to Christ, according to Balthasar, "in inversion." *Die antiromische Affekt. Wie lasst sich das Papstum in der Gesamtkirche integrieren* (Freiburg, 1974), 130.

ministries, his pastoral concern for their spiritual welfare, his pastoral admonitions and warnings, his shepherding of them into the heart of the Church testifies not only to their authenticity but also confirms the validity of the Petrine role of discernment to "test everything and hold fast to what is good." This Petrine affirmation of the movements was made explicit by the Pope's decision to convene a gathering of the new movements in Rome in 1998 on the eve of Pentecost.

The Pentecost 1998 Meeting of Ecclesial Communities with the Pope

"It is as though what happened in Jerusalem 2000 years ago were being repeated this evening in this square, the heart of the Christian world."[3] So spoke Pope John Paul II on May 30, 1998 on the eve of Pentecost when he addressed the huge gathering of ecclesial movements which had congregated with him in Rome at his request. Almost half a million strong had gathered in St. Peter's Square on the Vigil of Pentecost 1998, the year of the Holy Spirit. Half a million faithful, zealous Catholics singing, chanting, clapping. "The Holy Spirit is here with us!" the Holy Father exclaimed. "It is he who is the soul of this marvelous event of ecclesial communion."[4]

This event was historic in its plan and scope. The Pope had called the many Church movements and ecclesiastical communities to come together for the first time in Rome for Pentecost in the year of the Holy Spirit. Why? Because he saw their existence as a manifestation of the Spirit's work of renewal begun in the Second Vatican Council; furthermore, he believed that the time had come for them to reach maturity under the direction of the Church. These groups were, individually, already faithful to

---

[3] Pope John Paul II, "Message to the World Congress of Ecclesial Movements, 1998."
[4] Ibid.

Church teachings and traditions, and they had a strong love for and commitment to serving the Holy Father. But they had always operated independently of one another, and sometimes in tension, adding unfortunately (and unnecessarily, as the Pope saw it) to the divisiveness already plaguing the Church.

Much of that division was the result of the misinterpretation, distortion and abuse of what Vatican II actually said. But the Holy Father believed that, through the Spirit, the Council also spawned these new movements, for nothing less than to "renew the face of the earth," and now it was time to send them forth on the mission to which they were called.

Charismatic and Institutional

At a General Audience in 1998 Pope John Paul II had already explained that "the New Testament testifies to the presence of charisms and ministries inspired by the Holy Spirit in the various Christian communities. The Acts of the Apostles, for example, describe the Christian community of Antioch in this way: 'in the Church at Antioch there were prophets and teachers, Barnabas, Symeon who was called Niger, Lucius of Cyrene, Manaen a member of the court of Herod the tetrarch, and Saul.'"

> In the former, one might recognize a more charismatic aspect, in the latter a more institutional tone, but in both cases the same obedience to God's Spirit. Moreover, this interweaving of the charismatic and institutional elements can be perceived at the very origins of the Antioch Community.[5]

The Pope continued to explain that the Antioch Community was a living reality in which two distinct roles emerged,

---

[5]   Pope John Paul II, "The Spirit is the Source of Ministries" (General Audience, August 5, 1998), 113-116.

namely, prophets who discerned and announced God's ways, and that of doctors and teachers who properly examined and propounded the faith.

When the mother community in Jerusalem heard of this new community and the work they were doing among the pagans they sent Barnabas to visit them. Acts 11:23-24 records "he was glad; and he exhorted them all to remain faithful to the Lord with steadfast purpose; for he was a good man, full of the Holy Spirit and of faith."[6] The Pope stressed that "in this episode clearly there emerges the twofold method with which the Spirit of God governs the Church: on the one hand, he directly encourages the activity of believers by revealing new and unprecedented ways to proclaim the Gospel, on the other, he provides an authentication of their work through the official intervention of the Church, represented here by the work of Barnabas, who was sent by the mother community of Jerusalem."[7]

The Pope then affirmed with vigor the teaching of *Lumen Gentium*, §12, that there is no such thing as one Church according to a "charismatic model" and another according to an "institutional model." In fact, he underlined that such erroneous opposition between charism and institution is "extremely harmful."[8]

Moreover, in the very first encyclical of his papacy, *Redemptor Hominis*, John Paul II, reflecting on the heritage received from the Second Vatican Council and from his predecessors, remarked on a spirit of collaboration and shared responsibility among the laity, not only strengthening the already existing organizations for lay apostolate but also creating new ones that often have a different profile and exceptional dynamism.[9] In 1984 he stated,

---

[6] Ibid.

[7] Ibid.

[8] Cf. Pope John Paul II, "Address to Participants in the Second International Conference of Ecclesial Movements, March 2nd 1987," *L'Osservatore Romano*, English Edition (March 16, 1987), 12.

[9] *Redemptor Hominis*, §5.

One of the gifts of the Spirit of our time is certainly the flowering of the ecclesial movements which, from the beginning of my Pontificate, I have constantly indicated as a motive of hope for the Church and for humankind. They are a sign of the freedom of forms taken by the one Church, and they represent certainly a new reality which has still to be adequately understood in all its positive effectiveness for the Kingdom of God at work in history today.[10]

Movements and Ecclesiology

As he exhorted them to prepare for the new millennium, the Pope also called them to examine their concept of ecclesiology against the reforms called for in *Lumen Gentium*.

Does it leave room for charisms, ministries and different forms of participation by the People of God, without adopting notions borrowed from democracy and sociology which do not reflect the vision of the Church and the authentic spirit of Vatican II?[11]

As early as 1987 he had spoken to the movements and to the world when he declared, "the great flowering of these Movements and their characteristic manifestations of energy and ecclesial vitality are certainly to be considered one of the finest fruits of the vast and deep spiritual renewal promoted by the last Council."[12]

The Holy Father's thought is expressed more organically in the post-Synodal Apostolic Exhortation, *Christifideles laici*. He affirms their right to freely form associations, stresses the value of

---

[10] Pope John Paul II, *Insegnamenti* VII/2 (1984), 696.

[11] *Tertio Millennio Adveniente*, §36.

[12] Pope John Paul II, "Speech of March 2," *Insegnamenti* X/I (1987), 476.

group life as a sign of the communion and unity of the Church, explains the criteria for discernment and for recognition and calls them to ever greater communion and mutual cooperation.[13]

> In recent days the phenomenon of lay people associating among themselves has taken on a character of particular variety and vitality. In some ways lay associations have always been present throughout the Church's history as various confraternities, third orders and sodalities testify even today. However, in modern times such lay groups have received a social stimulus, resulting in the birth and spread of a multiplicity of group forms: associations, groups, communities, movements. We can speak of a new era of group endeavors of the lay faithful. In fact, alongside the traditional forming of associations, and at times coming from their very roots, movements and new sodalities have sprouted, with a specific feature and purpose, so great is the richness and versatility of resources that the Holy Spirit nourishes in the ecclesial community, and so great is the capacity of initiative and the generosity of our lay people.[14]

New Evangelization

Later in *Redemptoris Missio* the Pope underlined the task of the movements in the new evangelization:

> I call to mind, as a new development occurring in many Churches in recent times, the rapid growth of ecclesial movements filled with missionary dynamism. When these movements seek to become part of the life of lo-

---

[13] Pope John Paul II, *Christifideles laici*, §29-32.

[14] Pope John Paul II, "Angelus, August 23, 1987," *Insegnamenti* X/3 (1987), 240; Cf. *Christifideles laici*, §29.

cal Churches and are welcomed by bishops and priests within diocesan and parish structures, they represent a true gift of God both for a new evangelization and for missionary activity properly so-called. I therefore recommend that they be spread, and that they be used.[15]

It is not enough, however, simply to record this judgment. It is crucial to point out that there is a theology undergirding the Pope's conviction that the movements are "one of the most important fruits of the springtime of the Church foretold by the Second Vatican Council."[16]

Ecclesiological Novelty

We need to realize, then, that the movements are an "ecclesiological novelty." They are attempts to enact, in an especially clear and organic way, an ecclesiology of communion (by means of "the concurrence of diverse, but complementary vocations, walks of life, ministries, charisms, and tasks")[17] and to order this communion of believers dynamically towards the one mission of the Church and the needs of the new evangelization. The development of the ecclesial movements reflects a further aspect. They are strictly bound up with "a providential rediscovery of the charismatic dimension of the Church," in the conviction that the institutional and the charismatic are equally essential aspects of the Church's constitution and work together, in different ways, to build up the Church's life, to foster its renewal, and to promote "the sanctification of the people of God."[18]

---

[15] Pope John Paul II, *Redemptoris Missio*, §72.

[16] Pope John Paul II, "Message to the World Congress of Ecclesial Movements, 1998," *Laity Today* (1999), 16.

[17] John Paul II, *Christifideles laici*, §20.

[18] Pope John Paul II, "Address of His Holiness Pope John Paul II on the occasion of the Meeting with the Ecclesial Movements and Communities, 1998," *Laity Today* (1999), 222.

Convinced that the new ecclesial movements are an authentic flowering of Marian spirituality, the Pope, in a very personal and committed manner, has initiated an exposition into what it means to be a movement in the Church. In 1984 at Rome he addressed the Communion and Liberation movement on their thirtieth anniversary,

> It should be noted how the Spirit, in order to continue with the man of today that dialogue begun by God in Christ and continued in the course of all Christian history, has raised up many ecclesial movements in the contemporary Church. They are a sign of the freedom of forms in which the one Church is expressed, and they represent a secure newness, which still awaits being adequately understood in all its positive efficacy for the Kingdom of God at work in the present moment of history.[19]

The Pope signaled even at this early stage that he recognized the authenticity and the potential of the movements, and he recognized that much more reflection and study needed to be undertaken to fully appreciate that which God had raised up. In order to assist the Church to appropriate the new ecclesial movements and indeed to help the new movements to deepen their self-understanding the Pope reflected at the Pentecost gathering on the very idea of what is a "movement" or what constitutes a "movement."

In the opening letter which he addressed to the participants at the 1998 World Congress of Ecclesial Movements the Pope described the Church itself as a "movement," and, above all a mystery which reveals the Father's eternal love, from which go forth the mission of the Son and the mission of the Holy Spirit.[20] The

[19] Pope John Paul II, "Go Into all the World," Address to Communion and Liberation Movement, 1984. Supplement of *30 Days* (September 29, 1989), 14-15.

[20] Pope John Paul II, "Message to the World Congress of Ecclesial Movements 1998," 19.

Church, born of this mission is in *statu missionis*. She is a "movement" which enters into the history of man as person and of human communities. The "movements" in the Church have to reflect the mystery of this love, from which the Church was born and is constantly born; the various movements must live the fullness of the Life transmitted to humankind as gift of the Father in Jesus Christ through the action of the Holy Spirit. They must carry out as fully as possible the priestly, prophetic and kingly mission of Christ, which is shared by the whole People of God.[21]

Action of the Spirit

At the Pentecost gathering of 1998, the Pope told the assembled crowds,

> With the Second Vatican Council, the Comforter recently gave the Church… a renewed Pentecost, instilling a new and unforeseen dynamism. Whenever the Spirit intervenes, he leaves people astonished…. He brings about events of amazing newness; he radically changes persons and history. This was the unforgettable experience of the Second Vatican Ecumenical Council during which, under the guidance of the same Spirit, the Church rediscovered the charismatic dimension as one of her constitutive elements…. It is from this providential rediscovery of the Church's charismatic dimension that, before and after the Council, a remarkable pattern of growth has been established for ecclesial movements and new communities.[22]

---

21 Pope John Paul II, *Insegnamenti* IV/2 (September 27, 1981), 305.

22 Pope John Paul II, "Address of His Holiness Pope John Paul II on the occasion of the Meeting with the Ecclesial Movements and Communities, 1998," *Laity Today* (1999), 219.

Groups Present at Pentecost

More than fifty groups were represented at this event, among them L'Arche, Communion and Liberation, Neo-Catechumenal Way, Regnum Christi, Focolare, Charismatic Renewal. The Pope acknowledged that in their relatively young existence, many or most of them had been involved, to a significant degree, "in uneasiness and tensions… presumptions and excesses… numerous prejudices and reservations"[23] in the Church. But he called that a "testing period" for their fidelity, and challenged them to be united in faith and purpose.

"The Church expects from you," he declared, "the mature fruits of communion and commitment."[24] And, returning to one of his most persistent issues in preparing for the millennium, he gave them their mission.

> The world is dominated by a secularized culture that encourages and promotes models of life without God. Thus we see an urgent need for powerful proclamation and solid, in-depth Christian formation.[25]

He acknowledged that these members of movements and ecclesial communities represented "wonderful Christian families… true domestic Churches," and said that "many vocations to the ministerial priesthood and the religious life have blossomed" as a result of their charisms and faithfulness. So they are the natural missionaries to send out, "ceaselessly proclaiming the truths of faith, accepting the living stream of tradition as a gift and instilling in each person an ardent desire for holiness."[26]

---

23 Ibid., 222.
24 Ibid.
25 Ibid.
26 Ibid., 223.

Central Role of Liturgy

In recognizing that these movements reflect the charisms given by the Holy Spirit, the Pope pointed out that "true charisms cannot but aim at the encounter with Christ in the sacraments."[27] This is an absolutely vital point not to be missed in this discussion of the movements, because it brings it all back to the liturgy, something which has enriched the life of all the new ecclesial communities, and to which they too bring a new vitality of worship.

"Christ, sent by the Father, is the source of the Church's whole apostolate," states the Vatican II Decree *Apostolicam Actuositatem*. "Clearly then, the fruitfulness of the apostolate of lay people depends on their living union with Christ.... This life of intimate union with Christ in the Church is maintained by the spiritual helps common to all the faithful, chiefly by active participation in the liturgy."[28]

Pope John Paul noted,

The ecclesial realities to which you belong have helped you to rediscover your baptismal vocation, to appreciate the gifts of the Spirit received at Confirmation, to entrust yourselves to God's forgiveness in the sacrament of Reconciliation and to recognize the Eucharist as the source and summit of all Christian life.[29]

Need for Shepherds

At the Pentecost gathering the Pope further instructed the movements, guiding their zeal toward safe shepherding. "In the

---

[27] Pope John Paul II, "The Spirit is the Source of Ministries" (General Audience, August 5, 1998), 114.

[28] Cf. *Apostolicam Actuositatem*, §4.

[29] Pope John Paul II, "Message to the World Congress of Ecclesial Movements, 1998," 20.

confusion that reigns in the world today, it is so easy to err, to give in to illusions." He then invoked *Lumen Gentium* in calling these movements to submission to the Church's authority and direction.

> The Council wrote in clear words: "Those who have charge over the Church should judge the genuineness and proper use of these gifts, through their office not indeed to extinguish the Spirit, but to 'test all things and hold fast to what is good'" (*LG* §12). This is the necessary guarantee that you are taking the right road![30]

He asked the movements to follow faithfully the guidance of the Church "with generosity and humility" in practicing their particular charisms in their local Churches and parishes.

> May this element of trusting obedience to the bishops, the successors of the Apostles, in communion with the Successor of Peter never be lacking in the Christian formation provided by your movements!... The latter, helped by the experience of the laity, are in a position to judge more clearly and more appropriately in spiritual as well as in temporal matters.[31]

At this Pentecost gathering, Pope John Paul, with great solemnity, beseeched the Holy Spirit to renew in these movements the mission set upon the Apostles at that first Pentecost.

> Today, from this upper room in St. Peter's Square, a great prayer rises: "Come, Holy Spirit, come and renew the face of the earth! Come with your seven gifts! Come, Spirit of Life, Spirit of Communion and Love! The Church and the world need you. Come, Holy

---

[30] Cf. *Eucharisticum Mysterium*, §7ff.
[31] Cf. *Lumen Gentium,* §37.

Spirit, and make ever more fruitful the charisms you have bestowed on us. Give new strength and missionary zeal to these sons and daughters of yours who have gathered here.... Strengthen their love and their fidelity to the Church."[32]

Then the Holy Father urged the gathering to recall the model of Mary, "Christ's first disciple, Spouse of the Holy Spirit and Mother of the Church, who was with the Apostles at the first Pentecost, so that she will help us to learn from her *fiat* docility to the voice of the Spirit."[33]

Pope Exhorts Faithfulness

Docility and obedience, submission to the *magisterium*, these are lessons Pope John Paul is directing not just at the movements, but to the whole universal Church through this address to the movements. He is invoking Vatican II, its call for renewal of the sacred liturgy and its teaching about holiness through participation in the sacraments to reach beyond the movements, which he is here setting on the right path. He is reaching out for the whole Church to realize the dynamism that the Council really did instill in her, a dynamism that he refers to as "unforeseen" but which has, in the last thirty years, been largely unseen. Pope John Paul also sees the emerging movements and ecclesial communities as the work of the Holy Spirit, something that has emerged from "the unforgettable experience of the Second Vatican Ecumenical Council." And he declares now to be the time to realize the transformation it intended. He told the gathering, preparing them to put that life at the service of the Church, that they were the "provi-

---

[32] Pope John Paul II, "Message to the World Congress of Ecclesial Movements, 1998," 19.

[33] Ibid.

dential response"[34] of the Spirit to a world where "the faith of many is sorely tested, and is frequently stifled and dies."[35]

Movements within Vatican II Ecclesiology

Significantly the Pope situated the movements within the ecclesiology of Vatican II and the Council's teaching on the mission and vocation of the laity. Only in this way can one understand the full theological meaning of this phenomenon that, following the Council, has marked out a "new era of group endeavors" in the Church.[36] Even if the origin of some of these movements such as the Focolare go back to before Vatican II, the full theological significance can only be understood in the light of the Council's teaching.

They are deeply rooted in the heart of the Church and should not be reduced to specific forms of spirituality, as sometimes happens. They are so much more than this! The Pope recognizes this reality when he said the movements "offer themselves as forms of self-fulfillment and as facets of the one Church."[37] The Pope affirms that the Church itself is a movement and above all a mystery, the eternal mystery of the Love of the Father and his paternal heart from which emerged the mission of the Son and the mission of the Holy Spirit. Hence "movements in the Church should reflect the mystery of that from which they were born and continue to be born."[38]

The Pope called forth from the movements "ecclesial maturity"[39] which is expressed in clear self-awareness on the part of a

---

[34] Ibid.

[35] Ibid., 222.

[36] Cf. *Christifideles laici,* §29.

[37] Pope John Paul II, "Message to the World Congress of Ecclesial Movements, 1998," 17.

[38] Pope John Paul II, *Insegnamenti* (September 27, 1981), 2-3.

[39] Pope John Paul II, "Message to the World Congress of Ecclesial Movements, 1998," 19.

movement that it is an ecclesial movement. As Bishop Rylko states in his evaluation of the Pope's address to the Congress of Ecclesial Movements, "This is the point of departure: what does it mean to be a movement in the Church?"[40]

Charism at the Heart of the Church

Specifically this demands from the movements a realization that they are not on the fringe of the Church but they are of the Church, for whom they are a gift and a grace just as the Church is gift and grace for them. With such awareness, comes responsibility to use the charisms which have called them into existence. Vatican II addressed the theology of charisms and it is largely out of such roots that these new charismatic ecclesial movements were born during the post conciliar period. In *Lumen Gentium* we read that the Holy Spirit, "guides the Church towards the fullness of truth (cf. Jn 16:13), unifies it in communion and service, equips and directs it through hierarchical and charismatic gifts, and enriches it with his fruits."[41] Church movements are one of the expressions of the charismatic dimensions of the Church and as the Pope confirmed in an earlier address, "both the institutional and charismatic aspects are equally essential and contribute to life, renewal and sanctification, although in different ways."[42]

Inclusive Rather than Exclusive

The Pope reminded the movements that they should never close in on themselves with a sense of self-satisfaction, but guided

---

[40] Bishop Rylko, *Laus Deo*, 3 (2002), 3. Bishop Rylko, Secretary of the Pontifical Council for the Laity, was given responsibility (along with Cardinal Stafford) to pastor the Catholic Fraternity within the Church.

[41] Cf. *Lumen Gentium,* §4.

[42] Pope John Paul II, Address, 2 March 1987, n. 3.

towards mission by their very nature, they must continuously reach out to the world. The charism of a movement has a universal character which can attract people from different cultures, traditions and age profiles. Furthermore, although they are lay in character their very identity includes the capacity to gather within the same community people from various vocations and different states of life.

Discernment of Charisms

The issue of the individual charism of each ecclesial movement brings with it the question of discernment and Church verification. The Council clearly states:

> "Judgment as to their (charisms) genuineness and proper use belongs to those who preside over the Church, and to those whose special competence it belongs, not indeed to extinguish the Spirit, but to test all things and hold fast to what is good (cf. 1 Th 5:12 & 19-21)," so that all the charisms might work together, in their diversity and complementarity, for the common good.[43]

Locally based movements consequently require the approval of the diocesan bishop while international movements require approval from the Pontifical Council for the Laity. Such ecclesiastical recognition not only guarantees the authenticity of the charism and its implementation but it also enables the charism of the movement to become part of the spiritual patrimony of the whole Church. Pope John Paul II's insight in welcoming the arrival of the new ecclesial movements and his zeal and commitment to bring them into the heart of the Church has been not

---

[43] Cf. *Christifideles laici*, §24.

only a decisive and essential exercise of the Petrine charism but an authentic one. As Stafford puts it,

> there can be no persuasive exercise of the hierarchical office that does not presuppose the characteristic contemplative dwelling of the Holy Spirit and then of Mary. The unity-in-distinction between the divine Word (institutional) and the Spirit of the Father (charismatic) is sacramentally and archetypically revealed in the two disciples Peter and Mary. The Petrine-hierarchical-institutional dimension of the Church always presupposes the Marian-charismatic action of the Holy Spirit to which it owes its origin. The Marian dimension reaches its fulfillment in the Petrine-sacramental dimension of the Church. The Marian and Petrine dimensions presuppose the fusing together in the Church of objectivity and subjectivity, of the Word and of the Spirit.[44]

The Pope recognized this truth and has discerned that the new ecclesial movements, a subjective work of the Spirit, need to be "fused" within the objective reality of the institutional, hierarchical Church. To this end, he has called on his brothers in the episcopacy to work with him in bringing about this reality.[45]

The "Fides" News Agency interviewed Dr. Guzman Carriquiry, Under-Secretary of the Pontifical Council for the Laity about the purpose of the synod of Bishops which the Pope convened shortly after the Congress of Ecclesial Movements. He was fulsome in his praise of the Pope for his pastoring of the movements and for the calling of the seminar of the Bishops entitled "Ecclesial Movements and New Communities in the Pastoral Care of Bishops."

---

[44] James Francis Cardinal Stafford, Foreword to "The Ecclesial Movements in the Pastoral Concern of the Bishop," *Laity Today* (2000), 8.

[45] Pope John Paul II, "Message to the Participants in the Seminar on The Ecclesial Movements in the Pastoral Concern of the Bishops," *Laity Today* (1999), 16.

This event is a follow-up to the historical encounter of May 30, 1998 (which we now refer to affectionately as "May 30") between the Pope and representatives of more than fifty movements, at the close of a World Congress of Church Movements.... "May 30" was a re-proposal of the riches of Movements, their charism, their educational action, their missionary spirit without fear of being identified with the heart of the Church.... "May 30" was also the Pope's call for a new phase of maturity for Movements.[46]

One of the key speakers at the seminar was Bishop Stanislaw Rylko, Secretary of the Pontifical Council for the Laity. He pointed out:

The movements are a gift from the Spirit to the whole Church. And a gift always implies work: it challenges the recipient to responsibility. Because a response must be made to the gift: it must be fruitful.... It is well known that in the Pope's pastoral plans, the ecclesial movements occupy a special place: "One of the gifts of our time, which from the beginning of my pontificate I have pointed out as a reason for hope for the Church and for men."[47]

This warm and prophetic acceptance by the Pope of the new ecclesial movements as an authentic sign of the Holy Spirit vivifying the Church has been critical in their emergence and their acceptance within the structures of the Church. The Pope has been moved by the fervent spirituality, the centrality of *communio*, and the zeal to evangelize, all of which are key dimensions to the lifestyle of these new ecclesial movements.

---

[46] Cf. <www.legionofchrist.org/eng/articles/en99100802.html>.
[47] Ibid.

Undoubtedly, the unexpected arrival of the new ecclesial movements exudes promise and hope, and the Church, especially through the efforts of the Pope, has largely warmed to their potential and to the charisms they bring to vivify the life of the Church. Yet tensions persist notably between the local and the universal Church and it has sparked some heated theological debate from significant antagonists.

CHAPTER EIGHT

Universal and Local Church: The Perennial Tension

The emergence of the new ecclesial movements has also brought to the fore another delicate issue in the life of the Church, namely, the relationship between the local and the universal Church, between the local bishop and the Pope. This too needs to be given an overall historical setting so that one can appreciate the nuances of the current reality.

Historical Perspective

Ratzinger, in a paper that he presented at the World Congress of Ecclesial Communities in 1998, outlined an historical overview that is an excellent starting point for this survey. In his analysis, the early apostles proclaimed the message of Christ without any geographical restrictions; their mission field was the whole world, "to the ends of the earth" (Ac 1:8) and to make disciples of all men (cf. Mt 28:19). The apostles were not bishops of particular local Churches, but assigned to the whole world and to the whole Church; the universal Church thus preceded the local Churches, which arose as its concrete realizations.[1] Paul did not

---

[1] Cf. Joseph Ratzinger, *Called to Communion. Understanding the Church Today* (San Francisco: Ignatius Press, 1996), 75-104.

see himself as a bishop of a particular place, and the initial division of labor of Paul and Barnabas for the Gentiles and James and Cephas for the Jews was soon superseded. In brief, one can say that early Church history bears unequivocal testimony that the apostolic ministry was a universal one which in turn gave rise to the establishment of local Churches.

Organization and Structure

These new Churches required leadership at the local level and of necessity organization and structure naturally arose within the local situations. Thus two forms, the universal mission and the local apostolate, co-existed side by side in the nascent Church. This structure continued well into the second century when the demands of the local Churches saw the emergence of a tripartite division of bishop, priest and deacon. Irenaeus of Lyons testifies that the bishops now understood that they were the successors of the Apostles.[2]

However, with the development of the episcopal ministry, the ministries of the universal Church gradually disappeared in the course of the second century. According to Ratzinger, "this was a development not only historically inevitable but theologically necessary; it brought to light the unity of the sacrament and the intrinsic unity of the apostolic service."[3]

Yet danger was ever present: because there was a real temptation to perceive priestly ministry only in institutional or bureaucratic terms, the charismatic dimension could so easily be forgotten. Moreover, there was a real danger that the ministry of the apostolic succession could "wither away into a purely local ecclesial ministry."[4]

---

[2]   Irenaeus, *Adv. Haer.* V, 11:1.
[3]   Ratzinger, "The Ecclesial Movements; a Theological Reflection on Their Place in the Church," 37.
[4]   Ibid., 36.

Monasticism

In response to these dangers to the universal dimension, a new element appears in the life of the Church as early as the third century. It was called monasticism but Ratzinger has "no hesitation in calling this element a 'movement'." While it did not have a missionary impulse as characterized by its original founders such as Antony,[5] the desire to live the *vita evangelica* radically and totally created a new "spiritual fatherhood," one which supplemented "the fatherhood of bishops and priests by the power of a wholly pneumatic life."[6] Antony challenged the mindset of his time. As Quefflec points out,

> ...men like Antony had realized that it (the Church) was becoming too middle class and affluent, becoming preoccupied with Greek tinsel, becoming infected with heathen ideas and becoming political.[7]

Bishop Cordes, writing on this period states convincingly that

> the close and intimate bond with God that distinguished the desert fathers also prepared the spiritual ground in the Church for the theological assault on the heresy of Arianism.... Without the school of the desert, would not St. Athanasius (d. 373), the disciple and biographer of Antony, have been broken by the relentless persecution by his theological adversaries? ... the men who gathered round Athanasius constituted a phalanx against apostasy. In them the desert had lib-

---

[5]   See St. Athanasius, "Life of Antony," *Sources chrétienne* 400 (1994) especially in the introductory section: 'L'exemple de la vie évangélique et apostolique,' 52-53.

[6]   Ratzinger, "The Ecclesial Movements; a Theological Reflection on Their Place in the Church," 37.

[7]   Cf. H. Quefflec, *Saint Antoine du Desert*, 2nd Ed., Paris: 1988, 131.

erated the spirit that preserved, within the Church, faith in the co-essential divinity of the Son of God.[8]

In a further reflection on these first movements in the Church, Cordes perceptively identifies a critical, distinctive, feature in any movement of change.

> Renewal is not achieved without delimitation, without the definition of frontiers. Only by this means is it possible to be different. If the conscience of everyone is conformistically leveled, it is impossible to find the firm and undeviating point that alone can initiate change. Movements originate only if they have a different level than that of their surrounding environment.[9]

St Basil

Yet, St. Basil, who gave Eastern monasticism its permanent form, did not set out to create a separate institution alongside that of the Church. His Rule as he conceived it was not one for a religious order as such but an ecclesial rule, *Enchiridion* (manual) of the committed Christian.[10] A characteristic of the ecclesial movements is that they seek not for a community apart but for an integral form of Christianity. Basil is a wonderful model for the new ecclesial communities of today because he accepted the call to the episcopacy and thus in his own life he exemplified the charismatic aspect of the episcopal ministry, the inner unity of the Church lived by the bishop in his own life. The sociologist Max Weber sees this as an inevitable transition from radical to conservative.

---

[8] Paul Josef Cordes, *Charisms and New Evangelisation,* St. Paul's Publications, 1991, 23.

[9] Cordes, 24.

[10] Cf. J. Gribomont, "Les Regles Morales de S. Basile et Le Nouveau Testament," *Studia Patristica* 2 (1957), 416-426. See also H. U. von Balthasar (ed.), *Die Grossen Ordenregeln*, 48-49.

We find that peculiar transformation of charisma into an institution: permanent structures and traditions replace the belief in the revelation and heroism of charismatic personalities; charisma becomes part of an established social structure.[11]

A Certain Distance Needed

Crucially, Basil came to recognize that the movement to follow Christ in an uncompromising fashion cannot be totally merged with the local Church. In his small *Asketikon*, he sees the movement as "a transitional form between a group of committed Christians open to the Church as a whole and a self-organizing and self-institutionalizing monastic order." Gribomont likens the monastic community founded by Basil to a leaven, "a small group for the vitalization of the whole"; in Gribomont's assessment Basil is not only the founding father of the teaching and hospital orders "but also of the new communities without vows."[12] In Ratzinger's assessment, the monastic movement

> created a new center of life that did not abolish the local ecclesial structure of the post apostolic Church, but that did not simply coincide with it either. It was active in it as a life-giving force, a kind of reservoir from which the local Church could draw truly spiritual clergy in whom the fusion of institution and charism was constantly renewed.

He further asserts that just as the local Church,

---

[11] See Max Weber, *Economy and Society*, 1978.

[12] Cf. Gribomont, "Obéissance et Évangile selon S. Basile Le Grand," *La Vie Spirituelle*: Supplement 5 (1952), 192-215, esp. 192. See also Balthasar, *Die Grossen Ordenregeln*, 48-49.

necessarily determined by the episcopal ministry, is the supporting structure that permanently upholds the edifice of the Church through the ages... the Church is also traversed by the successive waves of movements that renew the universalistic aspect of her apostolic mission and thus serve to foster the spiritual vitality and truth of the local Churches.[13]

The charism of any authentic reformer has a mystical element yet mysticism is always problematic for the Church, because it is precisely here that the Church can encounter the explosive force of theological individualism. The mystic is tempted to disregard the communion of the Church in his journey towards God. His personal immediate relationship with God "appears as the Archimedean point of the life of faith, which cannot be called into question."[14]

The life of faith is detached from the tradition and can apparently dispense with the human mediation provided by the Church's ministry. This too has been a temptation of the new communities and movements that have emerged in the last century but I will refer to this in greater detail in the next chapter.

Ignatius of Loyola

Even mystics who were subsequently embraced by the Church, proved problematic at first to the existing *communio*. They were perceived as a threat because they showed little interest in the Church as an institution. Ignatius of Loyola was a classic example of this reality. In Ignatius, God created a man whose mission it was to open up in the Church an "official" way for an indi-

---

[13] Ratzinger, "The Ecclesial Movements; A Theological Reflection on Their Place in the Church," 39.

[14] Cordes, *Charisms and New Evangelisation*, 31.

vidual who wants to be conducted by God in person. *The Pilgrim's Story* (Autobiography) of Ignatius reveals the renunciation and the "expulsion" that he had to endure. What he stood for conflicted with current ecclesiastical practice. Others such as St. Philip Neri and his Oratorians, St. Alphonsus Liguori and St. John of the Cross all suffered similar treatment.

As shown earlier in the first chapter, the Reformation had thrown the ecclesiastical authorities as a whole into a state of uncertainty. Given the threat of individualism and the *devotio moderna* which challenged the mediating role of the Church, the preservation of the purity of the faith was paramount. Yet, by 1535, Ignatian spirituality had been accepted and inserted into the life of the Church. Stark seizes upon this to point out a salient feature of authentic protest movements within the Church.

> The Catholic protest movements have always protested without becoming Protestants,... they have fruitfully bored from within, instead of fruitlessly attacking from without... and they have been allowed to do so.[15]

That this held true was largely due to the role of the Pope, the successor to Peter. Ratzinger stresses that the Pope is not just the local bishop of Rome "but bishop for the whole Church and in the whole Church."[16]

> Ministries and missions that are not tied to "the local Church alone but serve universal missions and the spreading of the Gospel must always exist in the Church."[17]

---

[15] W. Stark, *The Sociology of Religion, a Study of Christendom* (London and New York, 1967), 387ff. See also W.J. Barry, and R.G. Doherty, *Contemplatives in Action, the Jesuit Way* (Mahwah, NJ: Paulist Press, 2002).

[16] Stark, 45.

[17] Stark, 46.

Danger of Imbalance

There is always the danger that a particularist view of the Church which exalts the rights of the local Church would damage the universality of the Church.

> In particularist ecclesiology the whole Church is present in a particular Church; in universalist ecclesiology, by contrast, the whole Church is present only in the integration of all the particular Churches. If one thinks of the universal Church from a particularist ecclesiology, one has the idea of the communion of Churches; through participation in this communion, the particular Churches express or "focus" the being of the entire Church. If, however, one thinks of the particular Churches from a universalist ecclesiology, one understands the local Church as a portion of the People of God, existing through incorporation into the Church universal.[18]

Nichols sees that it is important to suppress neither of these equally valid perspectives but to seek to hold them in balance. This is difficult to achieve because this very issue raises the relationship of authority and the precise nature of the Petrine ministry within the *collegium* of bishops. The emergence of the new ecclesial movements brings this matter to the forefront of current ecclesiological debate. The new movements have sought affirmation from Rome when their ministry has been thwarted or not recognized by the local bishop. This has raised the delicate issue of the universal and the local Church and the precise relationship of the bishop and the Pope.

The "Letter on Certain Aspects of the Church Understood

---

[18] Aidan Nichols, *Epiphany, A Theological Introduction to Catholicism* (Collegeville, MN: Liturgical Press, 1996), 220.

as Communion"[19] makes clear that in the situation among the Eastern Orthodox Communities, although their local Churches may be considered as true particular Churches, nonetheless their existence as such Churches is wounded because of their deprivation of full communion with the universal Church represented and realized through the Petrine officeholder.[20] The First Vatican Council stigmatized as heretical a unilateral concentration on either the total episcopate or the papacy. The Pope can in his own right speak infallibly, and does not need to appeal to a council but the bishops are not just papal administrators; the episcopate is also of divine right that no Pope can set aside. Church and Pope cannot be set over against each other but need to exist in a relational unity in order to complement each other. The Pope as guardian of the faith and practice does not displace the local bishop but "confirms, supplements and sometimes corrects their efforts."[21] At the same time, the local bishop, whose particular Church is itself the Church in miniature, brings the experience of an often far-flung community to the Petrine, from where their concerns can be mediated to the rest of the Church universal. The local and the universal Church interpenetrate in an unbreakable exchange, a kind of *perichoresis*, similar to that of the persons in the Trinity. Within the western tradition this is graphically captured in the Eucharist which is celebrated *una cum* (one with) the Pope as well as the local bishop.

Though the papacy is not a sacramental order, it can be called a charismatic order[22]; it is not separate from the regular ministry which all bishops share but it is unique in its mode of continuity and in the personal authority conferred by the charism of the papal office. Ultimately, this *perichoresis* is a mystery and requires a journey of faith into the mystery of unity, notwithstanding the tensions which are evident.

---

[19] *Letter on Certain Aspects of the Faith Understood as Communion*, Congregation of the Doctrine of the Faith, 1992.

[20] Nichols, 221.

[21] Ibid., 232.

[22] Ibid., 233.

Movements Test the Relationship
of the Universal and the Local

The recent arrival of the new ecclesial communities into this milieu highlights again the delicacy and the intricacy of the local and universal concept of Church and the sensitive nature of the relationship between the Bishop of Rome and his fellow bishops. The recent theological debate between then Cardinal Ratzinger and the recently appointed Cardinal Kasper indicates that the Church is also grappling to understand the true relationship between the local and the universal, between the papacy and the College of Bishops. The arrival of the new ecclesial movements has brought this issue to the forefront of theological debate. Undoubtedly, these new movements have caused some concern at local level because they have disturbed the peace and they have not always fitted smoothly into existing parish structures. Moreover, their zeal and commitment have at times led them to be somewhat elitist in their membership and in their attitude. Bishops have not always welcomed them and at times have intervened to thwart their plans.

One of the most significant was the conflict between the Communion and Liberation movement and Cardinal Carlo Martini in Milan, where he rejected the methodology of their pastoral program in his diocese.[23] Often these communities have appealed to Rome for approval, in this way circumventing the role of the local ordinary. In a nutshell, their emergence is a perfect example of the current theological debate about the relationship between the local and the universal Church. It is about what came first, the local Church or the universal.

---

[23] Robert Moynihan, "Valiant for God, the New Movements 1," *The Tablet* (February 20, 1988), 8.

Ratzinger's View

As former head of the Congregation of the Doctrine of the Faith, Cardinal Ratzinger's position was that the universal Church came first, and as the papacy is of the essence of the universal Church, then the papacy came first too. Moreover, Ratzinger contends that the contest in the West over the freedom of the Church from the state under Gregory VII (d. 1057) and the conflict with the mendicant orders in the thirteenth century highlighted the Petrine role as guarantor of spiritual resurgence. Only the universal Church can ensure the separation of the particular Church from the state and society. Today too, we are experiencing the phenomenon of apostolic movements coming "from below" and transcending the local Church: movements in which new charisms are emerging and animating the local pastoral ministry. Today too, such movements, which cannot be derived from the episcopal principle, find their theological and practical justification in primacy.[24]

All of this is more than just a question of historical sequence. It affects the way the Church's fundamental design is understood. It places the papacy *in charge* of the Church. Because they came after the universal Church, the local Churches, each led by its own bishop, are subordinate to the papacy. For all sorts of things they might want to do — indeed, believe in all conscience they ought to do — they need Rome's permission first. It is often not forthcoming.

It is all the more dramatic, therefore, that a serious challenge to this theory of Church structure has been mounted not from some progressive academic campus but by the head of the Pontifical Council for Christian Unity, Cardinal Kasper, who has challenged the basic Ratzinger proposition that the universal Church came first.[25]

---

[24] *Forum katholischer Theologie* 2 (1986), 81-96.
[25] Robert Leicht, "Cardinals in conflict," *The Tablet* (April 28, 2001), 607-608.

Kasper's Alternative View

The latest installment of Cardinal Kasper's argument with Cardinal Ratzinger (now Pope Benedict XVI) originally appeared in a German theological magazine.[26] When an English translation appeared in *America*,[27] provided by Professor Ladislas Orsy, SJ, of Georgetown University Law Center, Washington DC, some of the remarks attributed to Cardinal Kasper were publicly challenged by Cardinal Avery Dulles as having been embroidered in translation. So *The Tablet*, because of the importance of knowing exactly what Cardinal Kasper was saying, commissioned its own more literal translation from Robert Nowell.[28]

Professor Orsy later joined the debate himself arguing that the Vatican curia's behavior since the end of the Second Vatican Council in 1965 has largely nullified what was intended to be the Council's most important doctrinal achievement, its doctrine of collegiality. This nicely dovetails with the Kasper analysis. Both of them point to the urgent need to reinforce the weight given to the local Churches, in the internal affairs of each of them and in the government of the Church regionally and as a whole. And this is not just for the sake of good will but because it is necessary in order to respect the inalienable rights and responsibilities of local bishops. They are not delegates of Rome. They are empowered directly by their sacramental orders. Collegiality comes from Christ, not from the dispensations of the curia. And a Church without papacy *and* collegiality is unbalanced.

Kasper, in his historical review of the first millennium, concluded that the ecclesiology of this period "excluded a one-sided emphasis on the local Churches as well as a one-sided emphasis

---

[26] The German text of this article was originally published in the journal *Stimmen der Zeit* (December 2000).

[27] The translation appeared in *America* (April 23, 2001), 16-17.

[28] This translation appeared in *The Tablet* (June 23, 2001), 927-930.

on the universal Church."[29] In his judgment, the priority of the universal over the local has been a characteristic of the Latin Church since the onset of the second millennium, ever since the Latin Patriarchate (based in Rome) lost the counterweight of the Greek patriarchs (based in Constantinople and elsewhere) after the Great Schism of 1054. The West alone developed a new conception of Church that put the emphasis on universality. This caused a trend to develop which attributed all authority to the Pope. Undoubtedly this doctrine was crucial in the fight against conciliarism, the Protestant Reformation, state absolutism, Gallicanism and Josephism. The First Vatican Council with its teaching on the primacy of jurisdiction of the Pope, reinforced this doctrine as did the 1917 *Code of Canon Law*.

The Second Vatican Council sought to recover the beliefs and attitudes of the early Church and to harmonize them with the teachings of the First Vatican Council. The enactments regarding the sacramental character of episcopal ordination and episcopal collegiality bear testimony to this. Subsequently, the Extraordinary Synod of Bishops stated that communion was the central and foundational idea of the Second Vatican Council. Later, in 1992, the Congregation for the Doctrine of Faith, in a letter to the bishops objected to a one sided ecclesiology which attributed excessive weight to the local Churches, to the detriment of the universal. However, in Kasper's view, they went beyond the teaching of Vatican II by asserting that the local Churches exist "in and from" the universal Church and they proposed the ontological and historical priority of the universal Church. Congar also believed that Vatican II ecclesiology recognized anew the reality and the significance of the local Church.

This represents a movement away from an ecclesiology concerned simply with the universal Church and the expansion of one Church — the Church of Rome — throughout the world and for-

---

getful of the reality of the local Churches; in other words, an ecclesiology oriented towards a uniform universality which is pragmatically divided into dioceses. Yves Congar believed that this was the most fundamentally new and promising contribution made by the Council.[30]

Summary

The existence of new ecclesial movements brings into immediate relief the relationship of the local bishop with that of the Petrine office; furthermore, it tests the link between the universal and the local. Undoubtedly, there is unresolved tension here within this delicate balance of roles, responsibilities and rights. Given the calibre of theologians and Churchmen involved in the current debate, one can assume that clear definitions may not be forthcoming for some time. Pending a resolution to the universal versus the local debate, the new ecclesial movements are in somewhat unsettled waters. Their role is both within the parish and *supra* parish, and both within the diocese and *supra* diocese. This necessitates relationships with the local ordinary and with the Petrine. How the Church, both universal and local deals with them, will be critical to their future development.

---

[30] Yves Congar, *Le Concile de Vatican II* (Paris: Beauchesne, 1984), 24.

SECTION FOUR

ASSESSMENTS AND CONCLUSIONS

CHAPTER NINE

Hopes and Dangers

The aim of this book was to examine the reality of the new ecclesial movements in the Church and to come to some assessment of their impact to date. To accomplish this task I felt it was important to provide an historical backdrop to the arrival of the new movements. Thus the methodology chosen was an historical review of the charismatic trends that have always been a feature of the Church. This necessitated a global examination of significant renewal movements with more emphasis being given to some of the more major renewals such as the monastic movement, particularly the role of St. Basil, the Franciscan movement, and the prophetic direction of Cardinal John Henry Newman. Scrutiny of these pivotal reform movements, their struggle for acceptance by the institution, the dynamism which they brought, their unexpected arrival, their charisms which enriched the Church, their suffering and their faithfulness in spite of that suffering, and their legacies, all provided fascinating insight into the current phenomenon under review.

The charismatic reality has always been a feature of the Church as part of the Marian profile and this tradition has collaborated with the Petrine to energize and to protect the life of the Church. Although this relationship of the Marian and the Petrine has not been trouble free, the research shows that invariably the charism of truth leads them into unity and impels the

Church to new fruitfulness. The history of charisms and the role of the Pope in safeguarding the transmission of the charisms throughout the Church, and the prophetic Marian role in calling forth the primacy of the papacy, all shed critical light on the mutuality of the Marian and the Petrine dimensions of the Church.

Given that the membership profile of the new movements was largely lay in character it was also important to examine this predominantly lay spirituality within the tradition of the Church. Hence I provided an overview of the main developments in the understanding of the role of the layperson in the life of the Church. This in turn led to an examination of the ecclesiology of the Second Vatican Council which restored to the Church a renewed sense of *communio* and reclaimed a profound understanding of baptism which calls each member to know Christ and to make Him known. Specifically, I looked at the emergence of three of the new movements within this rediscovered ecclesiology, namely, the Neo-Catechumenate, Communion and Liberation, and Charismatic Renewal. I attempted to define the salient features of the new movements and to see their emergence within the evolving awareness of the Church herself as a movement.

Arising out of the research undertaken, I propose a number of conclusions which I have ascertained from the study of this new phenomenon. A good overview of the situation is provided by Jean Vanier, the Founder of L'Arche, who presented an excellent paper on new communities, new spiritual families and new movements which have risen up throughout the history of the Church.[1] These constitute a mixture of hopes and fears, possibilities and dangers.

---

[1]   In February 1997, Jean Vanier, the founder of the L'Arche communities, delivered a talk on "New Lay Movements: Signs of the Spirit or Christian sects." Jean Vanier examined how a movement can develop in relation to itself and to the wider Church. A new lay movement faces many challenges and needs wise guidance, both from within and from outside if it is to evolve healthily according to the Spirit and remain open. The talk was organized by *The Tablet*, a Catholic journal, and an abridged version of this text subsequently appeared in the 15th March 1997 issue (346-347). He articulates succinctly the dangers that face new movements and I have relied heavily on his experience in the conclusions which I present. Cf. also Internet reference <www.tasc.ac.uk/cc/briefing/9704/9704006.htm>.

Hopes and Dangers

Vanier states that some of these communities, movements and spiritual families have grown and are still with us today; others have died out. Each one responded to a need of the times. First came the hermits, then the monastic orders, then later the foundation of the Franciscans, the Dominicans, the Society of Jesus, and many teaching, missionary and service congregations. Some were founded in answer to new needs, others to rediscover values of faith and poverty that had been forgotten in a Church which had become powerful, rich, lax and intolerant; still others were founded in order to live a new spirituality, a new gift of the Spirit. Each one had a mission to do certain things (evangelize, teach, pray, etc.), to be a sign of the kingdom for the world; to lead people into deeper union with Jesus and to renew the Church. These spiritual families helped people grow towards greater compassion, freedom, and openness. All of these spiritual families, each with their own particular charism, appeared as a renewal for the Church.

Vanier points out that new families in the Church almost always begin small, poor, radical and enthusiastic. Frequently, there are amazing signs of Providence and beautiful stories of conversion in the early days. Under the guidance of a prophetic figure, members feel chosen by God for a specific mission, maybe even to reform and renew the Church. They then become recognized, approved, even admired and many come to join them. They acquire wealth and property, spiritual power and influence; this can be a dangerous moment for some communities, as the history of the Church shows. They become attached to power and influence; they feel they are the elite, perhaps the "real" Church. Over the years, however, a certain mediocrity can set in. There can be a desire to control people, to create structures that are heavy and which prevent the life of the Spirit and all new initiatives. Law and power can destroy freedom of the heart and of the Spirit. The question remains for all communities and movements, young and old, as they develop over the years: How can they remain alive, close to the Gospel message and the spirit of the beatitudes? Most of all, how can they remain close to the spirit of the founder(s)? What nourishment do they need to enable all their members to remain loving, ready to carry the cross of pain and to stay close to those in pain? How do they remain open to difference? How do they help their members to grow in inner freedom? How to encourage and not stifle initiatives?

There is always a danger that leaders of new movements, believing that they are inspired by the Holy Spirit, prevent a healthy evolution of the community, as if the founders had been inspired once and for all, and were infallible in every detail of the foundation and for all generations to come. Structures put into place during the founding years, possibly in reaction to particular cultural and ecclesial realities at the time, may not be relevant in later years. What was adequate in twentieth century Europe may not be adequate for the new millennium in Europe, Africa or Asia.

Concerns and Criticisms

A concerned and constructive critic of the new ecclesial movements is Raniero Cantalamessa. In particular, he is concerned about the negative and at times disparaging perception of the new movements, particularly Charismatic Renewal, as they are often depicted in Church publications. His considered opinion is that many of these publications view the new ecclesial movements "as conservative forces, if not downright reactionary."[2] This has caused the new movements to be confined to one part of the Church only and in the case of Charismatic Renewal to be considered "so alien that they (the Church) feel justified in keeping well clear of it."[3]

---

[2] Raniero Cantalamessa, "Remember Those Early Days: A Reflection on Charismatic Renewal," Ed.: International Catholic Charismatic Renewal Services. This paper was presented at the Gathering of Priests promoted by the Italian National Service Team for Renewal in the Spirit, Rome, 28 September 1999.

[3] Ibid.

Most damning of all the criticisms of the new ecclesial movements is that which emanates from Gordon Urquhart, a former Focolare member, who is now seriously disaffected with the burgeoning new ecclesial movements. He presents a searing attack upon three of the most energetic new movements in the Roman Catholic Church: Focolare, CL, and the Neo-Catechumenate.

> Many of their main characteristics reflect those of Mao's Red Guards — the fanaticism, the blind obedience, the sloganeering, the personality cult around the Pope, manipulation of the media, anti-intellectualism, denunciations, the formulation of rigid ideology, a younger generation mobilized in the struggle against their elders.[4]

Urquhart has his supporters in the media who castigate the new movements and seek to taint them with cult-like similarities. A *Time* magazine writer spoke as follows:

> The Vatican scholar is specifically concerned with these movements' authoritarian structure, and their use of ritual group confession, clandestine rites, and secretive ceremonies. In response, the well-connected defenders of these newly sanctified evangelicals have mobilized to play down such criticism.[5]

One such "well-connected defender" of the movements' integrity is Robert Moynihan, the editor of *Inside the Vatican*.

> Silence, fasting, cutting oneself off from one's former friends and associates to devote oneself to God, laboring to bring the Gospel to the ends of the earth, all of these behaviors are seen as fanatical, irrational, cult-like.

---

[4]   Gordon Urquart, *The Pope's Armada* (New York: Prometheus, 1999).

[5]   Rod Usher, *Time Magazine* 149 (January 27, 1999), No. 4.

But these are behaviors that Catholics honor and praise
in St. Benedict, St. Francis of Assisi and St. Thomas
More.[6]

There is a balanced and generally positive assessment by
Michael Walsh, a former Jesuit priest, in an article in *The Tablet*
magazine.[7] He argues that the recruitment and training methods
used are similar to those employed by religious life throughout the
centuries. Yet, he too critiques the new movements because he sees
them as being antagonistic towards each other.

Human Limitations

Obviously every new foundation reveals a new call, a new way
of incarnating and proclaiming the good news of Jesus. But in every
foundation there is a mixture of light and darkness; no movement
is entirely pure, totally holy or inspired in all its aspects. The ideal
and vision may be beautiful, holy and inspired, but the concrete
realities are relative to circumstances and to people as they are with
their beauty, inner fears, blockages and brokenness. There are always elements of pride, fear, insecurity and error in every new
movement. There is always tension between the effort to maintain unity and purity of a group with its spirituality through strong
leadership, and the need to allow for creativity, diversity and openness in order to help the movement as a whole to evolve according to the Holy Spirit as the times change. Each movement goes
through a crisis, a phase of purification and even division in order
to discover the truth and charism of the foundation and the truth
of the Gospel message.

For Catholic communities recognition or approval by the
Church means that their constitution safeguards the liberty of its

---

[6]   Robert Moynihan, *Inside the Vatican* (editor), in a *Time Magazine* article (1997).
[7]   Michael Walsh, "Sects Or Movements," *The Tablet* (July 8, 1995), 864-866.

members, and that the goals and government are in accordance with the Gospel message, that the movement shows reliable signs of the Spirit. Approval by the Church does not mean that everything is perfect. As the years go by, and as the movement is implanted in different cultures, it is imperative that a clear distinction be made between the fundamental spirituality and vision of the founder or foundress, which can be for all generations because they are rooted in the Gospel message, and the structures, rules and regulations, the ways of exercising authority, and of forming and accompanying new members. The latter are called to evolve according to circumstances. Lately there has arisen a huge difficulty around this very point in the Emmanuel Community, Paris. There is serious tension between the direction the new moderator wishes to lead the community towards and the structures established by the founder, Pierre Goursat. The history of the Church and the mistakes and evolution of many religious orders are there to show us that new movements and communities are called to be re-founded and to evolve in a healthy way.

Reception

This insertion into the local Church can take time because of a certain "closedness" in some areas and the fear of something new. Some new movements, because of their enthusiasm, poverty and radical faith seem to "rock the boat," revealing a fear of change. This happened in the Catholic Church after Vatican II. People are often set in their ways and their ideas and do not like change. That is why interventions by the Pope and the universal Church can be important for some new movements which were originally accepted in a particular diocese but then have been transplanted elsewhere. The Pope can sometimes see further than those in the local Church, but after necessary recognition by the Church it is important that these new communities become well inserted into the local Church, recognizing the authority of the bishop, and cooperating with other movements. On the other hand, some movements may need to be challenged if they have sectarian attitudes or are too closed in upon themselves. The danger is always that movements move towards success, power, riches and security, rather than towards fidelity to the Spirit and a life of faith and of trust lived in the spirit of the Sermon of the Mount. Numbers are not always a sign that the movement is of God.

Ordained Priesthood Within the Movements

Another significant aspect of the new ecclesial movements is the role of priests within them. The presence of the ordained priesthood is both a hope and a danger. Indeed, this question of the participation of priests in ecclesial movements is a very sensitive issue, one that the Pope himself addressed in a letter he sent to a meeting of Church movements organized by the Focolare movement.[8] The Pope acknowledged that many priests are "attracted by the charismatic, pedagogical, community and missionary drive which accompanies the new ecclesial realities."[9] Such experiences are useful because they "are capable of enriching the life of individual priests as well as enlivening the presbyterate with precious spiritual gifts."[10] Yet he reminded them that priests are called "to live the grace of the sacrament to the full which is why they are configured to Christ, head and shepherd, for the service of the whole Christian Community, in cordial and filial reverence to the diocesan presbyterate. They belong to the particular Church

---

[8] Pope John Paul II, "The Participation of Priests in Ecclesial Movements," *Catholic News Service*, 31, Pt. 10 (2001), 187-188. This meeting took place from June 26-29, 2001 at the headquarters of the Focolare movement in Rome. Cardinal J. Francis Stafford, President of the Pontifical Council of the Laity read the message to over 1,300 priests participating in the gathering.

[9] Pope John Paul II, "The Participation of Priests in Ecclesial Movements," *Catholic News Service*, 31, Pt. 10 (2001), 188.

[10] *Pastores Dabo Vobis*, 31.

and collaborate in her mission."[11] He further warned against priests who are members of movements becoming "narrow or closed-minded."[12] He called for them to be open to the Spirit and to "respect the other ways in which the faithful can take part in the life of the Church, encouraging them to become ever more persons of communion,"[13] "pastors of the whole."[14] Another area of concern raised by the Pope was the danger of a "drift toward a 'clericalization' of the movements."[15] Such a development could lead to a blurring and an eventual assimilation of the ministry of the priest to the lay state. It was important for all the members of the movements that in this interesting experience of communion none would lose "their distinct identity."[16]

Notwithstanding the possible dangers, the Pope exhorted priests to "live within a movement as an outstanding presence of Christ, head and shepherd, minister of the word of God and of the sacraments, educator in faith by means of his link with the bishop over and above the functions and offices he is called to assume."[17] He affirmed that "by belonging to them, priests can learn better how to live the Church in the rich experience of her sacramental, hierarchical and charismatic gifts that correspond to the many forms of ministries, states of life and tasks by which she is built up."[18]

Local and Universal

These considerations lead on to the relationship of the ecclesial movements and communities to the Pope and the Vati-

---

[11] John Paul II, "The Participation of Priests in Ecclesial Movements," 188.
[12] Ibid.
[13] Ibid.
[14] *Pastores Dabo Vobis*, 62.
[15] John Paul II, "The Participation of Priests in Ecclesial Movements," 188.
[16] Ibid.
[17] Ibid.
[18] Ibid.

can on the one hand, and to the bishops and episcopal conferences on the other hand. As with the new religious orders of the
past, these movements fit into Catholic life through direct relationship with the Holy See, and thus they raise once again the
age-old controversies concerning degrees of exemption from local episcopal control. Notwithstanding valiant efforts by the Pope
to promote the authenticity of the new ecclesial movements, it is
hardly a secret that some bishops are less enthusiastic about some
of the new movements than the Holy Father. Those in positions
of authority in the Church must be careful not to despise the prophetic voice of the Spirit while diligently testing it to see if it be
from God (1 Th 5:20-21). They must guard against the desire for
institutional self-preservation that leads to legalism and fear of
change. As Cardinal Suenens says in his book, *A New Pentecost?*

> The Church cannot dispense with a code of law or with
> legislation, but it must carefully steer clear of legalism
> and a mechanical view of its own life… the Gospel is,
> in the highest sense, the supreme law of the Church.
> The Word of God and the Spirit of Jesus are the ulti-
> mate authority in the Church and all hierarchy is at
> their service.[19]

Ironically the new ecclesial movements have also been castigated as examples of Catholic conservatism or neo-classicism,
directly opposed to the innovative and reformative spirit of Vatican II.[20]

It is important to try to look objectively at the issues involved
in this feature of Catholic life. On the one hand, the long pattern
of religious orders with degrees of exemption from local episcopal authority has provided the Catholic Church with a vitality that
it would surely not have had without them. There is a close con-

---

[19] Suenens, *A New Pentecost?*, 62.
[20] Cf. H Bourgeois, "Le Neo-Classicisme Catholique," *Études* (February 2001), 221-232.

nection between these relatively autonomous bodies and the Church's missionary impetus. Territorially determined units cannot easily develop and implement a missionary thrust elsewhere. The existence of these movements allows for both a practical flexibility and a framework for ecclesial insertion and supervision. On the other hand, the close alliance between a centralized papacy and international movements not under local Church authority can breed an elitist arrogance in the movements[21] and undermine the Church's collegial and episcopal structure, which is according to our faith *jure divino*.

These questions have obvious ecumenical repercussions. For instance, the Orthodox Church, which has a strong monastic tradition but no religious orders in the Western sense, is strongly hostile to this dimension of Catholic life, which it sees as a practical consequence of an exaggerated view of papal authority.

Challenge to Current Structures

The relative "successes" of the new movements present various challenges to our geographically based parochial and diocesan systems. In particular, they pose the question as to whether these frameworks can by themselves reverse the decline in faith-conviction and practice. The new movements bring the blessings and the dangers of intense religion and more explicit commitment. They are also free to specialize and to follow their own particular callings, concentrating their resources on specific areas of the apostolate. The astonishing variety among the new movements represents not only a great richness within the Church, but also a capacity to impact people and society in many different ways.

By comparison the world of dioceses and parishes can seem

---

[21] This criticism was leveled at the Neo-Catechumenate particularly in the Clifton Enquiry (cf. www.ourworld.compuserve.com/homepages/Ronald-haynes/nc-erpt.htm) and at Communion and Liberation (cf. Luigi Geninazzi, "An Interview of Luigi Giussani," *Avvenire*, Sunday Supplement *Agora* October 8, 1995, 6).

rather humdrum, maybe at times little more than the maintenance of essential services. Yet it is not hard to see that while new movements represent a new vitality within the Church, they cannot be the whole Church. New movements in a Catholic understanding exist to serve the existing organic unity of the Church. Thus, one of the criteria given in *Christifideles laici* for assessing lay associations of the faithful is their filial relationship to the Pope and to the local bishop (para. 30). It is wise for the new ecclesial movements to take seriously John Paul's guiding principles as listed in *Christifideles laici*, Articles 29 and 30. In Article 29 he speaks of the phenomenon of lay people forming new associations, the character of which is varied and vital. He says we can speak of a new era of group endeavors of the lay faithful. Article 30 sets out the criteria of ecclesiality for such groups, namely, the primacy given to the call of every Christian to holiness, the responsibility of professing the Catholic faith, the communion with the Pope and Bishops, conformity to and participation in the Church's apostolic goals, commitment to a presence in human society. Associations of lay faithful must become fruitful outlets for participation and solidarity in bringing about conditions that are more just and loving within society.

The challenge for new ecclesial movements and communities will be to remain faithful to the charismatic graces that God has given them and to ensure the full and mature use of the gifts of the Spirit and the fruits of the Spirit as a means of building the Church and of enabling it to be a more authentic sign to a world grievously in need of redemption and abundant life. In order for them to remain in this grace, their close association with the bishops of the Church and the See of Rome is an essential element of discernment of the particular leadings of the Spirit in the respective communities. Only when each individual part of the body is faithfully listening to the Lord can they then gather together to hear in a true and real sense not only what the Spirit is saying to the communities but also what the Spirit is saying through them to the wider Church.

The new ecclesial movements can learn from the history of

the religious orders in the Church because they have already traveled the pathway that has been well tested and can offer to these new movements of the Spirit wisdom for a lasting, fruitful journey. There is then a challenge to dioceses and parishes to welcome new movements that serve the life and communion of the Church and a challenge to these movements to be of humble service of the whole Body of Christ. Both need to acknowledge their dependence on each other.

In the view of the Pope the new ecclesial movements are a providential response to the needs of the modern era. There can be little doubt but that traditional moral standards and Christian values have come under severe attack and have lost ground in recent decades, particularly in the Western world. While I have used the term "secularization," other words may better reflect major factors in this decline of civilization, such as commercialization, consumerism and hedonism. It seems most likely that the diminishing Church attendance in many European countries, for instance, reflects a steady wearing down of Christian faith and its social embodiment in face of the overwhelming pressure of the media and the surrounding culture. This is the context in which Pope John Paul II sees the importance of the new ecclesial movements and communities within the Catholic Church.

This context explains the differences between the lay movements of the days of Pius XI and Pius XII and the new movements that are flourishing today. Such is the pressure of the neopagan world around us that only strong environments of faith and deep commitments stand much chance, first, of holding newly-converted young people and, secondly, reversing the tide so that the Church has more impact on society than society on the Church. If people are fed by the average television diet for twenty hours a week (a low estimate for most of the population), then how can we expect a seven to 10-minute homily and a 45-minute Mass each week to have greater influence on the thinking and the affections of even those who go to church regularly?

The new movements typically present a clear call to conversion of heart and life, and then provide an ambiance of faith support, a discipline to undergird daily prayer and regular study, and the vision of an alternative society. The new movements can then be seen as a modern mutation of forms of apostolic and consecrated life now extended to lay people. They express a more radical living of Christian faith than that required or expected of the faithful in general, with these more radical patterns being commonly expressed in forms of personal commitment avoiding the traditional language of vows.

The New Ecclesial Movements Attract Young People

The new movements and communities often have a strong attraction for young people. Youth generally flourish in large enthusiastic gatherings, but often struggle where they are only a handful. Geographical boundaries and corporate loyalties mean little to young people, so there is a challenge to parishes and dioceses to let go of possessive mentalities, and to the movements to respect and serve the Church in each area, rejecting all temptations to see themselves as the real communion of the Spirit.

The tensions between parishes and the new movements are heightened, not only by the greater enthusiasm characteristic of the latter, but also by the inclusion of married people and families in the ecclesial movements and new communities. Enthusiasm also tends to be a feature and to date the word and its connotations have had a mixed press. Originally it meant "being possessed by a god" but in reaction to the excesses in the English Civil War in the middle of the seventeenth century it became a negative word within the English language denoting religious fanaticism and outlandish behavior.[22] Indeed, it was a code word for the excesses of spurious revival since the days of the Reformation. Samuel Johnson defined it as "a vain confidence of Divine favor or communication."[23] In 1868, Disraeli advised Queen Victoria

---

[22] Finney, 26.
[23] John Paul II, "The Participation of Priests in Ecclesial Movements," 188.

against appointing Bishop Tait to Canterbury, with the delicious words, "there is in his idiosyncrasy a strange fund of enthusiasm, a quality which ought never to be possessed by an Archbishop of Canterbury." This feature of enthusiasm sometimes makes these new bodies more direct competitors of the parishes in a way that was not true with religious institutes and congregations comprised only of celibate members. Communion and Liberation is a particular example of this reality as the Milan experience in Italy indicates clearly.[24] Cardinal Carlo Martini has been one of the sharpest critics of Communion and Liberation and there have been numerous clashes over how pastoral programs should be carried out in the diocese. In particular, Martini and Communion and Liberation warred over what instruction in Catholic social doctrine should be given in the diocese. Martini's view held sway but it left a residue of hard feelings. Don Giussani, the founder of Communion and Liberation, believes that Catholicism has suffered from a Protestant virus that has resulted in subjectivism, moralism and a weakening of the organic unity of the Christian fact. The latter point refers to a lack of fidelity to the Bishop of Rome. Giussani believes that a local Church cannot stand up against a dominant culture; it can only suffer it. In his view, unity with the Pope is the only successful strategy for Christians if they are to counter successfully the dominant culture of the age.[25]

The New Ecclesial Movements Incarnate Core Aspects of Vatican II Theology

Examining the new elements in the lay movements and communities of today indicates a further development in the theology of the laity. Vatican II represented a clear development from the epoch of Pius XI and Pius XII with its grounding of the apos-

---

[24] Robert Moynihan, "Valiant for God, the New Movements 1," *The Tablet* (February 20, 1988), 196.

[25] Moynihan, 197.

tolate of the laity in the sacraments of baptism and confirmation, and its clear distinction between the apostolate grounded in baptism, not needing the permission of the hierarchy, and lay sharing by delegation in the apostolate of the ordained.

The vision of the laity in Vatican II is primarily one of being a witness and a leaven in the world. We get the flavor of this combination in *Lumen Gentium*:

> By reason of their special vocation it belongs to the laity to seek the kingdom of God by engaging in temporal affairs and directing them according to God's will. They live in the world, that is, they are engaged in each and every work and business of the earth and in the ordinary circumstances of social and family life which, as it were, constitute their very existence. There, they are called by God that, being led by the Spirit to the Gospel, they may contribute to the sanctification of the world, as from within like leaven, by fulfilling their own particular duties. Thus, especially by the witness of their life, resplendent in faith, hope and charity they must manifest Christ to others. In a special way they are challenged to illuminate and order all temporal things with which they are so closely associated that these may be effected and grow according to Christ and may be to the glory of the Creator and Redeemer.[26]

The important Synodal document *Christifideles laici* (1988) recognizes in its section on "The Ministries, Offices and Roles of the Lay Faithful" that "It is... natural that the tasks not proper to the ordained ministers be fulfilled by the lay faithful. In this way there is a natural transition from an effective involvement of the lay faithful in the liturgical action to that of announcing the word of God and pastoral care."[27]

---

[26] *Lumen Gentium*, §31.

[27] *Christifideles laici*, §23.

The New Ecclesial Movements Are Agents of Evangelization

Important, too, has been the emphasis on evangelization and the explicit proclamation of the Christian *kerygma*, stemming from Paul VI's *Evangelii nuntiandi* (1975). The new movements, especially those issuing from the Charismatic Renewal, have been in the forefront of proclamation of the Gospel by lay Catholics. The fruit of this ecclesial experience can be seen in the recent *General Directory for Catechesis* (GDC), which recognizes the need for an "initial" or "primary proclamation" aimed at producing a basic conversion to Christ (47-49, 51-52, 56b-57) and candidates for catechesis. There is undoubtedly an urgent need to mobilize effectively the laity in the area of evangelization. As Pope Paul VI noted, contemporary society is not likely to pay attention to what is taught by the hierarchy, unless that teaching is accompanied by a compelling personal witness. A personal witness to Christ is, par excellence, the role of the laity in our Church.[28] This point was reinforced cogently in *Redemptoris Missio*:

> People today put more trust in witnesses than preachers, in experience than in teaching, in life and action than in theories. The witness of a Christian life is the first and irreplaceable form of mission.[29]

Lay Catholics are already in daily contact with the unchurched. The laity have all sorts of natural ties to people who have no living contact with the Catholic Tradition. They have ready entry to many relationships and situations where no priest would be welcome. It is ironic that while Catholicism has a much stronger and richer theological basis for evangelization than evangelical Protestantism, the Protestants are the ones who are actually doing the lion's share of the evangelizing. The fact is that the

---

[28] Cf. *Evangelii nuntiandi*, §18.
[29] *Redemptoris Missio*, §41.

global evangelical missionary movement has grown explosively over the past decades. In just the past ten years, the number of evangelical Protestants in the Third World has doubled from around 150 million to about 300 million. This missionary explosion has been effected by an evangelistic workforce that is 99% lay. And even more meaningful is the fact that a large percentage of these lay Protestant evangelists are former Catholics.

Approximately 30% of today's thirty-five million evangelicals in the US are first or second generation former Catholics. That means that something like 11 million former Catholics identify themselves as Protestant evangelicals.[30] Among Hispanic Catholics in the United States, who now constitute nearly a third of American Catholics, five million have left the Catholic Church in the last ten years to join evangelical or Pentecostal Churches or other religious movements. In 1970, 90% of American Hispanics identified themselves as Catholic. In the early 1990's, only 70% so identified themselves.[31]

And this trend is not just true in America. Bishop Bonaventura Kloppenburg of Brazil has recently noted that Latin American is turning Protestant faster at the present time than Central Europe did in the sixteenth century.[32] Between 1960 and 1985, the numbers of evangelical Protestants have doubled in Chile, Paraguay, Venezuela, Panama, and Haiti; tripled in Argentina, Nicaragua, and the Dominican Republic; quadrupled in Brazil and Puerto Rico; quintupled in El Salvador, Costa Rica, Peru, and Bolivia; and sextupled in Guatemala, Honduras, Ecuador, and Colombia.[33] Guatemala may have already become the first Protestant country in Latin America since the year 2000.[34] In Brazil, the largest Catholic country in the world, there are more Protestants

---

[30] Ralph Martin, *The Catholic Church at the End of an Age* (San Francisco: Ignatius Press, 1994), 39.

[31] Martin, 38.

[32] Martin, 45.

[33] Martin, 42.

[34] Thomas S. Giles, "Forty Million and Counting," *Christianity Today* (April 6, 1992), 32.

in Church on Sunday than Catholics. There are 30,000 full time Protestant ministers and only 13,000 Catholic priests. Laymen preside at more than 70% of the country's Sunday liturgies.[35] The slums of Rio are filled with Protestant churches as Catholicism is rapidly becoming the faith of the middle and upper classes. "The irony is… that the Catholics opted for the poor and the poor opted for the evangelicals."[36]

Why are the Protestants such effective evangelizers? The analysis of both evangelical and Catholic observers in Latin America and in the United States is very similar. One of the explanations, given again and again, is that evangelicals mobilize their lay people for mission. Observers agree that popular Protestantism has a remarkable ability to mobilize all Church members for the missionary task. This sense of participation in mission leads to a sense of participation in worship and, sometimes, decision-making in the community.[37]

R. Kenneth Strachan, the late general director of the Protestant Latin American Mission, developed this influential principle for Latin Churches when he argued that the growth of any movement is in direct proportion to that movement's success in mobilizing its entire membership in constant propagation of its beliefs.

Proclamation of the Gospel must begin outside the Christian community but we cannot stop there. We must recognize that proclamation alone is not truly effective evangelization because proclamation alone does not usually make lifelong disciples. Lifelong discipleship requires the ongoing, lifelong support of the Christian community. To make disciples requires not only evangelists, but an evangelizing community as well. This is where the new movements have so much to offer. Providentially they reveal

---

[35] Martin, *The Catholic Church at the End of an Age*, 44-45.

[36] James Brooke, "Pragmatic Protestants win Catholic converts in Brazil," *New York Times* (July 4, 1993), 10.

[37] Andreas Topia, "Why is Latin America Turning Protestant?" *Christianity Today* (April 3, 1992), 3.

the Church by grace and vocation as the "sacrament in Christ, and so, sign and instrument of intimate union with God and of unity with the human race."[38]

Conversion and baptism give entry into a Church already in existence or require the establishment of new communities which confess Jesus as Savior and Lord. This is part of God's plan, for it pleases him "to call human beings to share in his own life not merely as individuals, without any unifying bond between them, but rather to make them into a people in which his children, who had been widely scattered, might be gathered together in unity."[39] To be fully Catholic, evangelism requires not just the evangelizing preacher, but the evangelizing community. Such a community is indispensable for making the Church existentially what she is already sacramentally. As Coda puts it, "In different yet convergent forms, it seems that the new ecclesial realities have arisen to actualize in a living form the ecclesiology proposed by the teaching of Vatican II."[40]

The New Ecclesial Movements Are Schools of Communion

Pope John Paul II acknowledged the movements as "schools of communion" in *Novo millennio ineunte*,[41] wherein we can catch a glimpse of the varied face of the Church, "a beginning, a barely sketched image of a future which the Spirit of God is preparing for us."[42] Central to this emerging icon is the epiphany of the communion between the hierarchical gifts and the charismatic gifts. Theologically it has always been accepted that charisms have played a unique and indispensable role in the life of the Church but as the Pope explained, the Second Vatican Council, "under

---

[38] *Lumen Gentium,* §1.

[39] *Lumen Gentium,* §9.

[40] Piero Coda, "The Varied Face of the Church: an Epiphany of Communion," *Being One* 10 (2001), 41.

[41] *Novo millennio ineunte,* §42.

[42] Ibid., §4.

the guidance of the Spirit, has rediscovered the charismatic dimension as constitutive of herself."[43] The Pope confirmed that the sacramental-hierarchic and the charismatic dimensions are "co-essential to the divine constitution of the Church founded by Jesus."[44] In articulating this he was recalling *Lumen Gentium* §4 which attributes the action of the One Spirit of Christ equally to both.

Crucially, this theological fact dismisses the false juxtaposition of the charismatic and the institutional. The role of the Holy Father in shepherding the new ecclesial movements into the heart of the Church and securing their acceptance by the institutional Church has been an outstanding example of the Petrine welcoming the authentic Marian and finding a home for it. Christ's words to Mary, "Woman, behold your son; son behold your mother" (Jn 19:26, 27) and the subsequent insertion of Mary into the home of the disciple have established the template.

Balthasar declared that an authentic charism is like a lighting flash from heaven, aimed at illuminating a unique and original point of God's will for the Church at a given time. This lighting flash makes manifest a new way of following Christ inspired by the Holy Spirit, and also a new illustration of revelation.[45]

The rediscovery of the co-essentiality of the hierarchic and charismatic gifts in the life and the mission of the Church has practical implications and consequences which are still unfolding. However, we do know that the acceptance of this reality demands a "rigorous and prophetic discernment, one which sees all the Church's members as protagonists, attentive to the signs of the times."[46]

---

[43] John Paul II, "Discourse" during the Vigil of Pentecost, 1998. Cited by Piero Coda in "The Varied Face of the Church: An Epiphany of Communion."

[44] John Paul II, handwritten message to the participants of the World Congress on Ecclesial Movements, 1998 in Pontifical Council of the Laity, *Movements in the Church* (Vatican, 1999), 13-20.

[45] Cf. Hans Urs von Balthasar, *Two Sisters in the Spirit: Therese of Lisieux and Elizabeth of the Trinity* (Milan: Jaca Book, 1973), 20-21.

[46] Piero Coda, "The Varied Face of the Church: an Epiphany of Communion," 44.

Coda proposes three responsibilities of openness on the part of all involved. Firstly, the pastors need to be open to the new charisms as manifested by the new ecclesial movements, "a real and sincere openness to what the Spirit wants to say to the Church, both profound and concrete, for her way of being and acting to-day."[47] This would avoid the temptation to wrongly insert the dynamism of the new charisms into pre-existing categories or es-tablished pastoral schedules and plans. Conversely the leaders of the new ecclesial realities need also to be open to each other and "above all else to the Church, whose daughters they are."[48] To do otherwise would be a betrayal of communion as the principle and the end of the New Evangelization.

The New Ecclesial Movements Are Authentic Charismatic Realities

Thus in the last decade or two, we seem to be moving into a third phase, in which the laity are not just leaven and witnesses by their lives but active proclaimers and mediators of the Gospel and life in the Spirit. In this development, the emergence of "charisms" is playing an important role. The reintroduction of this concept[49] has been followed by a multiplication of charisms and a richer vision of the equipment of the whole Church for her mis-sion. The charisms found among the laity are directly concerned with the building up of the Church, as clearly articulated in *Christifideles laici.*[50]

All these factors point to a new realization of the laity in their full Christian dignity, sons and daughters of God, fed by Word and sacrament, and empowered by the Holy Spirit precisely as ar-

---

[47] Coda, 45.
[48] Ibid.
[49] Cf. *Lumen Gentium,* §12.
[50] Cf. *Christisfideles laici,* §24.

ticulate believers. This development can be seen as an unpacking in "the Church's mission of salvation"[51] and of the implications of the dignity and the responsibilities of all the baptized. It would seem that the biblical renewal through which the Holy Spirit is leading the Church involves this rediscovery of the full implications of conversion-baptism and Spirit endowment-confirmation for all the members of the Church. In this, the new movements are catalysts for something wider and bigger than themselves.

As Cardinal, Ratzinger confirmed that the threefold division of the people of God into priests, religious and laity is fundamental[52] but within the ecclesiology of Vatican II he stressed that the episcopal and priestly role, while remaining representative of the sacrament and therefore responsible for the presence of faith, "will be less a monarch, more a brother in a school where there is only one teacher and only one Father." In his view, "the 'monarchic episcopate' has been misunderstood for a long time."[53]

Inculturation of the New Ecclesial Movements

Writing about the universal communion of the Churches, Tillard argues that, while the universal communion of bishops is of absolute importance for effecting the union of the Churches, these Churches have different customs, traditions and problems, different organizations, even different "souls."[54] At this point, Tillard adopts the use of the distinctly theological word "inculturation" in order to point out how recent a concept it is, growing out of the "new Churches" of recent missionary activity, where "…incarnation into the proper cultural values is still in its very beginning. Yet, since the beginning, the Church has spread by taking

---

[51] Cf. *Lumen Gentium*, §33.

[52] "Dialogue with Cardinal Ratzinger" in *Ecclesial Movements* (Vatican City, 2001), 227-8.

[53] Ibid.

[54] J.M.R. Tillard, *Église d'églises: L'ecclésiologie de Communion* (Paris: Éditions du Cerf, 1987), 325.

on characteristics which have come from the territories where they were born."[55]

In the "Church of Churches," there is no question of a fragmentation, but rather of the union of all in one communion of salvation. Writing specifically about the local Churches, Tillard applies his final remarks to the diversity of cultures and it is an apt comment on the emerging ecclesial movements.

> Uniformity suffocates *communion*, while certain divergences on fundamental points render it non-viable. Unity without diversity makes the Church a dead body; pluralism without unity makes of it a dismembered body. Shall we not grasp how, with the Spirit of God, they are to get along with each other in the healthy equilibrium that "communion of communions" implies?[56]

This is one of the most critical questions that the Church will have to address as she attempts to integrate the new ecclesial movements into the heart of the Church. William Bausch, in his recent book, *Brave New Church*, cites the second millennium as "the millennium of the papacy (and bishops and clergy)."[57] He believes the third millennium will be "the millennium of the baptized."[58] How the Church becomes fully an egalitarian communion of all the baptized will be influenced significantly by the new ecclesial movements.

---

[55] Tillard, 326.

[56] Tillard, 401.

[57] William Bausch, *Brave New Church, From Turmoil to Trust* (Twenty-Third Publications, 2001), 282.

[58] Ibid.

The Movements Are Coming to an "Ecclesial Maturity"

The birth and spread of such movements has brought to the Church's life an unexpected newness. Within their structures there is strong inter-personal community support for individual Christians living in a fiercely secular and even pagan society; often one will not find this support in institutional congregations and parishes. The Gospel is presented more effectively by vibrant communities to the urbanized world where old family and village structures no longer exist and where people are forced to live individualistic and isolated lives in an impersonal environment.

We can say with some certainty that the Church that turns the tide of secularization and neo-paganism will be made up of people who are living out their baptismal call to holiness, who are bonded in believing communities and who are deeply committed to serving God in the world. The pattern is already there among the Protestant "house" and "community" Churches and among the Catholic ecclesial movements and communities.

However, as the work of Tillard illustrates, it is important to see the new ecclesial movements not as a threat or as a deviation from the norm but as an exciting new expression of inculturation. The Church today continues to seek new ways to insert the Gospel truths into a variety of cultural contexts and in a host of authentic expressions. The ecclesial movements impregnate culture and society by their committed and faithful lifestyles, rooted in Gospel values. The Church is not only a model *of* communion, but a model *for* a richer historical development of that communion. The new ecclesial communities may indeed be a model or a blueprint *for* the shape of the Church of tomorrow.

Ecclesial Criteria

In his Pentecost 1998 address to them, Pope John Paul II reminded the new ecclesial movements of the criteria that guarantees their authenticity. He referred again to the Apostolic Exhortation *Christifideles laici*[59] which underlines the following:

1. There is an inescapable responsibility to confess the Catholic faith and to clearly show fidelity to the Church's *magisterium* in matters of faith and doctrine.

2. There is a call to be authentic witnesses of communion with the Pope, who is the center of unity between the universal Church and the bishop. Moreover, this principle is expressed at diocesan level in obedience to the bishop and in willing collaboration with other associations and movements. Church communion demands both an acknowledgment of a legitimate plurality of forms in the associations of the lay faithful in the Church and at the same time, a willingness to cooperate in working together.

3. The ecclesial movements are called to a dutiful and genuine compliance with, and participation in, the apostolic aims of the Church. Therefore each ecclesial movement should have a strong missionary thrust to the whole world and guard against closing in on oneself or one's circle.

4. The ecclesial movements are missioned to be a committed presence in society, to build it according to the spirit of the Gospel; this requires solidarity, defense of human rights, dignity of persons: they are called to work for the sanctification of the world from within as a leaven.

5. Most important of all, they are called to be schools of holiness where they grow closer to the image of the risen Christ and serve him among their brothers and sisters.

Conclusion

According to a recent editorial by *La Civiltà Cattolica*, the most serious and difficult challenges that the ecclesial movements

---

[59] *Christifideles laici*, §30.

pose to the Church today are the following: the legislative vacuum, dual membership, non-Catholics in their membership, and priests torn from their dioceses.[60]

a. The legislative vacuum refers to the fact that there is no overarching law because the present Code of Canon Law does not deal explicitly with the ecclesial movements, and this generates confusion. Canonical systematization will be particularly difficult.

b. The second concern is the presence in some movements of religious men and women belonging to other institutes: this "has provoked an identity crisis for some of them and has induced others to leave their own institutes or to establish a sort of dual membership."[61]

This phenomenon is observed especially among the Charismatics and members of the Neo-Catechumenal Way. It frequently happens, for example, that Jesuits or Franciscans become part of these movements. Fr. Raniero Cantalamessa, official preacher of the papal household, is a famous case of dual membership: he is a Franciscan friar, and at the same time he is part of the Charismatic movement, Renewal in the Spirit. There are many cases of dual membership among the Charismatics. In the Neo-Catechumenal Way, on the other hand, it happens more frequently that a religious abandons his own institute of origin and shifts completely to the movement founded by Kiko Argüello and Carmen Hernández. It is understandable that ancient and glorious religious families would not look with a kindly eye upon the exit of their own consecrated men and women, and the passage of these into new movements.

c. The third challenge "is constituted by the fact that some ecclesial movements… admit baptized non-Catholics": if these "were to become very numerous, they might influence the gen-

---

[60] The editorial, dated June 19, 2004 entitled "The ecclesial movements today" and signed by Jesuit Fr. Giuseppe De Rosa, appeared in *La Civiltà Cattolica* listing the "dangers" and "challenges" posed to the Church by many of these movements.

[61] Ibid.

eral assemblies to make substantial statutory changes, putting in danger the Catholic nature of the movement itself."[62]

This brings to mind the Focolare movement founded and headed by Chiara Lubich, which counts among its members thousands of non-Catholics and non-Christians, among whom are many Muslims and Buddhists. It is true that the non-Catholics belonging to Focolare do not enjoy any deliberative power, but the fear is that they might gain influence as a pressure group and weigh upon the public image of the movement and of the Church, in a relativistic sense.

More substantial is the case of the monastic community of Bose, the founder and prior of which is Enzo Bianchi. There are some non-Catholics who have full membership in this community: the Swiss Reformed pastor Daniel Attinger, two other Protestants, and the Orthodox monk Emilianos Timiadis, previously the metropolitan archbishop of Silyvría. And this is enough to make it impossible for Bose to receive canonical approval from the Holy See, not to mention the other obstacle constituted by its being a mixed community, with monks and nuns in the same monastery.

d. The most delicate challenge is that of the participation of priests in the movements. It must be remembered, in the first place, that some movements have created their own seminaries, in which the students are formed according to the charism of the movement and prepared to be priests at the service of the movement itself.

Then there remains the open question of the canonical incardination of these priests: if the movement has as its marks universality and missionary activity, which are recognized and approved by the Holy See in granting the movement the status of a public association, who should incardinate its priests? Generally, recourse is had to an instrumental incardination, in which a bishop well disposed toward the movement incardinates the priest into

---

[62] Ibid.

his diocese, while leaving him available — in general full time and with full freedom of movement — to the movement itself, through a written agreement. This means that a priest thus incardinated is at the service of the movement, wherever it may need him. But difficulties can arise if a bishop is succeeded by another who does not agree with this type of incardination, or if urgent and grave pastoral needs require the presence of the priest in the diocese: in this case, it can happen that the bishop tends to restrict the freedom of the priest and ignore the written agreement. Among other issues, such an agreement has more a formal than a juridical value, as it is not provided for in canon law.

Many movements correspond to this profile. The most visible case is that of the Neo-Catechumenal Way, with more than fifty *"Redemptoris Mater"* seminaries throughout the world, from which thousands of priests have emerged and been juridically incardinated in the dioceses, but are often, in fact, at the exclusive service of the Way. Analogous cases include the Community of Sant'Egidio, Focolare, the Marian Oases, the Missionary Community of Villaregia, and many more: all with priests at their service, ordained or contributed by friendly bishops. The solution proposed by *La Civiltà Cattolica* is that "the movements that are by nature universal and missionary should obtain the faculty of incardinating their own clergy,"[63] as is the case for the Franciscans, Dominicans, and Jesuits, and for the institutes of consecrated life in general.

In effect, among the movements that have arisen during the past few decades, some have already obtained the faculty of incardinating their own priests: the Legionaries of Christ, the Lefebvrists who re-entered the Catholic Church, the Missionaries of St. Charles Borromeo — linked with Communion and Liberation and with its superior general Fr. Massimo Camisasca — and, naturally, Opus Dei, as it is a personal prelature. The Neo-Catechumenal Way did try unsuccessfully, in the past, to obtain

---

[63] Ibid.

the status of a personal prelature. To date, it is accountable to the Pontifical Council for the Laity.

Many of the new movements, apparently, have characteristics that make them unsuitable for full approval by the Vatican Congregation for the Institutes of Consecrated Life. The Marian Oases, for example, apart from having a woman as superior general, have communities of men and women together: under these conditions, it is unlikely that they would obtain from the Holy See permission to incardinate their own priests.

History and the test of time will determine more definitively whether the above difficulties will be solved. Interestingly, Ratzinger when confronted with questions around some of these issues, responded with the words, "Organization must follow life."[64] The movements have been a surprise of the Spirit, an ecclesiological novelty and their import is still unfolding. The future shape of the Church is still not known and to some extent the laws and structures of the Church are always retroactive.

The concerns summarized by *La Civiltà Cattolica* are important because they reflect significant anxiety within faithful established sections of the Church who are uneasy at the way they see the Church going. However, at this interim period, from a global perspective, I believe the signs are in general very positive. Notwithstanding the criticisms and reservations that many significant Church leaders have expressed, aware that mistakes and at times grave errors have been made, nevertheless, Pope John Paul has recognized their emergence as "a providential response."[65] He has reminded them that not "all problems had been solved"[66] and there

---

[64] Adriadnus Cardinal Simonis (Archbishop of Utrecht) posed such a question in the dialogue with Cardinal Ratzinger which followed some of the presentations made at the seminar "The Ecclesial Movements in the Pastoral Concern of the Bishops," *Laity Today* (1999), 228.

[65] Pope John Paul II, "Address to the delegates on the occasion of the Meeting with the Ecclesial Movements and the New Communities (Rome, May 30th 1998)," *Laity Today* (1999), 223.

[66] Ibid., 22.

was a challenging road ahead. He called them to a deep "ecclesial maturity,"[67] one that would bear "mature fruits of communion and commitment."[68]

Angelo Scola, in a dialogue with Cardinal Ratzinger, at the close of the seminar on "The Ecclesial Movements in the Pastoral Concern of the Bishops," stated that the ecclesial movements had reached a second stage in their development. The first stage had been "aimed at making space separate from what we may call the institutional ecclesial reality for these new phenomena that the Spirit has produced in the Church."[69] He saw the second stage as "the need to recognize the substantial unity between these new charismatic realities... and the great reality called the apostolic succession or at any rate the institution. The Pope clearly said that this is the task for the future."[70] Having reached the first stage of acceptance by the Church, and having been given the space they needed to grow and develop, separate to, and yet parallel with the parish and diocesan structures, they now commence the next stage of their journey. This call to unity with the Church and with one another is the great challenge that lies ahead for the ecclesial movements.

Finally, Bernard Sesboué, SJ, a French theologian, in his book *N'ayez Pas Peur*[71] says that the Church today has particularly porous boundaries. He explains what he means. In many cases we cannot hope to convert people in the strictly confessional sense, but have to settle for conversions which Sesboué calls existential movements towards true life. Perhaps two scriptural motifs, "light of the world" and "salt of the earth" could illuminate the issue. "Light of the world" is the institutional Church as lighthouse, in-

---

[67] Ibid.

[68] Ibid.

[69] Angelo Scola in dialogue with Cardinal Ratzinger, "The Ecclesial Movements in the Pastoral Concern of the Bishops," *Laity Today* (1999), 250-251.

[70] Ibid., 251.

[71] Bernard Sesboué, *N'ayez Pas Peur: Regards sur L'église et les Ministères aujourd'hui*, Pascal Thomas-Pratiques chrétiennes, no. 12 (Paris: DDB, 1996).

spiring, leading, offering people the sure way home. "Salt of the earth" is the Church buried, half-anonymous, in society, forming opinion, offering hope to the desperate, putting love where otherwise there would be none: the kind of thing done by the new ecclesial movements in a host of milieux, across every continent in the world.

Both light and salt are necessary. If the new shape of the Church is to be more salt, less light, perhaps this redresses a historical imbalance. As Paul VI said: "We need to evangelize the culture and the cultures of humankind... not in a decorative way, as if applying a coat of paint to their surface, but in depth, penetrating to their very roots."[72] If we are to lead the way in this, clearly we need to change our own way of thinking and reacting.[73]

By concretely realizing the ecclesiology of Vatican II, the ecclesial movements are putting before the Church a model of Christian communion in which the different parts of the Church form an organic and mutually supportive unity. The spiritual movements of the past not only led to new apostolic endeavors but also to internal reform within the local Churches. They "eventually affected the whole Church, so too the new ecclesial movements will profoundly change the Church of our time."[74] Hopefully, the arrival of the new ecclesial movements will help show to the rest of the Church how "the Church herself is a movement."[75]

---

[72] *Evangelii Nuntiandi,* §20.

[73] Anthony Philpott, "The Church Will Rise Again," *The Tablet* (October 3, 1998), 1272-1274.

[74] Cf. Pope John Paul II's Homily at the first international gathering of the movements in Rome in 1981 quoted in *Movements in the Church,* 109.

[75] Ian Ker, "New Movements and Communities in the Life of the Church," *Louvain Studies* (Spring 2002), 69-95.